Philosophical Archaeology

SUNY series in Contemporary Italian Philosophy
———————
Silvia Benso and Brian Schroeder, editors

Philosophical Archaeology

With and Beyond Agamben on Philosophy, History, and Art

Ido Govrin

Published by State University of New York Press, Albany

© 2023 State University of New York

All rights reserved

Printed in the United States of America

No part of this book may be used or reproduced in any manner whatsoever without written permission. No part of this book may be stored in a retrieval system or transmitted in any form or by any means including electronic, electrostatic, magnetic tape, mechanical, photocopying, recording, or otherwise without the prior permission in writing of the publisher.

For information, contact State University of New York Press, Albany, NY
www.sunypress.edu

Library of Congress Cataloging-in-Publication Data

Name: Govrin, Ido, author.
Title: Philosophical archaeology : with and beyond Agamben on philosophy, history, and art
Description: Albany : State University of New York Press, [2023] | Series: SUNY series in Contemporary Italian Philosophy | Includes bibliographical references and index.
Identifiers: ISBN 9781438491578 (hardcover : alk. paper) | ISBN 9781438491592 (ebook) | ISBN 9781438491585 (pbk. : alk. paper)
Further information is available at the Library of Congress.

10 9 8 7 6 5 4 3 2 1

Contents

Acknowledgments		ix
Prologue		xi
Chapter One	The History of Philosophical Archaeology from Kant to Agamben	1
Chapter Two	Toward Agamben's Philosophy of History	39
Chapter Three	Ar[t]chaeology	83
Conclusion		119
Notes		121
Bibliography		173
Index		183

Acknowledgments

The road to this book's publication began nearly a decade ago as a dissertation, the preliminary draft of which was developed at the European Graduate School (Saas-Fee, Switzerland) and was subsequently written, at full throttle, in the Department of Visual Arts (Western University, Canada) under the supervision of David Merritt, Patrick Mahon, and Antonio Calcagno. I am wholeheartedly grateful for their sincere attentiveness and extraordinary generosity and wish to thank them for being thoughtful intellectual interlocutors during the entire length of my doctoral endeavor and beyond. I am likewise grateful to Kim Moodie for his kind, astute reflections on my work.

I wish to thank the School of Graduate and Postdoctoral Studies at Western for the Mary Routledge Fellowship and the Alumni Graduate Award—they granted me the precious time needed to develop the research for this book. The research that led to this book simply would not have been possible without the financial support of the Social Sciences and Humanities Research Council of Canada—thank you.

I am deeply grateful to my editor, Emily Anglin, for the patience, attention to detail, and valuable insights she provided in preparing this manuscript. I would like to express my gratitude to Silvia Benso, Brian Schroeder, and Michael Rinella at State University of New York Press for their vital help in bringing this book to press.

Eternal thanks to my extended family and, above all, to L, N, and Z—this book is lovingly dedicated to you.

Prologue

In his opening remarks to *The Signature of All Things: On Method*, Giorgio Agamben claims, building on an idea by Ludwig Feuerbach, that "the genuine philosophical element in every work, whether it be a work of art, of science, or of thought, is its capacity to be developed."[1] It is a tensive element within a work, a seed encapsulating future realizations, whose unique nature enables its interpreter to also become its developer.

Upon encountering Agamben's book for the first time, I noticed that this very element may be seen as a key to the logic and structure of that book itself. It is described by the term "philosophical archaeology," which today is associated mainly with the work of Agamben, who identifies his overarching research methodology with this term and works tirelessly to systematize it.

Philosophical archaeology essentially embodies one's relation to history and historiographic research—a method of historical inquiry at the core of which lies a "historical a priori." The historical a priori, conceptually similar to the *arché*, conditions the historical development of the phenomenon, whether this phenomenon is objective or manifests as a subjective self.

However, this is only a partial definition of philosophical archaeology's multifaceted nature. Overall, this book conceives of philosophical archaeology more broadly (the complexity of which will gradually be revealed as the book unfolds): it is, as stated above, a research methodology (a historiographic framework) in the humanities at large; a metaphor (allegory); (art) content or subject matter; a materially based historiography; a critical force that conceives of its (past) objects as (future) prototypes or blueprints; and lastly, philosophical archaeology embodies a certain conception of time that conditions a (philosophical) conception of history.

The virtue of philosophical archaeology as a critical methodology stems not only from the penetrating nature of its tools but also from the integration of threads drawn from various fields of knowledge.

Due to the methodological, philosophical, and historiographic characteristics of philosophical archaeology, theorizing it means (for me) not to write as if externally about philosophical archaeology but to make it (with words), to do it in practice (through language). In this sense, Agamben's corpus also becomes the site (or the research object) where I practice and execute philosophical archaeology in writing and where I use language as an artistic medium (à la *détournement*)—a performance that illuminates the development of philosophical archaeology and the manner in which it is constituted within Agamben's own multilayered, extensive oeuvre. Thus, by implementing an archaeology of philosophical archaeology, I apply the logic of philosophical archaeology to itself.

This book attempts to observe Agamben's work from within, exhibiting his philosophical edifices as if they were found objects in order to show how they recur throughout his corpus, sometimes inconsistently or even paradoxically, and how their functions change over time. It delicately exposes the archaeological structure of his philosophy and overarching corpus in order to illuminate it for what it is and to show how it relates to other pertinent thinkers (whether he is in agreement with them or otherwise).

Therefore, the structure and methodology of writing this book are essentially archaeological and nonlinear in the temporality they follow, often deliberately reflecting the archaeological paradigm of discontinuous knowledge (to which Italian culture and historiography are linked). Perhaps the book calls for readers who will allow themselves to willingly drift away along its routes—a drifting that will in turn allow a different structural logic to emerge. A course of thought that repeatedly returns, however convolutedly, to previously discussed topics shies away from "proving an argument" and instead (without renouncing its aspirations for thoroughness and coherence) seeks the unrepresentable and unapproachable by attempting to continuously reveal unnoticeable affinities. This kind of approach presents a different type of engagement with the object of research, one that consciously abstains from being too analytical or dogmatic, or from repeating (however differently) what has already been discussed widely in the literature.

This might call to mind the scholastic treatise that does not proceed in an argumentative fashion but rather indirectly through the digressive arrangement and development of (often contradictory) citations, interpretations, and remarks, so as to arrive at an unintentional end—in this sense, as will become apparent, it overlaps with Walter Benjamin's constellation-like practice of writing beyond discursive language that allows a coincidental (but nonetheless necessary) thought to present itself or, in Benjamin's words, to "shine out of the ruins of language."

Hence, one distinct quality of this manuscript is the manner in which it integrates a certain structural apparatus. This apparatus is made of a series of fourteen glosses that are integrated throughout. These glosses, in accordance with the Agambenian/Feuerbachian idea of the encapsulated philosophical element that awaits its development, comment on key issues/concepts that are crucial to a thorough comprehension of philosophical archaeology (and thus the book more broadly). In this respect, commentary is a discussion or expansion of a text in the form of writing (glosses, annotations) or images (diagrams, miniatures) as features that can form part of the original program of work but can also take on a secondary or extraneous nature. A gloss is a marginal or interlinear annotation of a word or wording in a text, commenting on, elucidating, or translating the words of the main text. In the history of commentary, glossing, and marginalia, the gloss (as an ancient genre of writing) is a creative form of intellectual work. The gloss focuses, in most cases, on a single object, formally shaping itself to its object while preserving the object's structure; however, the gloss multiplies and synthesizes meanings, ideas, and references without necessarily revolving around a central thesis, providing interpretive and philological access to its object. Most importantly, the gloss forms a relationship of "continuing discontinuity" with its object—it digresses from it in order to open it from within. It is therefore clear, I believe, why this structural apparatus became relevant to the task of writing this book.

Chapter 1 discusses the emergence of philosophical archaeology on the theoretical horizon of continental philosophy (beginning in 1793 with Kant) and further outlines its course to Agamben. This course is highly interwoven with Agamben's oeuvre, thus in order to thoroughly historicize philosophical archaeology's development in time, the outline also includes various references to other pertinent philosophical figures (Overbeck, Nietzsche, Benjamin, Foucault, to name a few) and the (in)

direct key concepts (paradigm, signature, potentiality, dishomogeneity, genealogy, *arché*, archaeology, historical a priori, to name a few) those figures developed. These thinkers, who practiced philosophical archaeology in their writings, contributed to the solidification of philosophical archaeology as a research methodology in the humanities and thereby together form a critical influence on the manner in which Agamben will eventually identify philosophical archaeology as his fundamental research tool and basis for his inquiries. A few questions guide this section: What is the Agambenian research methodology of philosophical archaeology? What comprises it? How does it operate? What results can it have? What subjects can it take? What enables and prevents it? Can one trace its history within Agamben's oeuvre or within those of others? What exactly is the component of it that can further be developed?

Further, a preliminary discussion is carried out regarding the temporal structure on which philosophical archaeology is based, followed by an attempt to further accentuate and develop the concepts of temporality and spatiality in history. The overall discussion of the temporal structure of philosophical archaeology leads to a look at Agamben's conception of time more broadly, explicating a theory of time in Agamben, which in turn conditions his conception of history (alongside his understanding of the nature of the force that propels history in different directions). Philosophical archaeology is further analyzed as a critical research methodology that enables one to inquire the "prehistory" (*Urgeschichte*) of history and thus to reveal the (achronological) historical a priori of a given historical phenomenon, including the historical phenomenon that is humankind. In this sense, philosophical archaeology not only provides one with a renewed perspective on the very research framework used in historical, anthropological inquiries; it also exposes the "becoming human of man," that is, its historical a priori (that includes the horizon of future possibilities) exemplified by humankind's ongoing articulation between language and world, and likewise, by humankind's philosophy. Thus, philosophical archaeology constitutes philosophy inasmuch as, time and again, it returns anew to the continuous event of the anthropogenesis.

In order to expand our understanding of Agamben's philosophical archaeology and conception of time, toward a broader philosophy of history, chapter 2 explores (via a biaxial formation) the interdependence and interrelatedness of three inseparable pillars: theology, philology, and aesthetics. These pillars are the driving forces behind Agamben's philosophical conception of history at large, working mutually and directly (but also somewhat discreetly) to inform his historical/archaeological studies. That these pillars are inseparable from one another means that the discussion must unfold in a collimated fashion—that is, as a multidirectional exploration that reveals the tripartite path a particular concept takes within Agamben's philosophy of history. In this chapter we will observe how concepts such as, for example, "citation without quotation marks" or "dialectical image" are discussed in one discourse (philology) only to find, when they are followed along the line they suggest, a conceptual joint that enables us to continue discussing them in another related discourse (aesthetics) and vice versa. Thus, this chapter must take a less schematic orientation—in other words, it offers a more nonlinear, multifaceted rendering of Agamben's oeuvre, yet again in line with the logic of philosophical archaeology itself.

The chapter begins with an in-depth analysis (deepening the previous discussion already initiated in chapter 1) of that which conditions and enables the unique formation of Agamben's philosophical archaeology: that is, the temporal structure of philosophical archaeology identified as (and in) the image of *messianic time*. The messianic conception of temporality and history is demonstrated, in this chapter, primarily by drawing on Agamben's reading of St. Paul's Epistle to the Romans (the theological-philological axis) and Walter Benjamin's "Theses on the Philosophy of History" (the philological-aesthetical axis). Thus, it traces the two ends of messianic time according to Agamben: from antiquity to modern thought—and particularly to the thought of Benjamin. According to Agamben, Benjamin's thought (among others) secularizes the messianic, and as such, enables us to properly think the philosophy of history in the present.

Agamben constantly "admits" the philosophical debt he owes to his predecessors; in particular, the abovementioned tripartite weaving (theology, philology, aesthetics) is a complex apparatus he inherits almost directly from the work of Benjamin. Thus, the chapter goes on to look at Benjamin's philosophy of history, articulated in the broader context of his thought and, principally, in terms of the aesthetic dimension and the possibility of messianic redemption it might encapsulate. The process of working out the messianic through aesthetic means is considered also in terms of an epistemology that, exceeding beyond discursive language, shines for a moment (as previously mentioned) "out of the ruins of language."

In chapter 3, the discussion slides along the length of the tripartite fault line and into the germane fields of contemporary art and art history/theory since a special place is reserved for these fields (or the aesthetic discourse at large) in Agamben's thought. His work, as he himself observes (and as others often criticize him for) again and again propels Western metaphysics toward impossible scenarios. That these scenarios are impossible indicates, essentially, their dependence on preexisting categories of the intellect in an attempt to resist any kind of forced domination or governance; but they also signify the unleashing of an unexhausted potentiality still not subsumed by the actual and the real. It is my belief that Agamben's "impossible project," in its entirety, is more than mere playful logic or impotent (political) manifesto. What lies at the core of this attempt is, perhaps more than anything else, the demand for an inimitable use of one's imagination, which directly evinces the centrality of aesthetics in Agamben's poetic-based methodology (or poetic experimentation) to approach philosophical problems.[2]

The chapter commences by discussing how, in relation to Agamben, the artistic present requires a constant deferred reflection—that is, messianic time. The messianic time of contemporary art, its beatitude (as Agamben defines it), is conditioned by a caesura that shows the pure representation and the silent core that are constitutive of an authentic work of art. This is an image of beauty that is weightless and postponed, existing in a standstill between passivity and activity (the caesura, according to Benjamin, puts a halt to the movement of thought)—a messianic moment of "de-creation," of "inoperativity," which thereafter unleashes, beyond discursive language, a new potentiality. This beatitude is made possible due to the unforeseen, nonlinear flow of time—like Benjamin's kaleidoscopic conception of history, time is an ever-changing temporal constellation charged with a redemptive, messianic force. Thus, art messianically enables us to "fracture" time and likewise prevents time from solidifying and forcing upon us a single perspective of reality.

The later discussion in chapter 3 is framed in the context of what seems to be a historiographic turn in contemporary art and thus offers a contextualization of the archaeological orientation in contemporary art with several references to artworks that are pertinent to the discussion.

With the intention to illuminate philosophical archaeology as a modus operandi, and to examine whether this artistic practice is in a position to distend history and historiography rather than vice versa, I have been led by the following questions: If examined from the perspective of contemporary art practices, is philosophical archaeology to any extent a research methodology that (in part or entirely) can or should be rethought, executed, or transformed into the different but related discourse of art? In what sense could philosophical archaeology be artistically used, or, better, regenerated as an integral, organic part of artistic practices and productions? How can an artistic act interpret and develop philosophical archaeology (as a relation to history), both theoretically and in practice? And consequently, how will it influence the knowledge generated relationally at the intersection of the foregoing discourses of the humanities?

In this chapter, the examination of materially based philosophy of history is at stake—it asks whether by means of manipulation of materials and production of artistic objects, an individual can conceive a new philosophy of history. The chapter shows how history's traditional, inert materials (documents, archives, etc.) become artistically charged with active potencies and are archaeologically transformed into sites of knowledge construction. Various cultural, archaeological projects reformulate a conception of time by materializing the past. Examining and interpreting the material object, beyond the constraints of language, these archaeological projects constitute a porous, multidirectional conception of time, and thus propel an epistemological difference between history and archaeology with regard to the object. In the hands of some contemporary artists, the return to the past becomes a technique for cultural production, capable of opening up new possibilities rather than a merely romantic, inspirational caprice. This return is thus transformed into a deferred present where past and future are constantly rewritten—is the present moment (against the dematerialization of the ephemeral art object) the only thing left that is possible to document?

GLOSS I—AGAMBEN'S METHODOLOGY

Before we move forward to chapter 1, let us offer a few additional notes (in the form of methodological principles) regarding Agamben's methodology, which will supplement our prologue and thus bring it toward a conclusion. First, for Agamben, method and theory (and likewise practice and theory) are inseparable, as each theory contains within itself the way or path to itself. Theory, he states, is practice, and thus any proper destruction (during the investigation) is also a construction, they are also inseparable.[3] Second, as Agamben claims, moreover, "method shares with logic its inability to separate itself completely from its context. There is no method that would be valid for every domain, just as there is no logic that can set aside its objects."[4] Third, Agamben modestly ascribes to Walter Benjamin the idea that doctrine may legitimately be presented only in the form of interpretation. It is in the context of this principle that Agamben frames his scholarly relatedness to Michel Foucault's work (as well as what may appear to be, across *The Signature of All Things*, nothing more than—albeit erudite—investigations on the method of Foucault, but in reality is much more). Fourth, Foucault once commented that his "historical investigations of the past are only the shadow cast by theoretical interrogation of the present."[5] Accessing the present is possible only by following the shadows these interrogations cast on the past. Foucault often draws relationships between his archaeology and historical inquiries—for him they are distinct but also connected; archaeology needs history and vice versa. And thus it is for Agamben, in accordance with philosophical archaeology's meditation on the relation between history and archaeology. He writes: "[E]very inquiry in the human sciences—including the present reflection on method—should entail an archaeological vigilance. In other words, it must retrace its own trajectory back to the point where something remains obscure and unthematized."[6] Fifth, in a statement (that I have previously mentioned), Agamben himself explains his own position on the interlocutory role of the interpreter: "The genuine philosophical element in every work, whether it be a work of art, of science, or of thought, is its capacity to be developed, which Ludwig Feuerbach defined as *Entwicklungsfähigkeit*."[7] This German expression is ambiguous: it signifies both a passive capacity as well as an active capacity; an expression that forms a buffer zone or a no man's land that cannot be exclusively appropriated by author or reader, original or annotated text.[8] Because of this principle, putting one's finger on a clear difference between the author of the work and its interpreter becomes as essential as it is difficult to comprehend. Elsewhere, Agamben writes about why he is fascinated with the search for the element liable to be developed—"[b]ecause if we follow this methodological principle all the way, we inevitably end up at a point where it is not possible to distinguish between what is ours and what belongs to the author we are reading. Reaching this impersonal zone of indifference, in which every proper name, every copyright, and every claim for originality fades away, fills me with joy."[9] Agamben once also referred to *Entwicklungsfähigkeit* as an adequate representation or definition for philosophy at large—something that exists in literature, art, or science, which lacks a concrete territory in and of itself but nonetheless exists as an element to be developed within it.[10] Philosophy always exists in exile and requires assembly. For Agamben, as we will see, the methodological principle of *Entwicklungsfähigkeit* corresponds with Benjamin's idea of "messianic time" that is prevalent throughout the length and breadth of "secular time," or to the hermeneutical idea according to which one is required to understand a certain author more than the latter understands itself.[11] And sixth, in his book on Agamben, David Kishik writes about Agamben's attempt to methodologically articulate a philosophy that is based on a different type of logic:

> Though he usually immerses himself in meticulous and systematic scholarly studies, Agamben likes to present his findings in the form of miniature sketches, images, or scenes—each of which can stand both still and alone. When he collects these vignettes into a monograph, they sometimes resemble a flip book, which gives the fleeting illusion of a moving image by the quick turn of the pages with the thumb and index finger. . . . Agamben speaks about 'brachylogy as a form of philosophy' without developing this idea any further. Brachylogy comes from the Greek *brakhus* and *logos*, or 'short speech.' . . . But if we consider this concept in logical rather than grammatical terms, . . . [b]rachylogy could also be said to stand for a form of philosophy without logical operations (*not, and, or, if/then*). . . . This is . . . that his thought does not pretend to lead us from point A to point B by means of an argumentative apparatus.[12]

Chapter One

The History of Philosophical Archaeology from Kant to Agamben

[1]

Chapter 3 of Giorgio Agamben's book *The Signature of All Things: On Method* is titled "Philosophical Archaeology" and outlines an overarching research methodology that essentially embodies one's relation to history and historiographic research.

Philosophical archaeology, as Agamben acknowledges, has developed based on a series of philosophical ruins in which "Jottings for the Progress of Metaphysics,"[1] Immanuel Kant's appendix to his own treatise of 1793, is considered to be its point of departure inasmuch as the term appears there for the first time.

Kant's essay struggles between, on one hand, the empirical, temporal nature of historical inquiry, and specifically, the history of philosophy that presents the empirical and thus contingent, successive order of how thinkers philosophized up to the present; and, on the other hand, the rational and necessary order of philosophical concepts, the ahistorical nature of philosophical thought or, in other words, the unconditional and thus a priori nature of a philosophical history of philosophy. A philosophical history of philosophy is thus conceived as a special kind of historical inquiry that becomes possible, in Kant's words, "not historically or empirically, but rationally, i.e., *a priori*. For although it establishes facts of reason, it does not borrow them from historical narrative, but draws them from the nature of human reason as philosophical archaeology [*als philosophische Archäologie*]."² Thus for Kant the idea of philosophical archaeology entails coming to know the means and ways by which philosophy is articulated by reason itself, as well as to know the history of philosophy as it is determined by the necessity of a priori principles.

Because philosophical archaeology is not merely an empirical history but also one that becomes possible a priori, and since philosophizing (specifically, in this case, about the history of philosophy) is a gradual development of human reason that could not have begun upon the empirical path, it fundamentally implies that (due to its paradoxical element) archaeology runs the risk of lacking a beginning and putting forth, as Kant writes, "a history of the thing that has not happened."³ Thus we can derive, Agamben deduces, that as an a priori history (which is, after all, a historical practice), philosophical archaeology's origin, the *arché* it seeks, can never be given in chronology nor be dated since it coincides with the complete development of reason; in other words, it is an *arché* that will be given in its totality only at the end of philosophizing, while currently its history is the history of the thing that has not happened. Philosophical archaeology is therefore a historiography of an incomplete gradation (a series of historical ruins, science of ruins—"ruinology" in Agamben's words) rather than of a given empirical whole, whose object or *archai* exist only as partial objects or ruins, given only as *Urbilder* or archetypes that can never be attained and serve merely as guidelines.⁴

GLOSS II—FIRST BEGINNING AND THE BEFORE OF THE BOOK

It should be noted that between writing the first *Critique* (1781) and the *Progress of Metaphysics* (1793), Kant wrote another relatively short text where the logic of "ruinology" is further articulated mainly in relation to the concept of the *arché* of historiography. There, he argues that a history of the first development of any phenomenon that has its original predisposition "in the nature of the human being" (reason, freedom, etc.) is fundamentally different from the history of the phenomenon "in its progression, which can be grounded only on records."⁵ Attempts to outline the *first beginning* of a certain (natural) historical phenomenon may legitimately include the insertion of conjectures regarding the phenomenon's *arché*, insofar as *nature* makes it. In this case, we assume it "was not better or worse than what we encounter now," thus the beginning need not be fictionalized. This, however, will be an illegitimate act in relation to outlining the *first beginning* of the history of human deeds, since "to let a history *arise* simply and solely from conjectures does not seem much better than to make the draft for a novel."[6]

As a genre-based semantic hinge, Kant's incidental comment about the novel (including its annexed footnote) enables us to reflect upon the (somewhat suggested) Kantian conception of temporality at the core of his framework of historicity or philosophical archaeology, as we have seen thus far. This also assists us in thinking about the influence Kant's conception of temporality has had on the manner in which Agamben articulates a conception of (messianic) time, which includes his understanding of the *arché* of philosophical archaeology. For example, in his relatively short meditations on literature, compiled under *The Fire and the Tale*, Agamben refers to Roland Barthes. Referring to any creative work, Barthes highlights the problem of the relation between "the fantasy of the novel" and the preparatory notes and fragments and about the similar relation between the fragmented novel and the proper novel. The period that precedes the finished work is named by Agamben, paraphrasing Barthes, as "the before of the book"[7]—a limbo, pre- or sub-world of fantasies, sketches, notes, copybooks, drafts, and blotters.[8] The problem with this world, according to Barthes, is that it is "poorly defined, and poorly studied"; to that Agamben adds that our culture is not able to give it a legitimate status nor to provide it with a sufficient visual vocabulary. The reason for this cultural situation stems from the thesis, put forward by Agamben, that "our idea of creation and work is encumbered with the theological paradigm of the divine creation of the world," according to which the world was created ex nihilo in an incomparable manner and not only that but was also instantaneously accomplished without hesitation and through an immediate act of the will. God thus had no preparatory draft nor initial matter for creation; and in fact, the very problem of the "before of the creation" is, in theology, a forbidden topic.[9]

In Romanticism we find the idea that fragments and outlines were superior to the completed work, and for this reason writers intentionally left their writings in a fragmented form.[10] The way in which we conceive the identity of the work has transformed radically in recent decades, a tendency that can be witnessed in the field of "ecdotics" (the science that deals with the edition of texts) where, in comparison with the past when the aim was the reconstruction of a single definitive critical text, nowadays we encounter the reproduction of all the layers of the manuscript without distinguishing the different versions. Thus the "text" becomes an infinite temporal process, toward both past and future, whose interruption at a certain historical point is purely contingent.[11] The caesura that ends the drafting of the work does not confer on it a privileged status of completeness; it just constitutes it as another fragment of a potentially infinite creative process. Thus, for Agamben, a draft (of a certain work of art) is not an ex nihilo act of creation but an ongoing process of fulfillment and transformation. The so-called "completed work," he writes, "is distinguished only accidentally from the uncompleted one." If each version of the work is a fragment, we can speak also about "the after of the book," that is, the process of retraction to previous "finished" works and the reworking of them in order to amend their flaws or clarify their meanings and aims (Augustine's *Retractationes* [of 427] and Nietzsche's *Ecce Homo* [of 1888] are just two of the most famous examples). This is the other side of the theological paradigm of divine creation according to which creation is an infinite continuous process that, if stopped by God, will be destroyed.[12]

The ontological status of the book and the work is governed by insufficient categories that our culture has accustomed us to think with. From Aristotle onward, according to Agamben, we think of the work (*ergon*) by relating two concepts: potentiality and actuality, virtual and real. We tend to think the potential and virtual as the "before of the work" that precedes the actual and real (completed) work. This means that in notes or outlines "potentiality has not been transferred to the act . . . [and thus remains] unrealized and uncompleted."[13] But, Agamben asks, "[I]s it not the case that every book contains a remainder of potentiality, without which its reading and reception would be impossible?" A work whose creative potentiality was totally exhausted would not be work but "ashes and sepulcher of the work." If an author can go back to his work, the reason is not, like the Romantics believed, that the fragments are more important than the work itself but that the experience of matter (or for the ancients, potentiality) is immediately perceivable in them.

The implications of the materiality of the book are vast and extend to both historical directions. The book as we know it today appeared in Europe between the fourth and the fifth century. The *codex* (technical term for "book," introduced with Christianity) replaces the *volumen* and the scroll (the norm in Antiquity). The disappearance of the volume also reflects the conflict between the church and the synagogue: the Torah as a *volumen* as opposed to the New Testament as a book (a shape no different than any profane book). The codex introduces the page, which was a real material and spiritual revolution for the West. The unrolling of the volume revealed a homogeneous and continuous space, while the codex presents a discontinued, delimited unity. This implies a different conception of time: from the cyclical (of Antiquity) to the linear (of the Christian world). Time of reading reproduces the time of life.[14]

[2]

The archetypal and unreachable characteristics of the (Agambenian/Kantian) *arché*, as herein conceived, imply that every authentic historical inquiry contains an "essential dishomogeneity," a constitutive gap between the *arché* it investigates (made of ruins or archetypes, not given in its totality within chronology) and the phenomenon's factual origin.[15]

GLOSS III—DISHOMOGENEITY

The idea of "essential dishomogeneity" mirrors the old philosophical problem of discontinuity. In the context of the following discussion, that is, a Foucauldian epistemological context, the problem of discontinuity establishes the background against which Foucault's archaeology (and later genealogy) must be thought, since his selection of different "moments" and the concentration on precise historical timeframes serve as the essential support for his analyses. The discontinuity element of Foucault's archaeology (which is characterized as Foucault's research methodology at least up until the beginning of the 1970s) designates not a historical investigation in the formal sense (a reconstitution of a historical field, outlining the continuous evolution of ideas), but, by bringing together diverse dimensions together, an attempt to "obtain the conditions of emergence of discourses of knowledge in general in a given epoch."[16] Such an attempt emphasizes the emergence of the new rather than the rediscovery of former conditions of possibility: "It is a discourse of historical emergence rather than philosophical origin."[17]

The idea of "essential dishomogeneity," according to Agamben, forms the basis of Foucault's essay "Nietzsche, Genealogy, History" (1971) where Genealogy (whose model Foucault finds traces of in Nietzsche, particularly in *Human, All Too Human* [1878], *The Gay Science* [1882] and *On the Genealogy of Morals* [1887]) is positioned against the search for an origin. At the historical beginning of things, the genealogist will never find "[T]he 'inviolable identity of their origin.' . . . [W]ill never neglect as inaccessible all the episodes of history. . . . [W]ill cultivate the details and accidents that accompany every beginning. . . . The genealogist needs history to dispel the chimeras of the origin."[18] The true object of genealogy (or genealogical research) is thus not the exact essence of things but, following the logic of the "essential dishomogeneity," what Foucault calls "descent" or "emergence, the moment of arising," which is qualitatively different from the empirical origin and what follows it historically. The question remains: what kind of object is "the moment of arising," and where exactly is it located if never at the "non-place of the origin"?

GLOSS IV—GENEALOGY

In "Nietzsche, Genealogy, History," genealogy is described as "gray, meticulous, and patiently documentary. . . . [It is a practice that] must record the singularity of events outside of any monotonous finality; must seek them in the most unpromising places, in what we tend to feel is without history."[19] Foucault distinguishes, among the terms employed by Nietzsche, between *Ursprung* (which is reserved, somewhat ironically, for "origin" albeit negatively) and the two terms that are more exact than *Ursprung* in recording the true object of genealogy: *Herkunft* ("descent") and *Entstehung* ("emergence, the moment of arising").

The genealogist who examines the descent (with its "subtle, subindividual marks") constructs, as Foucault quotes Nietzsche's term from *The Gay Science* (1882), "cyclopean monuments," not by a regression in time in order to restore "an unbroken continuity that operates beyond the dispersion of oblivion," nor by an attempt to demonstrate "that the past actively exists in the present, that it continues secretly to animate the present,"[20] but by revealing "the myriad events through which they were formed," and maintaining these events "in their proper dispersion" only to realize that "truth or being lies not at the root of what we know and what we are but the exteriority of accidents."[21] The search for the descent does not wish to secure foundations but conversely to destabilize what was previously considered founded to fragment what was thought unified; and if the genealogist "listens to history," he or she finds that "there is 'something altogether different' behind things: not a timeless and essential secret, but the secret that they have no essence," that their origin has no inviolable identity. Thus the genealogist rummages in history, in the "concrete body of becoming," not searching for any "distant ideality of the origin"[22] as the metaphysician does but for all the imprints left on the historical body up to the point of its destruction.

Genealogy ("seen as the examination of *Herkunft* and *Entstehung*"), writes Foucault, as opposed to history in the traditional sense is, for Nietzsche, a kind of "historical sense" that, contrary to a form of history that reintroduces a "suprahistorical perspective" and strives for a presentation of completed development based on its "belief in eternal truth, the immortality of the soul, and the nature of consciousness as always identical to itself,"[23] can evade metaphysics if it refuses the certainty of absolutes; but if otherwise—if "mastered by suprahistorical perspective," it can be bent by metaphysics to its own purposes. "The traditional device for constructing a comprehensive view of history and for retracing the past as a patient and continuous development must be systematically dismantled"—historical sense, as opposed to a historical tradition that aims at "dissolving the singular event into an ideal continuity," deals with events "in terms of their most unique characteristics, their most acute manifestations."[24]

For Foucault, one of genealogy's leading goals is to show specifically how the various "ways of life" come to be as they are and how they oppressively marginalize other people. The context of *Entstehung* ("*emergence*, the moment of arising") is that of power dynamics, systems of subjection and dominations, and it is always produced in a particular state of forces where a battle was won against certain concrete conditions—emergence is thus the entry of forces. A second leading goal is to develop interruptive knowledges that can lead to liberating options for those marginalized people. Having its roots in Nietzsche's thought, Foucault's genealogy accepts the former's insight that "formations of knowledge and values are always also formations of power (in Foucault's jargon, formations of power relations)"[25]; thus knowledge creation is a phenomenon that must be described in terms of power. Archaeological and genealogical studies are not mutually exclusive in Foucault's view; rather their different emphases are mutually supportive ("Archaeology focuses on the emergence and formation of various mutational, regulatory, and guiding structures. . . . Genealogy focuses on relations of power and their dynamic mode of operation").[26] Foucault's Genealogy thus has both political and ethical dimensions.

Although the theoretical discontinuity between Foucault's conception of archaeology (as in the archaeology of knowledge) and genealogy (as in the genealogy of power) might seem quite abrupt, in fact a closer reading (and cross-referencing other "secondary" sources by Foucault) might reveal a more gradual shift between them. Once "Nietzsche, Genealogy, History" is published, which is often seen as a marker for Foucault's introduction of the term *genealogy* (and his explicit focus on power) from the early 1970s onward, it seems that Foucault attempts to use the term in order to elaborate a certain perspective that archaeology alone could not capture, not as a complete replacement for the latter. Thus, crude periodization of Foucault's work, in this sense, is rather hard to maintain.[27]

Stephen Howard reflects upon the relation between archaeology and genealogy in Foucault as well as in Agamben, in an attempt to articulate the influence of Foucault's method on Agamben's work (especially since the latter formally declares such influence, being a stepping stone for his own methodology, in the preface to *The Signature of All Things*).[28]

Howard's argument is as follows: although Agamben claims to develop Foucault's archaeological and genealogical methodology at large (mainly in Foucault's works on governmentality, power, and biopolitics), the fact is that Agamben's methodology deviates significantly from Foucault's. How can that be?

In *Society Must Be Defended: Lectures at the Collège de France 1970–1971* (which marks Foucault's methodological shift around 1976), Foucault defines genealogy as the coupling of the two elements of what he terms "subjugated knowledge," that is, the buried historical conditions of possibilities of modern institutions (on the one hand) and disqualified knowledge of marginalized subjects (on the other hand). This coupling of, in other words, scholarly erudition and local memories contributes to a historical knowledge of struggles and the utilization of that knowledge in contemporary tactics. The aim of Foucault's genealogy is to de-subjugate historical knowledges, to reactivate local knowledges against scientific hierarchization of knowledge, and to free subjugated knowledge from its marginalized position and reactivate it for political ends. Foucault succinctly summarizes the relation between archaeology and genealogy: "Archaeology is the method specific to the analysis of local discursivities, and genealogy is the tactic which, once it has described these local discursivities, brings into play the subjugated knowledges that have been released from them."[29] Genealogy demands relentless erudition because it first requires archaeology's technical analysis; and after the analysis unveils the buried conditions of what had become the norm, genealogy then connects this analysis to the reactivation of marginalized knowledge. Foucault, as we have seen, builds upon Nietzsche's idea of *Entstehung* by claiming that *Entstehung* is the "entry of forces" and "play of dominations," thus norms have history and arise in particular contexts. The insurrection of subjugated knowledge made possible by the genealogical combination of archaeological erudition and a politically motivated reactivation of marginalized knowledge.[30]

Throughout his entire oeuvre and specifically in *The Signature of All Things*, Agamben conflates archaeology and genealogy; and his understanding of these terms distances his methodology from Foucault's. Although Agamben claims that their methodologies differ only in terms of the length of the historical shadow rather than in anything essential and intrinsic to their corresponding methodologies, it seems as if Agamben remains, methodologically, within the archaeological period of Foucault's thought. Agamben's patient scholarly attention to literary sources and manuscripts amounts to Foucault's idea of the work of the archaeologist. If this is true, asks Howard, can Agamben "be accused of ultimately indulging in what Foucault called the 'great, tender, and warm freemasonry of useless erudition'?"[31] His answer is no; and to demonstrate this, he looks into Agamben's method as manifested in *The Highest Poverty: Monastic Rules and Form-of-Life*, highlighting the political significance of Agamben's conflation of archaeology and genealogy (and thus showing that he is not merely an archaeologist in Foucault's sense).

Agamben's work in *The Highest Poverty* demonstrates that he does not subsume genealogy under archaeology but draws the two methods into equivalence or understands them as indistinct. In this book, Agamben had a political ambition—to return to a path not taken in the history of the West, to reactivate a conception of "use" that was available to the Franciscans but which they failed to develop. He accomplishes this through an archaeological reading of texts, a scholarly operation that should be in itself political. In what manner is this operation political? The answer lies, according to Howard, in the *methodological* importance of Benjamin to the Agambenian method (even though it might seem, in *The Signature of All Things*, that Foucault has the most significant influence; thus Foucault is less the source of Agamben's method than the subject of interpretation); in other words, Benjamin provides not only Agamben's undiscussed methodological principle (as stated in the introduction to *The Signature of All Things*) but also the key to Agamben's interpretation of the Foucauldian method.

Agamben's Benjaminian principle of "messianic-time" or "now-time" (explained and elaborated in a later chapter in this book) entails that archaeology (the patient, erudite attention to dusty texts) can itself have political effects, thus no further genealogical step is required (in contrast to Foucault's approach that combines, in his genealogy, archaeological erudition with the reactivation of marginalized knowledge). Howard writes: "In Agamben's conflation of Foucault's archaeology and genealogy, subjugated knowledges are reactivated not through genealogies of modern institutions and forms of knowledge; but through the archaeological analysis itself."[32] Agamben and Foucault differ in their account of the forces of history: for Foucault these are contingent forces, which determine the historical shift in the meaning of our notions, real forces that are the struggle of power; for Agamben the force of history is not a real, historical struggle over meaning, but rather the force of the *arché* (as origin) itself, which is neither chronological nor empirical per se, and which relates to Benjamin's idea of "messianic-time" and the eruption of the past into the present in an object's "now of knowability." Agamben's archaeology and genealogy is thus an interpretation of Foucault's methodology conditioned by the influence of Benjamin. Agamben's (Benjaminian) interpretations of the methodologies of archaeology and genealogy conflate what in Foucault are two distinct approaches. Foucault's genealogy aims for a more direct political intervention than his archaeology by "saving" oppressed knowledge, while Agamben's detailed readings manifest an archaeological method that intends to be in itself political without the need for a further genealogical step (as it already includes a [Benjaminian] temporal, historical, and thus political, element). Although Agamben considers Foucault and Overbeck (as we will now turn to) to be his sources for the concepts of "origin" and "emergence," which underpin his philosophical methodology, Howard's claim is that they stem more from Benjamin. Agamben's methodological transformation of Foucault requires the acceptance of Benjamin's conception of history if it is to share the political ambitions of Foucault's genealogy.

Agamben traces the discussion of genealogy's dishomogeneity (beyond Foucault and Nietzsche) back to the German theologian Franz Overbeck. According to Overbeck, genealogy's research object of "the moment of arising," which is a fringe or heterogenous stratum within the life of a historical phenomenon, "is not placed in the position of a chronological origin but is qualitatively other."[33] In his research on the origin of the patristic literature, he names it "prehistory" (*Urgeschichte*), although the prefix "pre" should not indicate chronology; it need not be understood as the most historically ancient past, since prehistory's past is not homogeneous with history's past and "is not tied to any specific site in time." The original (somewhat untranslatable to English) German prefix "*Ur*" is more apt in this instance since it is better equipped to convey prehistory's fundamental character, which is to be "the history of the moment of arising" rather than the history of its development, as well as the idea that prehistory is "a constitutive heterogeneity inherent in historical inquiry itself, which each time must confront a past of a, so to speak, special type." This means, for Overbeck, that every historical phenomenon splits itself into prehistory and history according to a qualitative difference that is not time dependent—a differentiation that is based on their different *qualities* thus requires "different methodologies and precautions." Agamben brings as an example to this required precaution the case of the division between the religious and the profane juridical spheres: should we hypothesize the existence of a more archaic stage beyond both spheres in which they supposedly are not yet separated, we will in fact be at risk of projecting upon the presupposed unified phase the characteristics defining both spheres, characteristics "[w]hich are precisely the outcome of the split. Just as. . . . [W]hat stands prior to the historical division is not necessarily the sum of the characteristics defining its fragments. . . . In this sense, too, prehistory is not homogenous with history and the moment of arising is not identical with what comes to be through it."[34]

The distinction between prehistory and history means that the historical efficacy of a phenomenon is bound up with this distinction, and that the dishomogeneity of every historical inquiry is thus a subjective datum that is, according to Agamben, embedded within the inquiry and guides it. Engaging this constitutive heterogeneity is crucial for whomever wishes to practice historical research and can be carried out as a critique of tradition and sources. This critique concerns, above all, "the mode in which the past has been constructed into a tradition," not in terms of chronological projections but in terms of the very structure of historical inquiry. It constitutes a critical view on a certain tradition in which the withdrawal to the past will eventually coincide with "renewed access to the sources" (previously unattainable due to the mechanism of "canonization" in Overbeck's terms) and will thus enable new epistemological possibilities in the present.[35]

Archaeology is thus a historical inquiry that has to do with the moment of a phenomenon's arising and that must not only engage anew with the sources and tradition but also must confront the various mechanisms through which tradition regulates and conditions what it transmits. The emergence of a historical phenomenon (its moment of arising, its *arché* as we have outlined it thus far) that archaeology seeks to reach cannot be localized in a remote past nor beyond this in a metahistorical, a-temporal structure. It represents a present and operative tendency within the historical phenomenon that conditions and makes intelligible its development in time. As Agamben concludes: "It is an *arche*, but, as for Foucault and Nietzsche, it is an *arche* that is not pushed diachronically into the past, but assures the synchronic comprehensibility and coherence of the system."[36]

Before continuing to elaborate on our investigation of archaeology as a historical inquiry, we need to further articulate the concept of the *arché* and to touch upon a few of its important elements to our discussion: (1) the tension between its chronological and morphological characteristics and the consequence this tension presents to the concept of temporality and history; (2) the philological history of the word *arché* in the philosophical discourse; and (3) the particular manner in which the structure of the *arché* is reflected within the cultural (operative) mechanism of the West.

GLOSS V—ARCHÉ

(1) In *Introduction to the Reading of Hegel: Lectures on the Phenomenology of Spirit* (originally published in French as *Introduction à la lecture de Hegel* in 1947), Alexandre Kojève puts forth the somewhat ironic idea that *Homo sapiens* has reached a final moment in its history in which there are only two possible options left open for it: on one hand, the "Post-Historical Animality" exemplified, according to Kojève, by the

American way of life (this was just an ironical-metaphysical remark) and, on the other hand, what he called "Japanese Snobbism," by which he meant a continuation of historical rituals devoid of any historical content.[37] We can try to imagine a third possibility of a relation to the past beyond Kojève's two suggestions, one in which a culture remains human, even after its history has supposedly finished, because it is able to confront its own history in its totality and find a new life in it. This is a conception that finds a historical phenomenon most interesting and alive when it is, in fact, finished. Once the history had reached its fulfillment, it can gain a new life precisely because one has managed to remain in the correct relationship with it, thus the ability to remain in a relation to the past means it is still alive and becomes present again.

This idea approximately resembles Walter Benjamin's idea of "the now of legibility" or "the now of knowability." Agamben explores this Benjaminian concept in relation to the *arché* (or the origin) in his essay "Walter Benjamin and the Demonic: Happiness and Historical Redemption,"[38] where two forms of historical consciousness are depicted: one that understands all human work (and the past) as an origin destined to an infinite process of transmission "that preserves its intangible and mythic singularity"; the other, as the inverted specular image of the first, liquidates and flattens out the singularity of the origin "by forever multiplying copies and simulacra."[39] These attitudes are not in opposition but rather are two faces of a cultural tradition in which the content of transmission and transmission itself are so irreparably fractured that this tradition can only ever repeat the origin infinitely or annul it in simulacra. The origin itself can be neither fulfilled nor mastered, the idea of the origin contains both singularity and reproducibility, and as long as one of them remains in force, according to Agamben, every intent to overthrow both is destined to fail. It is as if for Benjamin the revolutionary value that is implicit in the image of the eternal return can exasperate mythical repetition up to the point of bringing it to a halt.

In his book *The Origin of the German Tragic Drama*, Benjamin conceives of the origin not as a logical category but as a historical one:

> Origin [Ursprung], although an entirely historical category, has, nevertheless, nothing to do with genesis [Entstehung]. The term origin is not intended to describe the process by which the existent came into being, but rather to describe that which emerges from the process of becoming and

disappearance. Origin is an eddy in the stream of becoming, and in its current it swallows the material involved in the process of genesis. That which is original is never revealed in the naked and manifest existence of the factual; its rhythm is apparent only to a dual insight. On the one hand it needs to be recognized as a process of restoration and re-establishment, but, on the other hand, and precisely because of this, as something imperfect and incomplete. There takes place in every original phenomenon a determination of the form in which an idea will constantly confront the historical world, until it is revealed fully, in the totality of its history. . . . The category of the origin is not . . . a purely logical one, but a historical one.[40]

The idea of origin here is akin to Goethe's concept of Urphänomen:[41] it is not a factual event nor a mythical archetype but rather a vortex in the stream of becoming, manifesting itself through a double structure of restoration and incompleteness. In the origin, there is a dialectic that reveals every original phenomenon to be a reciprocal conditioning of "onceness" and repetition. In every original phenomenon, what is at play is an Idea that confronts the historical world until it is completed in the totality of its history (the theory of origin is tied to the theory of Idea).[42]

Benjamin speaks about his concept of origin as a transposition of Goethe's Urphänomen (which belongs to the domain of nature) to the domain of history; in other words, origin is in effect the concept of Urphänomen extracted from the pagan context of nature and brought into the Jewish context of history.[43]

Benjamin's explicit morphological awareness enables him to oppose the historical-chronological genesis to the morphological origin. This opposition highlights a possible polar tension working within the concept of temporality and/or that of history: on one hand, there is the historical dream of the traditional, historical quest for the first element of the iconic linear chain from which every other element can be drawn through proper transformation; on the other hand, the morphological gaze presents a radial structure where the various manifestations gather around the Urphänomen in a nonlinear way.

Agamben revisits the Benjaminian concept of the origin-as-vortex in "Vortexes,"[44] beginning with a similar, slightly deviated statement:

> The origin [*Ursprung*] stands in the flux of becoming as a vortex and rips into its rhythm the material of emergence [*Entstehung*]. . . . On the one hand, that which is original wants to be recognized as restoration and reestablishment, but, on the other hand, and precisely because of this, as something incomplete and unconcluded. There takes place in every original phenomenon a determination of the figure in which an idea will constantly confront the historical world. Origin is not, therefore, discovered by the examination of actual findings, but it is related to their pre- and post-history. The category of origin is not therefore, as Cohen holds, a purely logical one, but a historical one.[45]

Origin, for Benjamin, does not precede a phenomenon's becoming nor is separated from its chronology; origin autonomously dwells in a phenomenon but also derives its matter from it. Origin accompanies historical becoming, and like a vortex, is still present in it. The whirling origin that archaeological investigation tries to reach, writes Agamben, is an *arché*, a "historical a priori that remains immanent to becoming and continues to act in it. Even in the course of our life, the vortex of the origin remains present until the end and silently accompanies our existence at every moment."[46] For Agamben, the "correct" relation to the past[47]—this dialectic in the origin—echoes the *arché* in archaeology, which is not simply a historical fact that exhausts itself (as it is situated in a chronology) nor a meta-historical archetype but something immanent within history, internal to it, which cannot coincide with a precise chronological moment nor is simply a historical fact given in chronology.

(2) This conception is evident in the *arché*'s double meaning (in Greek),[48] which has its origin in the theological idea according to which God created the world but also continuously governs it. The word *arché* entered philosophical language around the time of Plato and Aristotle. Aristotle historically innovated the use of the concept in the sense of uniting both meanings into the same single abstract concept, and until the end of antiquity it remained, according to Reiner Schürmann, "a technical term for designating the constitutive, abstract, and irreducible element in being, becoming, and knowing,"[49] an abstract element that cannot be surpassed. The doctrine of origin, for Aristotle, "is a doctrine of a material substance from which things arise in order to return to it as

to their primordial element,"[50] but the *arché* itself is not an entity (nor supreme being) that creates and governs change, but only the common trait of the different types of causes.

In the second half of the twentieth century, three important attempts were made to theoretically wedge this dual meaning of the *arché*. The first was that of Schürmann in his interpretation of Heidegger in *Heidegger On Being and Acting: From Principals to Anarchy* (*Le principe d'anarchie: Heidegger et la question de l'agir*, 1982). He tried to separate the two meanings of the *arché*, to reach an *arché* only as a pure coming to being (to the present) without any pretention of commanding an historical development. This is, according to Schürmann, an anarchical interpretation of Heidegger, as Heidegger (perhaps paradoxically) was trying to reach an anarchical principle that would not command any historical development. The second attempt (and second interpretation of Heidegger) was that of Derrida, and his idea/methodology of deconstruction. He also tried to separate the origin from its commanding function; however, unlike Schürmann, who opposed the two, Derrida put in question the notion of the origin. For Derrida there is no origin, only trace, but precisely because of that, one can infinitely deconstruct. The third possibility of dealing with this dichotomy or duality comes from Foucault and his idea of the historical a priori: Foucault's critique of the origin in history and the favoring of the idea of the "point of emergence," that is, the point when something appears with no consequences or aspirations of commandment. He draws this idea most probably from Husserl's in *Origin of Geometry*, but while for Husserl this idea (of the historical a priori) means a universal category, for Foucault this implies a very concrete meaning (e.g., the Indo-European language as an historical a priori: it is a priori because it makes understandable concrete historical phenomena, and it is historical not because we have written evidence of its existence but because we have to presuppose that it had existed).

The earlier remark that the word *arché* was introduced into philosophical jargon roughly in the times of Plato and Aristotle requires slight amendment since one can retrace its appearance even farther back in time. In his essay on the *arché* (and its relation to the *apeiron*, the infinity, and the current sociopolitical order in the West), Stathis Gourgouris maintains that the word *arché* first appears as a philosophical principle in the well-known Anaximander fragment,[51] written around 570 BCE (although the word itself is already present in textual traces going back to Homer), where it is conjugated with a new concept: *apeiron* (infinity).

Reading Anaximander's fragment, Gourgouris makes the clear argument: "[T]he notion of *archē* (origin and rule) is first used philosophically in order to identify what has no origin and no end and over which there can be no rule."[52] He thus establishes two essential elements: The first is that the *archē* is infinite but at the same time is understood as the source of all things, a source not external to all things since (as finite things) they eventually decay and return to become source again. Source is not *Ursprung* in terms of being the one and only origin, but "an infinite space of interminably enacted beginnings of an indefinite array of 'things' that have one thing in common: they terminate."[53] The *apeiron* is not only limitless but also cannot be completed; the infinite is also incomplete. Thus, the paradox is that the incomplete/infinite enables the emergence of the complete/finite, an emergence that is a disturbance of the infinite, thus "the finitude of existence is thus justified by its very violation of the infinite." The infinite (*apeiron*) is not only the unlimited and incomplete but also whatever exceeds experience (*peira*) and cannot be empirically determined. Thus, the infinite (*apeiron*) cannot be empirically known; it is interminable and indeterminable—it has no *telos*, no finality, no termination: "it lacks de-finition, de-limitation, de-termination." The second of Gourgouris's elements is that the disturbance of the infinite by finitude also means that the infinite is not omnipotent, for it is thus crossed by time. Time decays things and by doing so opens infinity to their readmittance and return; thus, the infinite source is "a sort of repository, a burial ground, of what has come into the world and has gone out of it."[54] The condition of things entering the world, and necessarily going out of it, constitutes injustice (*adikia*). In other words, "Time itself constitutes an injustice, which the infinite, though an *archē*, can neither overrule nor alleviate."[55] Worldly things unsettle the "cosmic balance" that the relation between infinity and time attempts to maintain (i.e., infinity holds together a balance of contentious forces, where one *kratos* [power] cannot overcome another), since matter is subject to time and thus defies the infinite, but simultaneously, matter returns to infinity and thus defies time. "This unsettling of balance, this injustice, is life itself—the tragic life, from which there is no redemption."[56] This archaic Ionian imaginary, writes Gourgouris, for which finitude itself constitutes an injustice,[57] provides justice (*dikē*) by determining that one makes its own limits in the course of life "while submitting unredemptively to the ultimate limit of death."[58] Throughout man's life, potentially unlimited, one's infinite imagination partakes in the abyssal infinite and therefore is required to authorize one's own limits, to create or *poietize* (*poiein*) these limits.

Gourgouris quotes Jean-Pierre Vernant's reading of Aristotle[59] regarding the *apeiron*, according to which infinity is not another force in the cosmos, but the intermediary between the elements, what exists in the middle (*meson*) of them: "[T]he mediating space of the elements—the *medium* of a limitless abyssal terrain—on which the limit and capacity for self-limitation in every element is tested . . . [:] the limitless is a mediatory field that enables limits to be self-instituted."[60] Thus, the importance of the middle (*meson*) is not only figurative, as a mediatory space but should also be considered in geometric terms, as a central space from which all elements are equally distanced due to the balance they are forced to maintain at all times (recall Benjamin's elucidation [via Goethe] of the radial morphological structure of the concept of temporality and history); the geometrics of *meson*, of mediation and middle, thus "irrevocably alters an understanding of *archē* as the fixed point of origin and primary rule."[61] Not only is the *archē* not constituted as a primordial whole, but simultaneously it is cleft and permeated, and this condition renders it a condition of mediation. "The *archē* becomes a shared space of mediation that thereby disrupts the constitution or reconstitution of absolute singular (literally monarchical) rule/origin," and moreover, "the *archē*'s interminable generation from the matrix of the infinite is preserved by finitude, the same finitude that its necessity is expressed by the 'ordinance of time.' "[62]

(3) In *The Use of Bodies*, Agamben advances the claim that the structure of the *arché*, in Western culture at large, is determined and constituted by a "structure of exception"; in other words, the structure of exception has been revealed more generally to constitute in every sphere the structure of the *arché*. According to this idea, the originary structure of Western culture consists in an *ex-ceptio*, in an inclusive exclusion of human life.[63] The dialectic of the foundation that defines Western ontology is understood only as the function of this exception: "The strategy is always the same: something is divided, excluded, and pushed to the bottom, and precisely through this exclusion, it is included as *archè* and foundation."[64] The mechanism[65] at work is always the same (whether in relation to the juridico-political [*State of Exception*]; or between rule and governance and between inoperativity and glory [*The Kingdom and the Glory*]; or between the human being and animal [*The*

Open]): the *arché* is constituted by dividing the factual experience and pushing down to the origin—that is, excluding—one half of it in order then to rearticulate it to the other by including it as foundation. Thus, for example, "The city is founded on the division of life into bare life and politically qualified life, the human is defined by the exclusion-inclusion of the animal, the law by the *exceptio* of anomie, governance through the exclusion of inoperativity and its capture in the form of glory."[66] If the structure of the *arché* of our culture is such, claims Agamben, then philosophical archaeology is not a matter of thinking new articulations of the two elements (playing them against each other), nor a matter of an archaeological regression to a more originary beginning but one that may result from the deactivation of the machine. In this sense, following Agamben, first philosophy is always final philosophy.[67]

Moreover, according to Agamben, the anarchist tradition and (parts of) twentieth-century thought are pertinent but insufficient attempts to go back to a historical a priori in order to depose it. The practice of the artistic avant-garde and political movements of our time was often a miserably failed attempt to actualize a destitution of work, an attempt that ended up re-creating in every place the museum apparatus and the powers that it pretended to depose, which nowadays become even more oppressive insofar as they are deprived of all legitimacy. If it is true, as Agamben maintains, that the bourgeois is the most anarchic (Benjamin) and that true anarchy is that of power (Pasolini), then the thought that seeks to think anarchy (as negation of "origin" and "command," *principium* and *princeps*) remains imprisoned in endless *aporias* and contradictions. "Because power is constituted through the inclusive exclusion (*ex-ceptio*) of anarchy, the only possibility of thinking a true anarchy coincides with the lucid exposition of the anarchy internal to power. Anarchy is what becomes thinkable only at the point where we grasp and render destitute the anarchy of power."[68]

[3]

The term "archaeology," which nowadays (as stated previously) is largely associated with Foucault's investigations, appears in his texts (albeit in a somewhat different form) already in the preface to his renowned early work *The Order of Things* (1966).

GLOSS VI—ARCHAEOLOGY

The word "archaeology" belongs, at least philosophically, to Michel Foucault but no less also to Maurice Merleau-Ponty (and others, as we will see), who had already characterized his own thinking using the same terminology in the 1950s—one can thus speak of the prehistory of archaeology before it came to be prominently associated with Foucault.[69] Merleau-Ponty's proximity to Foucault lies in a concern for the profound spatiality of "archaeology" that is characterized by a lack, gap, hollow, or divergence. An increasing distance between them lies in their characterization of this lack in terms of transcendence or immanence.[70] Despite this distance (and their emphasis on spatiality at large), both Foucault and Merleau-Ponty refer to the past in their archaeological projects, a past that is somewhat still effective, still present, and one that "has always already been present": it is also a past that was never present and a past free for the future.

But as in most cases where we can identify someone who preceded the person previously thought to have conceptualized a certain matter, the case of the kind of past we are interested in here is no different. This past echoes, more or less, what Kant (1724–1804) called "a priori," what Husserl (1859–1938) called "transcendental subjectivity" or "Phenomenological Archaeology" (including Eugen Fink's writings on Husserl), and what Freud (1856–1939) called "the unconscious." These three thinkers thus also constitute the prehistory of the concept of "archaeology." Therefore, a concise summation of their ideas of archaeology is apposite and will be carried out in reverse chronology in order to come full circle to Kant, who is the main influence on Foucault's concept of archaeology [though Foucault is not always in keeping with Kant, and at times even contradicts Kant and Husserl (for example, his accusation of phenomenology being a "transcendental narcissism" or his wish to "free history from the grip of phenomenology."]][71]

According to Lawlor, by means of investigating the past, archaeology concerns itself in the transformation of the present. This concern comes from psychoanalysis (which is concerned, among other things, with curing the hysteric and not for investigating the past for its own sake), thus paradoxically archaeology is, in fact, interested in the future. This means another two characteristics of archaeology: on the one hand, as Freud says, the past that one returns to is always incomplete (and so the curing of the hysteria is always incomplete), thus the future cure is based (in addition to an incomplete past) on a reconstruction that is inventive; on the other hand, in order to find a future cure, the past must remain as a present and not really as a past—it must be conserved. Freud draws an analogy between the concept of the mind and ancient Rome, where everything is preserved, and thus the historical sequence of the mind is represented by juxtaposition in space; however, this is not a perfect analogy since in Rome there are intentional demolitions, whereas in the mind there are unintentional traumas (that can destroy remains of the past).[72] Although the past has an incomplete nature, the past remains intact in the unconscious (the processes of the unconscious are timeless for Freud, thus we should accept that there is an absolute memory, which is a memory not relative to consciousness). The idea of an absolute memory implies the fourth characteristic of archaeology: the displacement of the conscious subject. The analyst is like an explorer who finds ruins and who can operate in two ways: either to ask the inhabitant (patient) about the history and meaning of these remains or to encourage the inhabitant to excavate the scene; then things are deciphered (Freud's slogan is "stones talk"). This leads to the fifth characteristic: the dead monuments that nevertheless speak. In sum, the philosophical concept of archaeology is characterized by the following: its investigation of the past concerns the future; the past it investigates is incomplete. Yet, the past is conserved, juxtaposed, and simultaneous with the present. Present consciousness is not the object of archaeological investigation, and the object of interest is the monument that speaks for itself.

In his interpretation of Husserl, Fink defines Husserl's phenomenology in terms of the problem of Being or human access to Being through experiences. These experiences are not given (to consciousness) immediately but are mediated by tradition and forgetfulness, and in order to overcome this distance phenomenology engages in a regressive inquiry that aims at "re-establishing" what Fink calls "the initial knowledge forgotten in the buried traditions" and even aims at "returning to the immediate knowledge of the Being from which the traditions, even though they obscure, derived."[73] This regressive inquiry is not the psychical origin, a genesis of human thought, or psychological development. Instead, the phenomenological regressive's question concerning the beginning of knowledge attempts to grasp the human intellect in its movement toward the Being. The consciousness or subjectivity that phenomenology interrogates is transcendental and also includes the unconscious. Fink distinguishes *Wissen* from *Erkenntnis*, thereby anticipating Foucault's distinction between *savior* and *connaissance*.

Kant speaks of archaeology in (at least) three places: in *Anthropology from a Pragmatic Point of View*, the context is the "faculty of designation" and thus concerns signs; in *The Critique of Judgment*, he speaks about the "faculty of Nature" that concerns signs and traces (archaeology of nature distinguishes from natural history—the first describes *past* genera and species and thus passes through signs and traces, while the latter describes *present* ones and takes place by means of intuition); and in *Progress in Metaphysics*, as we saw earlier, he distinguishes between a mere history of philosophy (which presents the empirical and thus contingent order of how thinkers philosophized up to the present) and a philosophical history of philosophy (which is rational and necessary, thus a priori). Thus, Kant's philosophical archaeology concerns not the contingent, successive order of the history of philosophy but the rational and necessary order of philosophical concepts. Yet this order would still be historical since it would account only for this factual or singular set of concepts. Philosophical archaeology will constitute, with this necessary and yet factual order, a historical a priori. This archaeology, like that of nature, will proceed not by intuition but by means of signs. Kant's concept of philosophical archaeology implies that archaeology is a method of reading signs.[74]

The prehistory of the concept of archaeology, before Foucault and Merleau-Ponty, is summed up by Lawlor as follows: (1) archaeology concerns signs and traces of the past—that is—mediation, thus archaeology is not a form of intuition but a form of interpretation or regressive inquiry; (2) in the reading of signs, consciousness is displaced toward the unconscious that precedes it and had been conserved (and thus is incomplete). Therefore philosophical archaeology is a kind of an-archaeology—the complete origin is missing; (3) archaeology thus investigates the space of the unconscious, a spatial order that precedes consciousness or empirical/psychological genesis, thus is an order that can be called a priori; (4) although prior, this order is not an abstract a priori, but an a priori for these singular historical facts or signs; (5) in the investigation of this historical a priori, archaeology overcomes a kind of forgetfulness that implies it consists of memory; and (6) this memory is not really a memory of the past (it is not interested in the past for its own sake), but rather its interest is the future.[75]

Archaeology, in Foucault, means the description of a record. The word "record" does not designate a mass of texts that have been collected at a certain period for a certain social group but entails a discussion of rules. These rules define the limits of the forms of expressibility, conservation, memory, reactivation, and appropriation—these are the rules that a certain archaeology seeks to describe, and therefore to analyze, a discourse's conditions of existence.[76]

In an interview, Foucault refers to his conception of archaeology, understood as the science of an archive of a given period:

> By archeology I would like to designate not exactly a discipline, but a domain of research, which would be the following: In a society, different bodies of learning . . . refer to a certain implicit knowledge (*savour*) special to this society. . . . This knowledge is profoundly different from the bodies of learning that one can find in scientific books . . . but it is what makes possible at a given moment the appearance of a theory, an opinion, a practice.[77]

From this discussion derives the discourses' status of potential knowledge. Thus the Foucauldian archaeology means (in this sense, and not exclusively) an archaeology of knowledge where the archaeological metaphor signals knowledge as a substratum that "lies beneath a surface and needs to be uncovered before it can be understood."[78] It is the practice of an inquirer that deals with contingent historical facts regarding systems of knowledge, essentially through their lingual manifestations in written corpuses. These are not the formal rules of language, but the material rules that condition what can be said about the domain in question and thus condition the boundaries of a given "historical mode of thought"[79] or what Foucault calls the *episteme*.

Generally the concept of *episteme* is understood not as a worldview, theory, or framework but rather a set of elements from which a variety of conflicting worldviews, frameworks, and theories can be developed; in other words, the *episteme* reflects the relation that exists between discourses (a term that differs from another Foucauldian term, the *Archive*, which designates the set that encompasses these discourses).[80] The historiographic method of archaeology aims to reveal the differences or forms of nonidentity between the discourses rather than an underlying common identity that unites them.

Foucault's archaeology of knowledge does not have a purposely epistemological aim (reflecting upon the nature of knowledge in general), nor is it *épistémologie* in the French sense (thinking philosophically on the nature of scientific knowledge); rather it is a historical project that by going deep into a given field's cognitive structure, into its level of *savoir* (rather than operating merely at the level of *connaissance*, that is, the concepts and theories of particular sciences), also has epistemological repercussions.[81]

At the level of individuals, the *episteme* provides the locus from which individuals speak and know by limiting their potential for development. In *The Archaeology of Knowledge* (1969), Foucault gives a methodological reflection designed to provide historical accounts that "are not centered around the activities of human subjects and . . . have no place for a transcendental subject that is the source of historical meaning."[82] In his account of the "Foucauldian subject," Alain de Libera maintains that an unequivocal link exists between Foucault's rejection of the subject and his views on history, therefore criticizing (in the footsteps of Foucault) the role played by the sovereignty of consciousness (and by the sovereignty of subject) in history and opposing the idea of continuous history. He quotes from *The Archaeology of Knowledge* at length:

> Continuous history is the indispensable correlative of the founding function of the subject: the guarantee that everything that has eluded him may be restored to him; the certainty that time will disperse nothing without restoring it in a reconstituted unity; the promise that one day the subject—in the form of historical consciousness—will once again be able to appropriate, to bring back under his sway, all those things that are kept at a distance by difference, and find in them what might be called his abode. Making historical analysis the discourse of the continuous and making human consciousness the original subject of all historical development and all action are the two sides of the same system of thought. In this system, time is conceived in terms of totalization and revolutions are never more than moments of consciousness. In various forms, this theme has played a constant role since the nineteenth century: to preserve, against all decentrings, the sovereignty of the subject, and the twin figures of anthropology and humanism.[83]

Thus, according to de Libera, Foucault's archaeology not only aims to free history from the grip of the twin figures, that is, the constituent consciousness but also challenges the transcendental dimension as such.

∾

Archaeology, as we have seen, is presented in *The Order of Things* as an investigation into a dimension that is at once paradigmatic and transcendent, a kind of "historical *a priori*" where knowledge finds its structure and conditions of possibility (via the differentiation in the French language between *connaissance* and *savoir*).

But before we continue our reflection on the specific "historical a priori" dimension that Foucault's archaeology investigates epistemologically, let us elaborate more broadly on the concept itself (via Agamben's conception of it).

GLOSS VII—HISTORICAL A PRIORI

Based on discussions that were already started in earlier works (especially in *The Open*, 79–80), the second part of *The Use of Bodies* (titled "An Archeology of Ontology"), Agamben's final publication in his celebrated, decades-long series *Homo Sacer*, proposes to ascertain the current possibility to access first philosophy, or as Agamben synonymously paraphrases it, ontology.[84] First philosophy "opens and defines each time the space of human acting and knowing, of what the human being can do and of what it can know and say";[85] however, this space (the access to first philosophy) at least since Kant, has become so problematic that it is thinkable, according to Agamben, only in the form of an archaeology. Now, in Agamben's studies, any archaeological movement necessarily involves a relation, or is necessarily executed in relation, to language (that is beyond the obvious fact that a theoretical study is usually realized in and through language), thus ontology is considered by him as the originary place of the historical articulation between language and world and preserves in itself the memory of the anthropogenesis (the becoming human of the human being)—of the moment when that articulation was produced.[86] Anthropogenesis is not a completed event of the past but rather the event that never stops happening, a continuous process of the becoming human and remaining (or becoming) inhuman of the human being. First philosophy is the memory and repetition of this event: "It watches over the historical a priori of Homo sapiens, and it is to this historical a priori that archaeological research always seeks to reach back;"[87] and additionally:

> [W]hat is in question . . . in the Aristotelian ontological apparatus—and more generally, in every historical transformation of ontology . . . is the articulation between language and world that anthropogenesis has disclosed as "history" to the living beings of the species Homo sapiens. Severing the pure existent (the *that it is*) from the essence (the *what it is*) and inserting time and movement between them, the ontological apparatus reactualizes and repeats the anthropogenesis event, opens and defines each time the horizon of acting as well as knowing, by conditioning, in the sense that has been seen as a historical *a priori*, what human beings can do and what they can know and say.[88]

Shortly thereafter Agamben remarks succinctly: "In the preface to *Les mots et les choses* (1966), Foucault uses the term 'historical *a priori*' to define that which, in a determinate historical epoch, conditions the possibilities of the formation and development of knowledges."[89] He continues (in a long footnote):

> The expression is problematic, because it brings together two elements that are at least apparently contradictory: the *a priori*, which entails a paradigmatic and transcendental dimension, and history, which refers to an eminently factual reality. It is possible that Foucault had drawn the term from Husserl's *Origin of Geometry*, which Derrida had translated into French in 1962, but certainly not the concept, because while in Husserl the *historisches Apriori* designates a sort of universal *a priori* of history, it instead always refers in Foucault to a determinate knowledge and to a determinate time.[90]

The footnote continues:

> And yet, if it does not in any way refer back to an archetypal dimension beyond history but remains immanent to it, its contradictory formulation brings to expression the fact that

every historical study inevitably runs up against a constitutive dishomogeneity: that between the ensemble of facts and documents on which it labors and a level that we can define as archeological, which though not transcending it, remains irreducible to it and permits its comprehension. Overbeck (as was articulated, somewhat similarly, earlier) has expressed this heterogeneity by means of the distinction, in every study, between prehistory (*Urgeschichte*) and history (*Geschichte*), where prehistory does not designate what we usually understand by this term—that is, something chronologically archaic (*uralt*)—but rather the history of the point of emergence (*Entstehungsgeschichte*), in which the researcher must settle accounts with an originary phenomenon (an *Urphänomen* in Goethe's sense) and at the same time with the tradition that, while it seems to transmit the past to us, ceaselessly covers up the fact of its emergence and renders it inaccessible.

One can define philosophical archeology as the attempt to bring to light the various historical *a prioris* that condition the history of humanity and define its epochs. It is possible, in this sense, to construct a hierarchy of the various historical *a prioris*, which ascends in time toward more and more general forms. Ontology or first philosophy has constituted for centuries the fundamental historical *a priori* of Western thought.[91]

According to Agamben, from an archaeological perspective that herein attempts to reopen access to a first philosophy, the fact is that it is precisely the impossibility of a first philosophy that has become the historical a priori of the present time, beginning with Kant. This impossibility (which Kant called *Metaphysics*) is the true Copernican turn of Kantian critique (rather than the position of the subject).[92] Foucault, claims Agamben, had tried to rescue the survival of the impossibility of metaphysics with the stronghold of the transcendental (that is, "Being"), but the transcendental "necessarily entails a displacement of the historical a priori from the anthropogenesis event (the articulation between language and world) to knowledge, from a being that is no longer animal but not yet human to a knowing subject."[93] First philosophy becomes philosophy of knowledge.

Philosophers such as Nietzsche, Benjamin, Foucault, and Benveniste sought a way out of the transcendental by shifting the historical a priori back from knowledge to language, by isolating each time a dimension that called into question the pure fact of language, the pure being given of the enunciated, before or beyond their semantic content. "The speaking being or enunciator has thus been substituted for Kant's transcendental subject, and language has taken the place of being as historical *a priori*."[94]

Moreover, according to Agamben, language has superimposed itself over being. Language no longer functions as a historical a priori that determines and conditions the historical possibilities of speaking human beings but becomes totally identified with being, puts itself forward as a neutral ahistorical or posthistorical effectuality that no longer conditions any recognizable sense of historical becoming or any epochal articulation of time. This means that our time is not determined by any historical a priori; in other words, we find ourselves in a posthistorical time. From this perspective, Agamben's attempt is to trace out an archaeology of ontology, or to make a genealogy of the ontological apparatus that has functioned as the historical a priori of the West.[95]

It was previously said, regarding the epistemological dimension that Foucault's archaeology investigates, that this "historical *a priori*" dimension manifests the history of (a certain) knowledge's conditions of possibility; it is an epistemological field that Foucault termed *episteme*: not so much a place where ideas are historically revealed but where an inquiry attempts to discover "on what basis knowledge and theory became possible; within what space of order knowledge was constituted; on the basis of what historical a priori . . . ideas could appear,"[96] in other words, an unconscious category of the intellect that conditions the formation of knowledge. Furthermore, it was said, that Foucault's oxymoronic "historical *a priori*" attempts to underscore, according to Agamben's interpretation, that (although conditioning the historical experience) it is not a metahistorical origin that founds and determines knowledge, but the *episteme* is itself a historical practice.[97] That is, "The a priori that conditions the possibility of knowledge is its own history grasped at a specific level."[98] It is a concrete, ontological level of existence, a "brute fact" of its existing in a given time for a given society, the brute fact of its "moment of arising" (or, in Overbeck's terms, "prehistory").

Yet how could the a priori itself be embedded in a historical constellation? And how is it possible to gain access to it? Agamben asserts that the idea of the "historical *a priori*" as such originates more from Marcel Mauss's discussion of the idea of *mana* in his book *A General Theory of Magic* rather than from Kant's philosophical archaeology:

Mauss defines this historical transcendental as 'an unconscious category of understanding[,]' . . . suggesting in this way that the epistemological model required for such knowledge cannot be entirely homogeneous with that of conscious historical knowledge. . . . But as with Foucault, it is nevertheless clear that for Mauss the a priori, though conditioning historical experience, is itself inscribed within a determinate historical constellation. . . . In other words, it realizes the paradox of an a priori condition that is inscribed within a history and that can only constitute itself a posteriori with respect to this history in which inquiry—in Foucault's case, archaeology—must discover it.[99]

[4]

In *The Signature of All Things: On Method*, Agamben claims that Foucault did not question the unique temporal structure that seems to be indicated by the idea of a "historical *a priori*." Yet the past that is in question here, echoing previous ideas of such a past that we have seen so far (such as Kant's, Nietzsche's, and Overbeck's), is a unique type of past that neither predates the present (as origin) nor is plainly exterior to it. In his attempt to articulate the specific temporal structure of this past, Agamben assembles a series of paradigmatic examples from which I will concentrate on a few distinctive ones. These examples will serve us as a preliminary sketch to a later discussion regarding Agamben's conception of time as the basis for his conception of history.

The first example, relatively limited in scope, is that of Henri Bergson's conception of the phenomenon of déjà vu as it appears in his book *L'Énergie spirituelle* (1919). Bergson understands déjà vu as a phenomenon in which memory does not follow perception chronologically but occurs simultaneously with it and thus is able to produce "false perceptions" that he defines as "a memory of the present." This is a kind of memory that "is of the past in its form and of the present in its matter."[100] Similarly, according to Agamben, the condition of possibility in the "historical *a priori*" that the archaeologist is seeking to reach is not only contemporary with the present and the real but is an inherent and continuous part of them. The temporal structure of the "historical *a priori*" exemplifies a unique conception of the past that therefore enables the archaeologist pursuing such an a priori to "retreat, so to speak, towards the present." It is as if every historical phenomenon splits into prehistory and history ("a history of the sources and a historical tradition"), which are "in actuality contemporaneous, insofar as they coincide for an instant in the moment of arising."[101]

Similarly, another example (as a matter of fact, merely a note in Agamben's text, but an important one in the overall context) concerns Walter Benjamin's suggestion (in convolute N—Theory of Knowledge, Theory of Progress) that "the entire past must be brought into the present in a 'historical apocatastasis.'"[102] Benjamin's reference to eschatological reality (when a restitution of the origin will take place at the end of time), while characterizing it as historical, means a temporal structure that is similar to the "historical *a priori*."

Lastly, an elaborated example to the temporal structure of the ("historical *a priori*") past is that given in the work of the Italian philosopher Enzo Melandri. Reflecting upon the philosophical relevancy of Foucault's archaeology, writes Agamben, Melandri notices that while the codes and matrices of our culture are usually explicated by referring to a higher code that includes a mysterious explanatory force (this is the model of the "origin"), Foucault's archaeology suggests reversing the process, or better, "to make the explication of the phenomenon immanent in its description."[103] This means refuting any metahistorical structure (or metalanguage in Foucault's case, due to the centrality of language in his perimetric analysis) and, instead, favoring the model of the "historical *a priori*" while seeking (Melandri) to analyze its structure "vis-à-vis the Freudian opposition between the conscious and the unconscious." In order to perform his analysis—ultimately in order to arrive at his own conception of archaeology—Melandri first departs (just as Foucault) from a point rooted in Nietzsche, in particular his concept of "Critical History,"[104] indicating a history that criticizes and destroys the past in order to enable life in the present. However, Melandri, according to Agamben, generalizes Nietzsche's concept by connecting it to Freud's concept of regression, thus granting his concept of archaeology (which is based on a "Dionysian" regression in time) the role of the healer or the redeemer. Melandri writes:

> [Critical history] must retrace in the opposite direction the actual genealogy of events that it examines. The division that has been established between historiography and actual history

is quite similar to the one that, for Freud, has always existed between the conscious and the unconscious. Critical history thus has the role of a therapy aimed at the recovery of the unconscious, understood as the historical 'repressed.' . . . [This archeological process] consists in tracking genealogy back to where the phenomenon in question splits into the conscious and the unconscious. Only if one succeeds in reaching that point does the pathological syndrome reveal its real meaning. So it is a matter of *regression*: not to the unconscious as such, but to what made it unconscious.[105]

In contrast to the pessimistic vision of regression (which is "incapable of overcoming the original infantile scene"), Melandri's archaeology seems to be capable of a regression back to the point where the dichotomy between history and historiography (or conscious and unconscious when he relates his discussion to psychoanalysis) was produced, a regression not to a previous state (bringing the repressed back to consciousness) but to the moment that constituted it as such, to "the source of the split." In this sense, it is the opposite of rationalization, an archaeological operation, Agamben quotes, that "requires a 'Dionysian regression.' . . . To understand the past, we should equally traverse it *à reculons* [i.e., backwards]."[106] This "Dionysian regression" is an advance in time, a singular manifestation of the past's temporal structure, that turns its back to its final destination. It is the inverse, complementary advancement to that of the *Angelus Novus*—Walter Benjamin's well-known advancing "angel of history" described in his ninth thesis on the philosophy of history.[107] While Benjamin's angel advances toward the future as it gazes at the past, Melandri's angel regresses toward the past as it gazes at the future. Both advance toward an unidentifiable final destination—though we know that the destination of these two images of historical process is the present. At the end point of the archaeological regression, at the point where the split (between conscious and unconscious; actual history and historiography) produces the condition of our present experience, we realize that our way of representing the moment before the split is governed by the split itself and that we should not presuppose or expect (or try to represent) a kind of "golden age" beyond the dichotomy that is devoid of repressions. Rather, "before or beyond the split, in the disappearance of the categories governing its representation, there is nothing but the sudden, dazzling disclosure of the moment of arising, the revelation of the present as something that we were not able to live or think."[108]

Before we continue to follow Melandri's psychoanalytic path in our attempt to describe the archaeological regression and the special temporal form that we are interested in, we should make a few more prefatory remarks about Agamben's conception of time at large.

GLOSS VIII—THE CONTEMPORARY

An early indication for thinking about the time structure of philosophical archaeology can perhaps be found in an earlier text by Agamben titled *What Is the Contemporary?*[109] Constructing his arguments on the basis of Nietzsche's ideas of historical time, and specifically on Nietzsche's understanding of the contemporary as the untimely, Agamben writes that those who are truly contemporary, who truly belong to their time, are those who neither perfectly coincide with it nor adjust themselves to its demands; but precisely because of this condition, they are more capable than others of perceiving and grasping their own time. Contemporariness is, then, a singular relationship with one's own time, which adheres to it but also keeps a distance from it. Those who coincide too well with their time, those who are perfectly tied to it in every respect, are not contemporaries precisely because they do not manage to see it, they are not able to firmly hold their gaze on it.

Those who are contemporary, according to Agamben, are the ones who firmly hold their gaze on their own time so as to perceive not its light but rather its darkness. To perceive this darkness is not a form of inertia or passivity, but rather it implies an activity and a singular ability. This ability amounts to a neutralization of the light that comes from present time in order to discover its obscurity, its special darkness. The ones who can call themselves contemporary are those who do not allow themselves to be blinded by the lights of the century and so manage to get a glimpse of the shadows cast by those lights and their intimate obscurity. But there is a reverse and complementary movement or perception: it is to perceive, in the darkness of the present, the light that strives to reach us but cannot—this is what it means to be contemporary. It is, first and foremost, a question of courage because it necessitates the ability not only to firmly fix one's gaze on the darkness of the era but also to perceive in this darkness a light that, while directed toward us, infinitely distances itself from us. Our time, the present, is in fact not only the most distant but that which cannot reach us at all. Attempting to grasp it requires courage, and indeed as Agamben writes elsewhere (though in the broad context of the church, in reference to Benedict XVI's resignation of office—only the second resignation in the history of the Catholic Church): "Courage is nothing but the capacity to keep oneself connected with one's own end."[110]

There is another aspect, according to Agamben, to this special relationship with temporality in which we can see how contemporariness carves itself into the present "by marking it above all as archaic. Only he who perceives the indices and signatures of the archaic in the most modern and recent can be contemporary."[111] Being *archaic* amounts to being close to the *arché*, that is to say, the special type of origin that was already herein discussed, an origin that is "contemporary with historical becoming and does not cease to operate within it, just as the embryo continues to be active in the tissues of the mature organism, and the child in the psychic life of the adult. Both this distancing and nearness, that define temporariness, have their foundation in this proximity to the origin that nowhere pulses with more force than in the present."[112] In order to "enter" the present, we must perform archaeology, a practice that does not, however, regress to a historical past in a mere genealogical fashion but returns to that part within the present that we are absolutely incapable of living:

> What remains un-lived is therefore incessantly sucked back towards the origin without ever being able to reach it. The present is nothing other than this un-lived element in everything that is lived. That which impedes access to the present is precisely the mass of what for some reason (its traumatic character, its excessive nearness) we have not managed to live. The attention to this 'un-lived' is the life of the contemporary. And to be contemporary means, in this sense, to return to a present where we have never been.[113]

However, we should not naively assume a supposedly one-directional, archaeological movement in time. Our conception of contemporariness must also assume time's ability to repenetrate or refold back onto itself as if to form a porous structure—being able to think time as splitting into several times, thus introducing to it an essential dis-homogeneity, a kind of caesura in which time is being inscribed. But, claims Agamben, "precisely by means of this caesura, this interpolation of the present into the inert homogeneity of linear time, the contemporary puts to work a special relationship between the different times. If, as we have seen, it is the contemporary who has broken the vertebrae of his time, then he also makes of this fracture a meeting place, or an encounter between times and generations."[114] Thus the contemporary is not only the one who manages (via the double, two-sided movement in time) to capture, in the present, the darkness and the light that can never reach its destiny but is also

> the one who, dividing and interpolating time, is capable of transforming it and putting it in relation with other times. He is able to read history in unforeseen ways, to 'cite it' according to a necessity that does not arise in any way from his will, but from an exigency to which he cannot not respond. It is as if this invisible light that is the darkness of the present cast its shadow on the past so that the past, touched by this shadow, acquired the ability to respond to the darkness of the now.[115]

[5]

If we have conjured a somewhat psychoanalytic vocabulary, it is to help us form an analogy to the archaeological regression. The idea, writes Agamben, that the present might be given in the form of a "constitutive inaccessibility" is bound up with Freud's theory and understanding of what repression essentially means. In the context of psychoanalysis, repression is discussed through the event of trauma according to which an experience is repressed due to its traumatic character or because the conscious mind is unable to accept its consequences. Throughout the latent period of its repression, as if it had never taken place, the event nonetheless keeps on living, somewhat in secrecy, only to reappear later in the form of "neurotic symptoms or oneiric content." Only a successful analysis, according to Freud, can go beyond the symptoms back to the repressed event and heal the patient. The present's form of "constitutive inaccessibility" is further supported by the (psychoanalytic) idea, brought up by Agamben and set forth by Cathy Caruth in *Unclaimed Experience: Trauma, Narrative, and History*, that latency is constitutive of historical experience and that one can experience a (preserved) traumatic event precisely and only through its forgetting. In other words, the inherent latency—the inherent forgetting—within the traumatic experience itself, made it available to be experienced from the outset. This is the trauma's historical power, and thus "history can be grasped only in the very inaccessibility of its occurrence." From these ideas (and previous ones we mentioned, such as Bergson's conception of déjà-vu), Agamben concludes, with reference to archaeology, that both memory and forgetfulness

> are contemporaneous with perception and the present. While we perceive something, we simultaneously remember and forget it. Every present thus contains a part of non-lived experience. . . . This means that it is above all the unexperienced, rather than just the experienced, that gives shape and consistency to the fabric of psychic personality and historical tradition and ensures their continuity and consistency.[116]

In both cases (of psychoanalysis and archaeological regression), the past, which was never really experienced and therefore "technically cannot be defined as 'past,'" remains as a present—either in the form of neurotic symptoms (as in the Freudian schema) or, in the case of genealogy, in the form of canonization that only patient work focusing on "the moment of arising" (rather than searching for an origin) can gain access beyond tradition. Yet contrary to the analytic work of psychoanalysis, which if successful withdraws to the originary event and brings back to consciousness all the content that has been repressed in the unconscious, the archaeological regression withdraws further and reaches a threshold where memory and forgetting (or lived and nonlived experiences) both communicate with and separate from each other. In its withdrawal, genealogical inquiry does not search for the phenomenon's origin but focuses on its "moment of arising"; it does not wish (as in Freud) to restore a previous stage but, as Agamben writes,

> to go back not to its content but to the modalities, circumstances, and moments in which the split, by means of repression, constituted it as origin. . . . It does not will to repeat the past, . . . it wills to let it go . . . in order to gain access beyond the past to what has never been. . . . Only

at this point is the un-lived past revealed for what it was: contemporary with the present. It thus becomes accessible for the first time, exhibiting itself as a "source."[117]

For Agamben, this is why contemporaneity is rare and difficult, and why archaeology constitutes the only path of access to the present.

[6]

The course we took thus far showed us that in regard to the specific temporal structure implicit in philosophical archaeology, we deal not so much with a past (in its conventional sense) but with a "moment of arising," a "historical *a priori*" dimension of a certain historical phenomenon that cannot be identified as the phenomenon's diachronic origin but as an active tendency within it that conditions its development in time. The "historical *a priori*" designates a sequential past, yet not simply as an older prehistoric unified phase nor as an ahistorical structure; as a past that still commands in the present, it is an operative force within the historic phenomenon that guarantees its intelligibility and consistency. Philosophical archaeology is thus "a 'science of signs,' an inquiry into the signatures left by the origin on the living body of history."[118]

The "historical *a priori*" dimension is qualitatively different from the historical dimension. Like the child in psychoanalysis (which is a continuous active force within the life of the adult) or the "big bang" (which we assume took place and the effects of which we can feel, though we cannot locate chronologically), the "historical *a priori*" is not an event or substance that precedes the phenomenon diachronically or that can be dated or chronologically situated. Neither is it a metahistorical construct that narrates the phenomenon from the outside, as in the common sense of an origin. Lacking a concrete time and space, it is a heterogeneous fracture existing between history and prehistory, a field of bipolar historical tensions that spreads between the phenomenon's *arché* and its becoming, between arch-past and present.

The "historical *a priori*" dimension is synchronic, contemporaneous with the present and the real, and therefore the archaeologist withdraws, so to speak, toward the present. Gaining access to the present, beyond memory and forgetting (or rather "at the threshold of their indifference"), beyond their inverse, reciprocal operation on (and in) time, is archaeology's aim; and that is why the space opened toward the present is "projected into the future" while intertwining with it. Gaining access to the "historical *a priori*" can only be obtained by returning back to the point where it was covered over and neutralized by tradition (or in Melandri's terms, to the split between conscious and unconscious, history and historiography), only once the archaeological work has cleared away the blocked access to history. Once the archaeologist reaches this phase or dimension, the past that was never really experienced (and thus remained a present) becomes a real or true present; in other words, the future will be realized as a "past that will have been," and the *arché* will become accessible once it is realized as the past that "will have been," and only in this form "can historical consciousness truly becomes possible." Hence the "historical *a priori*" (the *arché*) elucidates the phenomenon from within. To quote Agamben: "The moment of arising, the *arche* of archaeology is what will take place, what will become accessible and present, only when the archaeological inquiry has completed its operation. It therefore has the form of a past in the future, that is, *future anterior*."[119]

From an epistemological perspective, the "historical *a priori*" dimension, through various processes of canonization, conditions the potential to constitute knowledge of and by the phenomenon while at the same time being conditioned itself as it is embedded within historical constellations. Fulfilling the paradox of an a priori condition embedded within history, it is thus paradigmatic and transcendent. Once the archaeologist, through a critique of origins, reaches this dimension that is covered and concealed by the long-lasting effect of tradition, the past that was never really experienced becomes accessible for the first time, and with it, its buried epistemologies.

The relation between archaeology and history becomes clear, writes Agamben, by realizing that archaeology moves backward through the course of history, representing a regressive force that retreats toward the point where history becomes accessible for the first time, in accordance with the temporality of the future anterior. Only then will this relation (just as in the Abrahamic theological doctrines where the work of redemption precedes in rank that of creation [while making it comprehensible and meaningful] and although seems to follow the latter, it is in truth anterior) reveal itself as an archaeological a priori condition that is embedded within history, making it possible. It is a relation of separation and, at the same time, unification. Benjamin, writes Agamben, "made redemption a fully historical category," making clear that "not only is archaeology the immanent a priori of historiography, but the gesture of the archaeologist constitutes the paradigm of every true human action."[120]

Chapter Two

Toward Agamben's Philosophy of History

A: The Theological-Philological Axis (*Messianic Time*)

[1]

Agamben's philosophical archaeology, as it is conceived with its postulations and purposes, its paradoxical necessity and precarious logic, its temporal structure and spatial architecture, *archai* and multiple nows, constitutes a comprehensive conception of history that is based on, and determined by, a certain understanding of time deeper and more elaborate than revealed thus far. Paraphrasing Agamben's own words, we can therefore ask: what is the Agambenian conception of time that is profoundly implicit in the Agambenian conception of history?

In *Infancy and History: On the Destruction of Experience*, Agamben addresses this very question to Marx in an attempt to clarify why historical materialism has failed to elaborate a conception of time that compares with its concept of history, and as a result, retained a conservative temporal framework that supposedly withheld the fulfillment of a promised, yearned-for revolution. Based on the assumption that every conception of history is accompanied by a certain experience of time that conditions it, and likewise that every culture adheres to a particular experience of time that requires a corresponding alteration of this experience once a new culture or revolution is undergoing, Agamben claims that Marx's dictum of "changing the world" also required the changing of time. This was a change that unfortunately never occurred since Marx made recourse to ancient theses and the concept of time dominant in Western culture.

The traditional experience of time (based on its vulgar representation as a precise and homogenous continuum) has thus diluted the Marxist revolutionary concept of history.

Thereafter, in order to show how Marx reached his conception of time, the (vulgarly represented) time of the West is historically drafted (albeit briefly) by Agamben.[1] He describes the evolution of the Western conception of time beginning with the Greco-Roman epoch, which conceived of time as circular and continuous: "Circular movement, which guarantees the unchanged preservation of things through their repetition and continual return, is the most direct and most perfect expression (and therefore the closest to the divine) of the zenith of the hierarchy: absolute immobility."[2] For example, in Plato's *Timaeus*, time is measured by the cyclical revolution of the celestial spheres and defined as a moving image of eternity. Aristotle, in the *Physics*, confirms the circular nature of time, which has no direction and no beginning, middle, or end; and in the *Problemata*, Aristotle concludes that from this perspective we cannot say whether one lives before or after, for example, the Trojan War. However, the fundamental character of the Greek experience of time, which for two millennia dominated the Western representation of time, is its precise, infinite, quantified continuum. Aristotle defines time as "quantity of movement . . . and its continuity is assured by its division into discrete instants [the now], analogous to the geometric point. . . . The instant . . . is a pure limit which both joins and divides past and future. As such, it is always elusive, . . . in dividing time infinitely, the now is always 'other'; yet in uniting past and future and ensuring continuity, it is always the same."[3] This is the instant's paradoxically nullified character and the basis for the radical "otherness" of time and for its "destructive" character. Western man's incapacity to master time and its obsession with handling it, according to Agamben, originate from this Greek conception of time as a quantified and infinite *continuum* of precise fleeting instants; thus man, based on this representation of time, has no real experience of historicity.[4] Greek philosophy deals with time often through *physics*—things in the world are "inside" time (that is, objective and natural); each thing inhabits a place, so it inhabits time. Time (with its destructive character), for the Greeks, destroys things. Thus, Herodotus in *Histories*, which marks the beginning of the modern conception of time, writes that he "puts forth the fruit of his researches, so that time may not erase men's undertakings"[5] and by that confirms the ahistorical nature of the ancient concept of time.

The next major metamorphosis in the conception of Western time, analyzes Agamben, was initiated with the rise of Christianity. The Christian experience of time is the antithesis to the Greco-Roman one, as it conceives of time as a straight line. The world is created within time, from Genesis to the Apocalypse, while (according to French historian Henri-Charles Puech) "its duration comprises neither the eternal nor the infinite, and the events which unfold within it will never be repeated."[6] Moreover, this conception of time has direction and purpose, and a central point of reference, that is, the incarnation of Christ. The eternal repetition of paganism, where nothing is new, is replaced with the idea that everything happens only once—that every event is unique and irreplaceable. The history of humanity is the history of salvation and the progressive realization of redemption whose foundation is God. Christianity, claims Agamben (somewhat problematically), thus lays the foundation for the experience of historicity, although the (ancient) idea of time as continuous and quantifiable has not been abolished, just displaced from the movements of the celestial stars to that of man's interior duration. Nonetheless, this interiorized time remains the continuous and quantifiable time of Greek thought. The ancient circular representation of Greek metaphysics returns to Christian thought: eternity, the regime of divinity, with its static circle, tends to negate the human experience of time; the discrete, fleeting instance intercepts the wheel of eternity.[7]

A further development in the conception and representation of time, as Agamben describes it, was introduced by the modern age. The modern conception of time is a secularization of rectilinear, irreversible Christian time, albeit devoid of the notion of an end or any meaning except for regulating our sense of before and after. This homogeneous, rectilinear, and empty representation of time is a result of modern mechanics, which, according to Agamben, prefers rectilinear over circular motion. Notions of before and after were vague and empty for antiquity and for the modern seem to have meaning in and of themselves.

As Nietzsche grasped:

> The idea governing the nineteenth-century concept of history is that of "process." Only process as a whole has meaning, never the precise fleeting *now*; but since this process is really no more than a simple succession of *now* in term of before and after, and the history of salvation has meanwhile become pure chronology, a semblance of meaning can be saved only by introducing the idea [. . .] of a continuous, infinite progress.[8]

Under the influence of the natural sciences, progress becomes the guiding category of historical knowledge, and behind the apparent triumph of historicism[9] in the nineteenth century lies a hidden negation of history that is modeled on the natural sciences.[10]

The last, crucial transformation (prior to Marx) occurred, as one can expect, with Hegel. Hegel based his idea of time on the Aristotelian model of the precise instant, conceiving the *now* as a point. This now ("which is nothing other than the passage of its being into nothingness" and vice versa) is eternity as true present. "The conjunction of spatial representation and temporal experience which dominates the Western concept of time is developed in Hegel as a conception of time as negation and dialectical dominion of space."[11] For Hegel, the instance (or time) is a negation of negation. "Time," he writes, "is the thing existing which is not when it is, and is when it is not: a half-glimpsed becoming."[12] In the Hegelian system, according to Agamben, time is the necessity and destiny of the unfulfilled spirit, which must *fall* into time, and history is essentially a gradual process. Both time ("whose essence is pure negation") and history can only be grasped as total social process.[13]

Marx's conception of history is different. He understands history not as something into which man *falls* but as man's original dimension as species-being, as being with the capability of generation, producing itself from the start as a universal individual. History is not determined (as in Hegel and the historicism that derives from him) by an experience of linear time as negation of negation but by *praxis*, by a concrete activity as essence and origin of man. Praxis is the founding act of history, the means by which the human essence becomes man's nature and nature becomes man. History is man's *nature*—man's original belonging to himself. "*Man is not a historical being because he falls into time, but precisely the opposite; it is only because he is a historical being that he can fall into time, temporalizing himself.*"[14]

Agamben concludes the historical layout by claiming that although Marx never elaborated a theory of time adequate to his conception of history, it is clear that it cannot be reconciled with the Aristotelian and Hegelian concept of time as a continuous and infinite succession of precise instants. The fundamental contradiction of modern man is that he has yet to develop an experience of time adequate to his idea of history; thus man is split between his being-in-time (as an elusive flow of instants) and his being-in-history (as the original dimension of man). The modern conception of history is twofold: diachronic reality and synchronic structure; and this double structure exemplifies the impossibility for man to take possession of his own historical nature.[15]

Man can experience a new concept of time, in our time, according to Agamben. He gives a preliminary hint for this cognitive change—it might be (as an ancient Western myth makes it humankind's original home) pleasure. Against the (previously mentioned) modern conception that the Western experience of time is split between continuous linear time and eternity, there must be, Agamben claims, the true site of pleasure that is neither precise, continuous time (as Aristotle also understood it, as heterogeneous in relation to the experience of quantified, continuous time) nor eternity. Pleasure is outside of any measurable duration but likewise its place is not in eternity; in other words, the form of pleasure is perfect, whole, complete, and does not occur in a dimension of time. The true site of pleasure is thus history. It is only as a source to happiness "that history can have a meaning for man. . . . For history is not . . . man's servitude to continuous linear time, but man's liberation from it: the time of history and the *cairós* in which man, by his initiative, grasps favourable opportunity and chooses his own freedom in the moment."[16] The full, discontinuous, finite, and complete time of pleasure is set against the empty, continuous, and infinite time of vulgar historicism; the chronological time of pseudo-history is set against the cairological time of authentic history.[17]

In a final return to Marx, true historical materialism (ideally) objects to continuous progress along infinite linear time and instead is ready to stop time because it acknowledges that pleasure is man's original home. This is the experience of time in authentic revolutions, experienced as the halting of time and the interruption of chronology. Yet how can one exactly conceive pleasure as a new conception of time, outside of both measurable duration and eternity? What is the pleromatic and cairological time of pleasure, appearing as the liberating time of history? What exactly does Agamben mean by "the halting of time"?

[2]

Agamben conceives of the halting of time (the authentic, liberating time of history) as exemplified by the idea of messianic time. Interpreted as the paradigm of historical time par excellence, messianic time is discussed, in Agamben's corpus at large, based on a hybridization of two illuminating historical manifestations of it: the one, in contemporary thought, is positioned in Benjamin; the other, as its origin, is traced back to an apostolic text of Paul.

In Benjamin's "Theses on the Philosophy of History" one finds the idea of Jewish messianic intuition. In this text, Benjamin criticizes the conception of time that is based upon continuous and quantified properties, seeking a concept of history where instead of the nullified present of the metaphysical tradition, one can posit an "untraditional" present in which time stands still and has come to a stop. Against the notion of historical progress, Benjamin puts forward the idea that makes the continuum of history explode;[18] against the empty, quantified instant, he advances "the time of the now" constructed as a messianic cessation of happening. This "full time" is, for Benjamin, the true site of historical construction. The messianic time of Judaism becomes (for Benjamin and others) a model for the conception of history.[19] We will come full circle back to Benjamin's understanding of the essence of history, but in order to do that, we first need to turn to that which Agamben identifies as the origin of Benjamin's conception positioned, as said above, in Paul.

[3]

Agamben dedicates *The Time That Remains: A Commentary on the Letter to the Romans* specifically to the idea of messianic time. The book is based on a seminar given by Agamben in which, throughout its six-day course, each day was dedicated to an individual part of the Epistle to the Roman's opening sentence: "*Paulos doulos Christou Iēsou, klētos apostolos aphōrismenos eis euaggelion Theou*" (Paul, a servant of Christ Jesus, called to be an apostle and set apart for the gospel of God.)[20]

The overture is dedicated to "*Paulos doulos Christou Iēsou*" (Paul, a servant of Christ Jesus) and includes Agamben's declaration that the book attempts, in part, to restore Paul's Letters to the status of the fundamental messianic text for the Western tradition, since antimessianic tendencies were operating (through translation and commentary acts) within the church and the synagogue in the past two thousand years to cancel out Paul's Judaism, to decontextualize it from its originary messianic framework.

In order to closely examine and demonstrate Paul's Jewish messianic context, one needs to realize messianic institution's paradoxical task of confronting an *aporia* concerning the very "structure of messianic time"—in order to understand the Pauline message, one needs to be able to fully experience such time; thus, we need to understand the meaning and internal form of the time he defines as *ho nym kairos*, "the time of the now," then raise the question of how messianic community is possible.

The first step Agamben (unsurprisingly) takes in the unfoldment of *ho nym kairos* is to contextualize it in terms of language. Paul's language (of the Letters) is Greek rather than translated Aramaic (as in Matthew and Mark); not belonging to any school or model, it "flows directly out of his heart" and is a "classic of Hellenism." Paul was part of a Jewish diaspora community that thought and spoke in Judeo-Greek (as is the case with Ladino and Yiddish), read and cited the Torah in the Septuagint. The community was subject to distrust since it was imbued with Greek culture and read the Torah in the language of Aristotle and Plato. "Yet," claims Agamben, "there is nothing more genuinely Jewish than to inhabit a language of exile and to labor it from within, up to the point of confounding its very identity and turning it into more than just a grammatical language: making it a minor language, a jargon, or a poetic language. And yet, in each case it is also a mother tongue."[21] Being neither Greek nor Hebrew and neither *lashon-ha-qodesh* (Hebrew for "sacred language") nor a secular idiom, is what makes Paul's language so interesting and what allows for its relation to the structure of messianic time.

Furthering the lingual trajectory, Agamben's hypothesis supposes that the words of the incipit (first verse only, comprising ten words in total (*"Paulos doulos Christou Iēsou, klētos apostolos aphōrismenos eis euaggelion Theou"*) contract within themselves the complete text of the Letter, recapitulate it (recapitulation is an essential term of the vocabulary of messianism).[22] Thus, the understanding of the incipit guarantees the understanding of the text as a whole.

Furthermore, language plays a significant role not only in the illumination of the opening sentence of the Romans but also for each individual word Paul makes use of. In the Hebrew context, the archetype for *metanomasia* (the changing of a name of a character) is found in Genesis 17:5, where God intervenes and changes the name of Abraham and Sarah by adding a single letter. Paul also changes his own name, from Saulos to Paulos, having, so it seems, a "new harmony" in mind—from Saulos, which is a regal name, to Paulos, which is insignificant, from grandeur to smallness (Paul in Latin means "small, of little significance"), defining himself as "the least of the apostles." Paul is a surname, the messianic *signum* (surname; *ho kai* in Greek, or *qui et* in Latin, is the formula that normally introduces a surname, "who is also called") that the apostle takes upon himself as he fully assumes the messianic vocation. Agamben writes: "*Metanomasia* realizes the intransigent messianic principle articulated firmly by the apostle, in which those things that are weak and insignificant will, in the days of the Messiah, prevail over those things the world considers to be strong and important."[23] The messianic separates the proper name from its bearer, thus we have only nickname or surname; Paul is also linked to the word *doulos* ("slave") in the sense that slaves did not have any juridical status in antiquity, thus did not have a proper name. The apostle, like a slave, transformed from a free man into "the slave of the Messiah," loses his name and thus calls himself by a simple surname.

Tracing the semantic history of the term *doulos* (servant, slave, the "slave of the Messiah"), New Testament lexicographers are habitually contrasting its juridical meaning (acquired in the classical world) to its religious connotation exemplified by the Hebrew word "Eved" (acquired in the Semitic world). In Paul, however, *doulos* refers to a profane juridical condition and the transformation this condition undergoes in relation to the messianic event. *Doulos* is opposed to *eleutheros* (free): "'Slave of the Messiah' defines the new messianic condition for Paul, the principle of a particular transformation of all juridical condition."[24]

Another instance where language plays a crucial role in the illumination of individual words, now also in relation to the overall attempt to cancel out Paul's Judaism, is the word *Christou*: from the Vulgate onward, Agamben writes, several terms are not translated from the Greek but are substituted with a loan translation: apostle for *apostolos*; evangel for *euggelion*; and Christ for *christos*. One should remember that *christos* is not a proper name but is, already in the Septuagint, the Greek translation of the Hebrew term *mashiah*, messiah. Paul is not familiar with Jesus Christ but rather with Jesus Messiah, and he never uses the term *christianos* (which at any rate only means "messianic")—"A millenary tradition that left the word *christos* untranslated ends by making the term Messiah disappear from Paul's text. . . . We will therefore always translate *christos* as 'Messiah.'"[25]

Agamben concludes as follows: "Our seminar . . . seeks to understand the meaning of the word *christos*, that is 'Messiah'. What does it mean to live in the Messiah, and what is the messianic life? What is the structure of messianic time?"[26]

To address these questions, Agamben's next phase revolves around the word *klētos*—"calling." It is positioned at the center of the verse, as a conceptual pivot, echoing the fact that the messianic calling is a central event in Paul's individual history. *Klēsis* (vocation, calling) indicates the particular transformation (or change, almost an internal shift) that every juridical status and worldly condition undergoes because of its relation to the messianic event and by virtue of being "called," a transformative movement that (according to the apostle) means a nullification (by vocation).

A worldly thing is nullified due to a special characteristic of vocation according to which vocation calls for nothing and to no place (*"The messianic vocation is the revocation of every vocation"*[27]), but instead the vocation calls the vocation itself, as if it were an urgency that worked it from within and hollowed it out, nullifying it in the very gesture of maintaining and dwelling in it. This is what it means to live in messianic *Klēsis*. Accordingly, Paul's messianic life concerns the ultimate meaning of *Klēsis* expressed by the formula *Hōs mē* ("as not").

The meaning of comparison (or of the comparative), expressed by the particle *Hōs*, was for medieval grammarians not something of an expression of identity or simple resemblance but rather was interpreted (in the context of the "theory of intensive magnitudes," according to which every possible object of experience possesses a determinate "degree" of reality) as an intensive tension that plays one concept against another. The Pauline *Hōs mē* is a special type of tensor; it does not push a concept's semantic field into that of another but sets it against itself in the form of the "as not." Thus, the messianic tension does not tend toward elsewhere, nor exhaust itself in the difference between two things; according to the principle of messianic *Klēsis*, a condition is set in relation to itself, thus it revokes the condition and undermines it without altering its form.

In Paul, the messianic nullification performed by *Hōs mē* is completely inherent within *Klēsis* and does not happen to it a second time, nor does it add anything: "Factical *Klēsis*," writes Agamben, "set in relation to itself via the messianic vocation, is not replaced by something else, but is rendered inoperative."[28]

To further unfold the structure of messianic time, Agamben addresses the term *apostolos* (which comes from the Greek verb *apostellō*, to send forth)—an emissary of the Messiah Jesus and the will of God for the messianic announcement.[29]

Why does Paul define himself as an apostle rather than a prophet?[30] The explanation for Paul's self-definition, according to Agamben, lies in the differences between the two figures. The prophet has an unmediated relation to the "*Ruah Yahweh*" ("the breath of Yahweh") and speaks on his behalf;[31] the apostle, on the other hand, on his mission, searches independently for the words of the message. This is the first difference between them.

The second difference concerns their relation to the future: the prophet always speaks about a time to come, a time not yet present, while the apostle only speaks upon the arrival of the Messiah, when prophecy is kept silent as it is now truly fulfilled. The time of the apostle is thus the present, and is the reason why Paul's technical term for the messianic event is *ho nym kairos*, "the time of the now."[32]

The apostle must be distinguished from another figure, the visionary, with whom he is often confused, just as messianic time is often confused with eschatological time. The messianic announcement is often confused not so much with prophecy (which concerns the future) but with apocalypse (which contemplates the end of times). The apostle, however, does not live in the time of the *eschaton* (the end of time). The difference then between messianism and apocalypse, between the apostle and the visionary, is that the visionary sees the day of judgment, the last day, and describes what he sees, whereas the messianic is not the end of time but *the time of the end*.[33] The messianic is the relation of every moment, every *kairos*, to the end of time and eternity. The apostle is not interested in the last day but in the time that contracts itself and begins to end: or, in other words, the time that remains between time and its end. The messianic time, the time that the apostle lives in and is interested in, is neither the ordinary present (*Haolam hazzeh*, chronological time, the time between creation and the last day) nor the time that will come after the end of the world (*Haolam habba*, the time after the world, the apocalyptic *eschaton*).[34] The apostle is interested in the remnant, in the time that remains between the two times, "when the division of time is itself divided."[35] Therefore, messianic time should not be mistaken for eschatological time, thus making the specificity of what constitutes messianic time unthinkable. As opposed to attempts to understand the Christian conception of time (time oriented toward eschatological salvation, toward final end) as antithetical to modernity's conception of time and history, Paul's messianic time questions the very possibility of a clear division between the two worlds.

Additionally, the time between the Resurrection and the end of time (i.e., the time that remains, the messianic time) means a radical transformation of our experience of time—it cannot be conceived in chronological terms but as time within (chronological) time, a time that transforms chronological time from within. Agamben writes (elsewhere): "On the one hand it is the time that time takes to end. But on the other hand it is the time that remains, the time which we need to end time, to confront our customary image of time and to liberate ourselves from it."[36] The time in which we believe we live in makes us powerless spectators of our own lives; the messianic time, however, is the time we ourselves are, when we grasp that we are nothing but that time. This is the only real time, and to experience it we need to go through a transformation of ourselves and of our ways of living.

How should messianic time be represented? The secular time, the *chronos*, spans from creation to the messianic event, that is, the resurrection of Jesus in which thereafter time contracts itself and begins to end. This contracted time, which Paul calls "the time of the now," lasts until the *parousia*,[37] the full presence of the Messiah, which coincides with the end of time (and which is nonetheless a point in time that remains indeterminate even if it is imminent). According to this description, messianic time does not, however, coincide with either the end of time nor with secular chronological time (but is not outside chronological time either). Messianic time is that part in secular time that undergoes an entirely transformative contraction. Thus, messianic time might be better represented as a "caesura which, in its dividing the division between two times, introduces a remainder into it that exceeds the division."[38] In this schema, messianic time is part of secular time (but exceeds it chronologically) and is part of eternity (but exceeds the future time). It is situated as a remainder with regard to the division between the two worlds. The problem with this representation of time is that it is based on spatial order (in the form of lines, points, and segments) that renders unthinkable the lived experience of time (the confusion between *eschaton* and messianic time is a prime example of that): spatial representations represent perfectly but make it also unthinkable; whereas reflecting upon the lived (or real) experience of time makes it thinkable but unrepresentable. Where does this gap between representation and thought, image and experience, come from? Is another representation of time possible?

In order to resolve this perplexity, Agamben draws on the idea of *operational time* formulated in full by the French linguist and philologist Gustave Guillaume in his work *Temps et verbe*, which deals, in this sense, with the temporality of verbs. According to this idea, writes Guillaume, "the human mind experiences time, but it does not possess the representation of it, and must, in representing it, take recourse to constructions of a spatial order."[39] The representation of time as an infinite line made out of two segments (past and future) separated by the cutting of the present (a representation he names "time-image") is inadequate, according to Guillaume, since it presents time as if it were always constructed but does not show time in the act of being constructed in thought. One needs to represent something not only in its achieved state but also in its various phases through which thought had to pass constructing it, thus: "Guillaume defines 'operational time' as the time the mind takes to realize a time-image."[40] According to Guillaume, language (which he investigates from the point of view of the Aristotelian distinction between potential and act) can organize the constructed image by referring it back to the operational time in which it was constructed; and in regard to the chronological representation of time, the process of forming the time-image can be cast back onto the time-image itself (adding a projection to this process). The result is a chronogenetic time, "a time which includes its own genesis,"[41] a new representation of time that is no longer linear but three-dimensional (pure state of potentiality, process of formation, and the state of final construction).

In his introduction to Guillaume's book, Canadian linguistic Walter Hirtle maintains that in his attempt to reach a deeper level of language, Guillaume determines an insight that provided the cornerstone for all of his later theorizing, that is, "that something is potential *before* it is actual."[42] This led Guillaume to theorize about how we think the possible and the real, realizing that in order to represent an event (in subjunctive mood) one needs to give it precedence, must think it prior to thinking it as real (in indicative mood). The only time this becomes possible is the "'thinking time' required by the mental process of representing a verb."[43] Thus, the system of mood, as Guillaume names it, means that it is essentially a single, subconscious operation of thought, determined by the underlying principle of analysis: *operative time*. The grammatical system is a mechanism in the mind that produces successive morphemes (i.e., the smallest grammatical unit that carries meaning, in a certain language) at different moments in the operation of thought, "as a potential meaning determined by its relative position in the operation involved."[44] Each morpheme is defined according to its position in the micro-stretch of time required for a mental process to unroll. The operative time of the system determines the "notional chronology" of the morphemes involved and their respective potential meaning as the consequences of their position within the system. The processes of language, for Guillaume, thus determines everything that can be understood regarding it. Language resides in the depth of the mind as an organized set of possible processes. The potential and the actual in language thus link in a subconscious morphogenetic process in order to produce a word, showing that a word (once described as a "miniature of art") must be assembled by the speaker before being used in a sentence. Guillaume's perspective of operative time enabled him a holistic view of language in which the potential and the actual are parts of a single phenomenon. Exploring further the passage from the potential to the actual, from system to sentence, Guillaume analyses the grammatical systems within the word, specifically those concerned with representing time within verbs (which he termed *chronogenesis*). His studies indicated that "all the individual grammatical systems of a language can be seen as particular cases of one general system of representation."[45] He thus looked for the most general system that provides the underlying structural mechanism of the word and finally found it in the most transparent of all words—the article. The mental operation underlying the system of the article consists of double movement: the first, from the universal to the particular; the second, following on the first in operative "thinking," from the particular to the universal. To each movement corresponds a sign: for the first (contractive movement), the indefinite article (*un*, a); for the second (expansive movement), the definite article (*le*, the). This form of the movements or this mechanism, for Guillaume, "could provide a representation of any variable relationship based on quantity . . . and he evoked it to depict the relation within the verb between time as an infinite stretch and time as a finite stretch (the present)."[46] This all-embracing language mechanism reflects one of the basic capabilities of human thought: the ability to generalize and to particularize.

Guillaume further writes: "Science is founded on the insight that the world of appearances tells of hidden things, things which appearances reflect but do not resemble. One such insight is that what *seems* to be disorder in language hides an underlying order—a *wonderful* order."[47] Guillaume speaks in terms of spatiality both in regard to things and order, thus it comes as no surprise to encounter his claim that "already to be found in *Temps et verbe* is the idea that time is constructed in terms of space on *n* dimensions."[48] The monograph exemplifies, according to Guillaume, the construction of time on the model of space, according to the principle that time is not representable by itself but requires to base its representations on spatial characteristics. The representation of time, the chronogenesis, is a spatialization of time. When the human mind does not carry out the representation of time according to these measures, time has no representation; it does not mean that it does not exist but rather that it exists in thought only as our experience does: "The human mind . . . has the experience of time, but has no representation of it (it must, therefore, invent this representation, which will be a spatialization, representability being a property of space, and of space alone)."[49]

Once applied to the problem of messianic time, the paradigm of operational time implies another time that is not entirely consumed by the "previous" representation of time,[50] as if man produces, with regard to chronological time, an additional time that prevents him from perfectly coinciding with the time out of which he is able to make images and representations. The idea of operational time demonstrates our inability to coincide with our image of time since it effects a gap between our experience and conception of the present moment. This is not a time added from the outside of chronological time nor a time supplement; it is a time within time, an interior time that measures the disconnection (and being out of sync, being noncoincidental) from our representation of time,[51] but precisely because of this, allows for the possibility of taking hold of it. The space that the messianic time opens between ourselves and our representations of time permits us access to this transformative force at every instant, and thus we take hold of chronological time in a manner determined by the messianic event.

Agamben offers a definition of messianic time: "Messianic time is *the time that time takes to come to an end*, or, more precisely, the time we take to bring to an end, to achieve our representation of time."[52] It is an operational time pressing from within chronological time, working and transforming it internally, "the time we need to make time end: *the time that is left us [il tempo che ci resta]*.[53] Operational time, the time that remains, is what's left of time (as a remnant) once it has exhausted itself in the actual. Whereas our representation of chronological time separates us from ourselves as impotent spectators, messianic time, an operational time in which we take hold of ourselves, is the only time that we ourselves have, the only real time.[54]

Agamben reaches a point in the analysis where he can now better articulate the structure of messianic time in Paul. The messianic event is decomposed into two times: Resurrection (the second coming of Jesus) and *parousia* (the full presence of the Messiah), both occur at the end of time. This decomposition implies the paradoxical tension between an *already* and a *not yet* that defines the Pauline conception of salvation, meaning that the messianic event has already happened (salvation has already been achieved) but in order to truly be fulfilled requires an additional time (thus not yet). This unusual scission introduces a constitutive delay or deferment into the messianic.[55] The Pauline decomposition of presence thus finds its true meaning from the perspective of operational time: as operational time, as the amount of time needed to end representations of time, the messianic *ho nym kairos* ("the time of the now") can never fully coincide with a chronological moment internal to its representation (the end of time as a time-image represented by a final point on a continuous line of chronology). But as an image devoid of time, it can never be grasped and thus tends to infinitely defer itself. The fallacious and inadequate representation of the end lies in changing operational time into a supplementary time added onto chronological time in order to infinitely postpone the end. Parousia does not mean the "second coming" of Jesus (a second messianic event that follows and subsumes the first one); it does not signal a supplement added to something in order to complete it nor a supplement that follows that can never reach fulfillment. Parousia for Paul highlights the innermost structure of the messianic event, inasmuch as it comprises two heterogenous times (kairos and chronos, operational time and represented time)[56] that are coextensive but that cannot be added together. Agamben writes:

> Messianic presence lies besides itself, since, without ever coinciding with a chronological instant, and without ever adding itself onto it, it seizes hold of this instant and brings it forth to fulfillment. . . . The Messiah has already arrived, the messianic event has already happened, but its presence contains within itself another time, which stretches its *parousia*, not in order to defer it, but, on the contrary, to make it graspable. For this reason, each instant may be, to use Benjamin's words, the 'small door through which the Messiah enters.' The Messiah always already had his time, meaning he simultaneously makes time his and brings it to fulfillment.[57]

Messianic time is further illuminated by Paul via two complementary notions: *Typos* and *Recapitulation*. Typos means "figure,"[58] "prefiguration," or "foreshadowing," and is used by Paul to establish a typological relation between every event from past time and *ho nym kairos*, messianic time. The important thing, however, is not this symmetry but the transformation of time implied by this typological relation. The problem here is mainly concerned with a tension that clasps together and transforms past and future in an inseparable constellation. The messianic is not just one of two moments in this typological relation, *it is the relation itself*. The two ends of the *Olam hazzeh* (chronological history) and the *Olam habba* (apocalyptic *eschaton*) are contracted into each other without ever coinciding—this contraction is messianic time.[59] For Paul, the messianic is not a third era situated between two times but rather a caesura that divides the division between times and introduces a remnant, a zone of undecidability, in which the past is dislocated into the present, and the present is extended into the past. Since it is impossible to clearly distinguish between the two times (worlds), since chronology is mutating, one likewise cannot spatially represent the messianic event in a traditional fashion. Messianic time, according to Agamben, is neither the complete nor the incomplete, neither the past nor the future, but the inversion of both.[60] This inverse movement is perfectly rendered in the Pauline typological relation as an area of tension in which two times enter into a constellation that the apostle called *ho nym kairos*. The past (the complete) rediscovers actuality and becomes unfulfilled, and the present (the incomplete) acquires a kind of fulfillment.

A recapitulation of all things, from creation to the messianic "now," is what messianic time does. This recapitulation of the past produces a *plērōma*, a saturation and fulfillment of *kairoi* (messianic *kairoi* are full of chronos but abbreviated, summary chronos) that anticipates eschatological *plērōma* when God "will be all in all." Messianic *plērōma* is therefore an abridgment and anticipation of eschatological fulfillment. The *plērōma* of *kairoi* is understood as the relation of each instant to the Messiah (each *kairoi* is immediate to God and not just the final result of a process, as in the case, writes Agamben, with the model of Marxism inherited from Hegel). Each time is the messianic now, whereas the messianic is not the chronological end of time "but the present as the exigency of fulfillment, what gives itself 'as an end.'"[61]

The widespread view of messianic time as oriented solely toward the future is fallacious. For Paul, the moment of salvation is not solely about the future: on the contrary, recapitulation means that *ho nym kairos* is a contraction of past and present, that the entire past is summarily contained in the present, and that we will have to "settle our debts" with the past. The Pauline gesture has a double movement as it produces a tension (toward what lies ahead) on and out of what lies behind. This is why Paul, caught in this double tension, can neither seize hold of himself nor be fulfilled.[62]

In the "Epistle to the Ephesians" (Eph 1:10), Paul writes: "For the economy of the plenitude of time, all things, both in heaven and on earth, recapitulate themselves in the messiah."[63] Messianic time thus recapitulates all times, summates the whole history, and now appears in the messianic now. The whole past is summarized and unfolds itself as a "figure," not in the sense of simple foreshadowing but as "a constellation and a contraction of the two times, so that the whole past, the whole of history is, so to say, summarily contained in the present, and the claim of a remnant to posit itself as a whole finds here its foundation."[64] The summarized past of the messianic pertains to a special kind of memory where at its core one finds "the economy of salvation," that is, a past that is exclusively individual past, thus a past that potentially opens up for man a new (past) possibility that enables him to "take leave from this past."

Paul (as previously mentioned) uses the verb *Katargeō*, a compound of *argeō* (that derives from the adjective *argos*) meaning "inoperative, not-at-work (*a-ergos*), inactive." The compound thus means "I make inoperative, I deactivate, I suspend the efficacy." Before Paul, it was in use as the form *argeō* in the Septuagint as a translation of the Hebrew word that signifies rest on Saturday or the sabbatical suspension of work. In Greek, the positive equivalent of *katargeō* is *energeō* ("I put to work, I activate"). The etymological opposition with *energeō* demonstrates that *katargeō* signals a taking out of *energeia*, a taking out of the act. In the opposition (that Paul uses) between *dynamis/energeia*, potentiality/act, the messianic enacts an inversion, that is, a moment when potentiality passes over into actuality and meets up with its *telos*. It does not happen in the form of force or *ergon* but in the form of *astheneia*, or weakness. Paul formulates this principle of messianic inversion in the potential/act relation: "'Power [or potentiality] realizes itself in weakness' [*dynamis en astheneia teleitai*] (2 Cor 12:9); and "'when I am weak, then am I powerful.'"[65]

In accordance with the Greek principle according to which privation (*sterēsis*) and im-potentiality (*adynamia*) maintain a kind of potentiality, Paul likewise believed that messianic power does not wear itself out in the *ergon* but remains powerful in it in the form of weakness. Messianic *dynamis* is constitutively "weak," but precisely for this reason it enacts its effects. This is the messianic inversion of the potential/act relation. The messianic power is realized and acts in the form of weakness, not by annihilation or destruction but by deactivation or rendering inoperative, thus giving potentiality back (to whatever was worked on) in the form of inoperativity[66] and ineffectiveness and restoring it (the thing worked on) to the state of potentiality (in order, at the later stage, to fulfill it): "That which is deactivated, taken out of *energeia*, is not annulled, but conserved and held onto for its fulfillment. . . . [K]*atargēsis* is not the destruction of being (*aphanisis tes ousia*), but the progression toward a better state."[67]

Luther, writes Agamben, translates the Pauline verb *katargein* as *Aufheben*—the word that harbors the double meaning of abolishing and conserving found at the center of Hegel dialectics.[68] Thus, a genuinely messianic term becomes a key term for dialectics, and in this sense Hegel's dialectic is nothing more than a secularization of Christian theology (i.e., Hegel used a messianic weapon against theology furnished by theology itself). If this genealogy of *Aufhebung* is correct, then not only does Hegelian thought involve hermeneutic struggle with the messianic (in the sense of it being a conscious interpretation and secularization of messianic theme) but so does modernity (as the epoch situated under the sign of the dialectical *Aufhebung*).[69]

B: The Philological-Aesthetical Axis (or, the Benjaminian Agamben)

[1]

As elucidated thus far, Agamben's philosophical archaeology always involves a messianic moment of thinking. This moment, although originally theological, is prevalent throughout the length and breadth of secular time. Secular time incorporates another time, messianic time, that (illustrated via Guillaume's idea of *operational time*) operates in it from within—messianic time enables chronology by the construction of "time images" (or "time representations") that only at that point are still charged with potentiality (*"the time which is left to us"*). Messianic time is in opposition to historical dialectics of progress, since the messianic is the pure potentiality of the present moment.

Recall that messianic time is formulated by Agamben not only from a theological-grammatical perspective but also (as described in chapter 1) from a logical-structural perspective on the basis of Benjamin's discussion of the origin and temporality/history (via Goethe). According to Benjamin, this messianic conception of time—this concept of temporality and history—shows a structure with bipolar tensions: linear chronology (which supposedly ends in an origin) and a radial form whose manifestations all revolve around an *Urphänomen* in a nonlinear manner. Based on a dialectic of "oneness" and repetition, the origin is (at the same time) inside and outside chronology, it is (at the same time) independent and inseparable from chronology. Like the *arché*, the origin is a historical a priori that remains immanent within history, within the phenomenon.[70]

But beyond these two perspectives, Agamben's conception of the messianic is further secularized based on additional aspects of Benjamin's work. *The Time That Remains* ends with a "threshold" (or *"Tornada"* as Agamben refers to it). In this final passage, we come full circle (likewise, in our attempt to analyze messianic time as the paradigm of historical time, to formulate a concept of time that will condition a concept of history) back to Agamben's positioning of the messianic concept in modern thought, particularly that of Benjamin. In Benjamin, the concept of messianism is (in part) further secularized—now reappearing particularly along a philological-aesthetical axis. This section thus shows how this Benjaminian axis had further influenced Agamben's philosophical conception of history.

[2]

Benjamin's image of the hunchback dwarf, taken from the "Theses on the Philosophy of History," assists him in portraying the text of the philosophy of history as a chessboard upon which a crucial theoretical battle unfolds, guided by a hidden theologian concealed within the text. Who is this hunchback theologian?

In order to answer this question, according to Agamben, we have to better understand the philological role of citation in Benjamin's work. Citation serves a strategic function; it is the mediator that enables secret meetings between past and present generations, as well as between past and present writings, thus citation is required to perform in secrecy. *Sperren*, in German, is translated as "spacing"—it refers to the method in typography of substituting italics with a script that places a space between each letter if that word is to be highlighted. Benjamin himself uses this method, which, from a paleographic standpoint, represents the opposite of how authors use abbreviations (in order to be read in full or because some words should not be read at all). As Agamben writes: "These spaced words are, in a certain way, hyperread: they are read twice, and, as Benjamin suggests, this double reading may be the palimpsest of citation."[71] In the second thesis, Benjamin writes: "Like every generation that precedes us, we have been endowed with a w e a k messianic power."[72] He refers, so it seems, back to Paul and his conception of the weakness of messianic power. Thus, the hidden Pauline text within the *theses* makes Benjamin's use of words and typography a form of citation without quotation marks, and this hyperlegibility (this hidden Pauline presence within Benjamin's *Theses*) is what is signaled discreetly by this spacing.

Now we can better identify the hunchback theologian who secretly guides the puppet of historical materialism in Benjamin's text. It is this entity, concealed between the lines of the philosophy of history (as a form of "citation without quotation marks"), that secretly guides the puppet's course; or to deploy a different perspective, it is that which is included within the grand narratives of modernity and Marxism that, although advancing rationality, secularization, and progress, is nonetheless guided by a hidden messianic theological power.

Benjamin's concept of the "image" (wherein the past and present are united in a constellation, and wherein the present recognizes the meaning of the past and the past finds its meaning and fulfillment) relates to Paul's "typological relation," where past and future enter a similar constellation: where a moment from the past must be recognized as the typos (figure) of the messianic now.[73] The fact that Paul writes, "He who is an image of the one who was to come," causes Benjamin to speak of an image and not a figure; additionally, Benjamin's own words "the true image of the past f l e e s by," propels Agamben to claim that Benjamin took from Paul the idea that the image of the past runs the risk of disappearing completely if the present fails to recognize itself in it. Note that elsewhere in reference to Paul, Agamben mentions Benjamin, who writes (as we recall) that "every day, every instant, is the small gate through which the messiah enters."[74] The accurate quote, taken from Benjamin's addendum to the "Theses on the Philosophy of History," reads as follows: "For every second of time was the strait gate through which the Messiah might enter."[75] Benjamin's conception of messianic time is an emphasis of the redemptive potentiality of the nonchronological present that, in the context of the Pauline epistles, bears a relation not only to Judaism but also to the Church.[76] As Agamben shows in *The Church and the Kingdom*, since messianic time does not mean chronology but a qualitative change in how time is experienced, in the original positioning of the Church it makes no sense to speak in terms of chronology—there is no time for delay. Thus Paul, when addressing the Thessalonians, speaks about the "Day of the Lord" in present tense; or in the Gospels, when referring to the Messiah, he is called *ho erchomenos*, "he who comes," he who never ceases to come.[77] Messianic time (the term Agamben was using in *The Time That Remains* to replace the term "kairology" in *Infancy and History*) is set in opposition to the historical dialectic of progress and its logic of deferral, for example, the future coming of the Messiah who will redeem mankind and bring history to an end. Instead, both Agamben and Benjamin conceive of the messianic event as a potentiality of the present situation, or, as Benjamin once described his surrealist alarm clock, a clock that rings "sixty seconds every minute."

Further to the philological perspective of the messianic concept: Benjamin's concept of "the now of legibility" (or knowability) defines a genuinely hermeneutic principle (in opposition to the idea that any work may become the object of infinite interpretations at any given time) according to which every text contains a historical index indicating both its belonging to a determinate epoch, as well as its only coming forth to full legibility at a determinate historical moment. In *The Arcades Project*, writes Agamben, Benjamin included the following note (N3, 1) that confided his "most extreme messianic formulation," a note that also serves Agamben as his final conclusion to *The Time That Remains*:

> Each now is the now of a particular knowability (*Jedes Jetzt das Jetzt einer bestimmten Erkennbarkeit*). In it, truth is charged to the bursting point with time. (This point of explosion, and nothing else, is the death of the *intentio*, which thus coincides with the birth of authentic historical time, the time of truth.) It is not that what is past casts its light on what is present, or what is present its light on what is past; rather, an image is that wherein what has been comes together in a flash with the now to form a constellation. In other words: an image is dialectics at a standstill. For while the relation of the present to the past is purely temporal, the relation of what has been

to the now is dialectical: not temporal in nature but imagistic [*bildlich*]. Only dialectical images are genuinely historical—that is, not archaic—images. The image that is read—which is to say, the image in the now of its recognisability—bears to the highest degree the imprint of the perilous critical moment on which all reading is founded.[78]

GLOSS IX—MESSIANIC LANGUAGE

As becomes clearer, Benjamin's philosophy of history is analyzed by Agamben not only "messianically" but also (and perhaps always, as these perspectives are complementary and interwoven) from a perspective based in language. One therefore finds a comprehensive discussion of Benjamin's philosophy of language, its connection with the problem of history and its messianic intention, in Agamben's early essay "Lingua e storia. Categorie linguistiche e categorie storiche nel pensiero di Benjamin."[79] The essay commences with a fragmented quote from Benjamin's preparatory notes to "Theses on the Philosophy of History":

> The Messianic world is the world of a total and integral actuality. The first instance of universal history occurs there. Today this term can only denote a type of esperanto which cannot be realized until the confusion of Babel is cleared up. It presupposes a language into which every text can be wholly translated. . . . Or rather, it is itself this language; not in written form, but as it is joyously acted out.[80]

Benjamin's argument, writes Agamben, messianically conflates language and history, maintaining that the history of redeemed humanity is the only universal history that amounts to its language (i.e., universal post-Babylonian language), and that this language comes in the form of joyous celebration rather than writing.

The conflation of historical and linguistic categories, according to Agamben, should not come as a surprise—in fact, it could be already be grasped in the Middle Ages (in the seventh century) when, for example, Isidore of Seville claims (in the *Etymologies*) that "history pertains to grammar,"[81] or in an even remoter reference, Augustine's *De ordine*, where one finds the claim: "Whenever something memorable was to be written down, it necessarily pertained to grammar. Grammar was thus linked to history . . . a discipline . . . not so much for historians but for grammarians."[82] Every historical process of handing down refers to the domain of the "letter," since the Augustinian conflation is based on a broader definition of grammar, one that also includes (beyond the obvious lingual structural analysis) "the infinite dimension of historical transmittal."[83] The letter, for Augustine, is essentially "an historical element." This conception is a sequel to the long tradition of the ancient world that reflects on language in terms of being a twofold system that incorporates names (as pure denomination) and discourse (in Marcus Terentius Varro's words, "a river from a spring"[84]). Man's use of words is a result of his historical participation in this river. That is, history mediates and conditions the foundation of language for man, who receives names (that proceed him) only through a process of them being handed down to him, them hierarchically *descending* to him within a historical process. Whether descending from a divine or profane source, the crucial thing here is that "the origin of names escapes the speaker. . . . As long as man has no access to the foundation of language, there will be a handing down of names; and as long as there is a handing down, there will be history and destiny."[85]

Benjamin's conflation of language and history thus means, writes Agamben, that "man's historical condition is inseparable from his condition as a speaker, and is inscribed in the very modality of his access to language, originally signaled by a split."[86] The original field of language, as articulated by Benjamin in his essay "On Language in General and the Language of Men" (1916), is that of names exemplified (according to the story of Genesis) in the Adamic language. This "pure language" is not our customary (and bourgeois, according to Benjamin) idea of language according to which a signifying word transmits meaning from one subject to another but a language where the name communicates itself absolutely—in the name, "the spiritual essence which communicates itself is language."[87] Nothing is communicated in the Adamic language beyond the name itself; in other words, spiritual essence and linguistic essence coincide, and in such a "pure language" the problem of the unsayable, which characterizes human language, does not exist, thus it corresponds with the religious concept of revelation, which does not know any "unsayable."

The original sin of man means, in this sense, language's fall from its perfect status of nonsignifying names to the signifying word as a means of exterior communication and, moreover, man's making of language a means and a sign, a process that ended up in a Babylonian mayhem. This fallen condition of language is later on thought from the perspective of messianic redemption via Benjamin's essay "The Work of the Translator" (1921). In this essay, Benjamin attempts to explicate the relation between the original, paradisiacal language and the multiple of languages that comprise it in terms of part and whole, claiming that a thing can only be understood not by an individual language but by the fusion of its various meanings as pure language. In other words, a meaning conveyed and explained by supposedly only one language is impossible as it exists merely as a potential waiting to be harmonized with all other languages, in what Benjamin terms the "messianic end of their history." Both history and linguistics move forward toward their messianic fulfillment; once this point arrives, language will be a "'word without expression,' which is liberated from the weight and the alienation of sense."[88] At the same time, however, once this state is reached, all communication and sense will extinguish themselves.

What is a word, asks Agamben, that no longer means and is no longer destined for the historical handing down of a signified? How can people speak purely, and how can they understand the word without the mediation of the signified? For Agamben, that which remains unsayable and unsaid in every language is precisely that thing it wants to say but cannot: "the pure language, the inexpressive word"; the field of names is that meaning it tries to convey but cannot bring as such into speech. Languages signify and have sense because they mean, but what they mean—that is, pure language—remains unsaid. The unsaid of meaning sustains, in each language, the tension between a language and its historical evolution; and it is what destined the language for its historical development. The biblical myth of the fall of Edenic language, according to Agamben, should be understood exactly in this way.[89]

The relationship between the various historical languages and their one common feature remains dialectical—on the one hand, they need to cease their meaning to say it, but on the other hand, this is exactly what they cannot do without (at the same time) abolishing themselves, since this capacity is only accessible to the totality of their messianic end: "Inasmuch as the pure language is the only one which does not mean, but says, it is also the only one in which that 'crystalline elimination of the unsayable in language,' can be realized."[90]

Benjamin suggested, according to Agamben, that universal language (or history) should not be understood in terms of being an "Ideal" or an infinite duty that crosses all historical evolution, nor that the inexpressive word should be understood in terms of an infinite task (that could never be fulfilled) toward which the historical experience of speaking man is moving. Agamben justifies this claim by interpreting Benjamin as a thinker who merges the transformation of Marxist classless society into an infinite task, with an analogous transformation of the Kantian idea into an ideal; and just as classless society is never actually realized, so the ideal language never reaches the level of the word. A classless society (which was, for Benjamin, genuinely messianic) is not the end of historical progress but its interruption, so often missed and finally fulfilled.[91] According to Agamben's interpretation of Benjamin, contemporary hermeneutics (which looks for the unsaid and the infinity of meaning) tries, in fact, to fulfill the unsaid and the infinity of meaning rather than to conserve them, which is the exact opposite of true textual hermeneutics. Accordingly, for Benjamin, "if the letters . . . commit human language to an historical handing down and an infinite interpretation, we can suppose . . . that the universal language represents rather the definite cancelation and resolution of human language."[92]

"Like the origin,"[93] writes Agamben, for Benjamin "the language of names is not, then, an initial chronological point, just as the messianic end of languages, the universal language of redeemed humanity, is not a simple chronological cessation. Together they constitute the two faces of a single 'idea of language.' "[94] The universal language can only be, for Benjamin, the idea of language, "not an ideal (in the neo-Kantian sense) but the very *Platonic idea* of language which saves and contains in itself all languages."[95] This "idea of language" no longer presupposes any other language; it has nothing more to say but simply speaks. At this radical point of transparency there is no distinction in the language between "field of names" and signifying words or between the intended and the said, and the language reaches its messianic end. Accordingly, universal history "knows no past to transmit, but it is the world of an 'integral actuality'. Language here disappears as an autonomous category. . . . [M]en no longer write their language, but they act it out like a celebration."[96] Language (that is, universal language) had become so close to man (and his history) that they seem, like never before, to perfectly coincide, in the same way as lovers who have no more room for any image, letter, or grammar to reside between them.

[3]

We will now attempt to show the connection and interrelatedness between Benjamin's conception of the messianic (and the philosophy of history, at large) and a few ideas (such as montage, image, [semantic] void, melancholy, and angels) that characterize his writings on art, thus leaning closer to the aesthetical pole of the philological-aesthetical axis. Illuminating the connection between these domains will assist us (among others) in better formulating the "Benjaminian Agamben" as well as in laying the groundwork for the chapter that follows (nodding toward, in particular, the possibility of epistemology beyond discursive language to be carried out by artistic means).

Benjamin, as it is well known, wrote increasingly on aesthetics and particularly on (imagery-core) photography. Thus, it comes as little or no surprise that the previously encountered idea of "citation without quotation marks" is also referred to in these terms, that is, as the idea (or method) of "dialectical image."[97]

GLOSS X—CINEMATIC MONTAGE AND HISTORY

A note (N1, 10) in *The Arcades Project* states the following: "This work has to develop to the highest degree the art of citing without quotation marks. Its theory is intimately related to that of montage."[98] What is a montage-based method of "citation without quotation marks"? How does it relate to history? And perhaps more importantly in the context of this chapter: how does Agamben, via Benjamin, conceive it?

Agamben refers to the artistic method of montage and its relation to history not only in the *Arcades Project*[99] but also in his essay on the poetic characteristic of Guy Debord's cinema. The specific function of the image that Agamben identifies in Debord's work (though not exclusively) is what ties cinema and history together—its operation no longer as an immobile entity. The image is not an archetype nor is it outside history, rather (similarly to Benjamin's "dialectical image" as Agamben writes) "it is a cut which itself is mobile, an image-movement, charged as such with a dynamic tension."[100] The mobility of the image pertains also to painting, according to Agamben, who conceives of it as a still charged with movement, a still from a film that is missing. The kind of history that Agamben thinks about, in this regard, is not our accustomed chronology but messianic history, which he defines (in this essay on Debord) by two major characteristics: a history of salvation ("something must be saved") and an eschatological history ("something must be completed, judged") where something happens right here but in another time and outside chronology but without entering some other world. This characterization renders the messianic incalculable but simultaneously makes every moment (and image) "the door through which the Messiah enters,"[101] (paraphrasing Benjamin) right here, right now.

This messianic historical situation equates, for Agamben, to Debord's compositional technique in the field of cinema, that is, montage. The conditions of possibility ("transcendentals" in the philosophical jargon) for Debord's montage, Agamben explains, are double: *repetition* and *stoppage*. There is no need to shoot the film anymore, he writes, "just to repeat and stop," thus montage is shown as such. Debord's montage is understood by Agamben as an epoch-making innovation in cinema; it ushers in the time in which cinema is made using images from cinema. Repetition for Agamben, building upon the works of previous thinkers, is not the return of the identical as one would imagine but "the return of the possibility of what was"—it restores past possibility and renders it possible anew. Repetition here relates to memory as the latter does not repeat the past as such but restores possibility to the past. This is, according to Agamben, the theological dimension that Benjamin ascribes to memory when he writes that "memory makes the unfulfilled into the fulfilled, and the fulfilled into the unfulfilled."[102] Images thus charged with a historical and messianic importance because they are able to deliver potential possibilities to that which is impossible by definition, "toward the past." The centrality of the act of repetition in Debord's montage comes from the opening it produces between the possible and the real as a "zone of undecidability" into which what might become possible again happily enters. The second transcendental is stoppage—the power to interrupt, "the 'revolutionary interruption' of which Benjamin spoke,"[103] which brings cinema closer to poetry than to prose, since both cinema and poetry, writes Agamben, exclusively share the concept of the caesura and the enjambment: "This is also why Hölderlin could say that by stopping the rhythmic unfolding of words and representations, the caesura causes the word and the representation to appear as such. To bring the word to a stop is to pull it out of the flux of meaning, to exhibit it as such."[104] This is exactly how stoppage works in Debord's practice, as constitutive of a transcendental condition of montage. The cinematic power of stoppage works on the image itself, causing it to become separated from continuous narration and to be shown as such. Both repetition and stoppage form a single system of montage in Debord; according to Agamben, together they accomplish the messianic act of cinema.

Benjamin uses "image" in a broader sense than we are often accustomed to, using it as more than a visual image ("recognized" but never "perceived") and thus escapes what seems to be a paradoxical term (i.e., "dialectical image," an image at once frozen and dialectical). His philosophical-historical method (further formulated as "dialectics at a standstill") brings together two parties in dialogue and into dynamic contact—that is, dialectical images represent the conjuncture of past and present and are considered by Benjamin as the only genuine (historical) images. A dialectical image is charged with an energy that is capable of "blowing elements out of the historical continuum" once they achieve a special legibility that Benjamin calls the "now of knowability/legibility." Agamben notes that "Walter Benjamin writes that the historical index contained in the images of the past indicates that these images may achieve legibility only in a determined moment of their history,"[105] as well as characterizing Benjamin's idea of the dialectical image as "the fulcrum of [Benjamin's] theory of historical consciousness."[106]

Agamben reformulates the historical indexicality of the image in somewhat different terms than Benjamin. "For Benjamin," writes Agamben in *The Signature of All Things*, "history is the proper sphere of signatures. Here they appear under the names of 'indices' ('secrets,' 'historical,' 'temporal') . . . often characterized as 'dialectical.'"[107] The precarious, dialectical, and fleeting characteristics of the image become clearer once restored to their proper context—the theory of historical signatures. Since an image is always accompanied by an index or signature, it is constituted temporally and becomes legible precisely by that index or signature. For this reason, the success of a historiographic research (which necessarily has to do with signatures) is determined, for Agamben, by the researcher's ability to read ephemeral signatures and follow their subtle and obscure thread. Before further elaborating on this point, we ought to unpack a few ideas that comprise the intertwining elements of paradigms and signatures (beyond the first glimpse we previously offered), mainly by providing a background for Agamben's conception of them.[108]

GLOSS XI—PARADIGMS AND SIGNATURES

(1) Agamben's dealing with paradigms (or prime examples)[109] begins specifically on the background of the discussion of the relationship[110] between the whole and the part, the common and the proper,[111] or

the general and the particular. This antinomy of the general and the particular "has its origin in language,"[112] where we name a particular object and thus transform it into a member of a general class defined by a property held in common. This procedure closely resembles the formation of political communities; thus, both politics and language are caught between universality and singularity. The concept of the paradigm nonetheless escapes this antinomy: "Neither particular nor universal, the example is a singular object that presents itself as such."[113] An example is simultaneously both a simple member of a set and the defining criteria of that set. By providing its own criteria of inclusion, the example remains ambiguously positioned alongside the class of which it is most representative, neither fully included in a class nor fully excluded from it. The paradigm is always both suspended from its group and belonging to it. Thus, the separation of exemplarity and singularity is false or impossible. All groups are immanent to their paradigmatic members, never presupposed.[114]

Based on Aristotle's description of the special logical movement of the example (which he distinguishes from both induction and deduction),[115] Agamben writes that the paradigm constitutes a peculiar form of knowledge that calls into question the particular-general relation as a model of logical inference. The paradigm is a mode of knowledge that moves between singularities. It refutes the general and the particular as well as dichotomous logic in favor of a bipolar analogical model.[116] As the example moves from particular to particular, its epistemic character remains unconnected to general categories of any kind and thus must be understood as analogical inasmuch as analogy is a cognitive process in which particulars are associated without reference to generalities. The example is the deactivation of a particular from its normal usage such that it both constitutes and makes intelligible "the rule of that use, which cannot be shown in any other way."[117] Paradigms make intelligible the analogical form of knowing, which can neither be explained with reference to an origin nor conveyed by way of rules. Herein lies its power to illuminate the present.

Following Agamben, a paradigm is at once embedded in a given historical situation and a tool for better understanding "the present situation." These paradigms must then walk a fine line between past and present, and for this reason they require the most careful understanding—at once historical and hermeneutical—if they are to achieve their end.[118] In other words, paradigms draw on historical occurrences of the past, while being crystallized and concretized in the real time of the present, though directed toward a future point in time when the (future) present will be rendered inoperative and free to be reused.

(2) Signature is the mode of distribution of paradigms through time and discourses, thus it is the exposition of intelligibility (the signature is akin to the paradigm and contains a few elements that refer back to the logic of the paradigm). It is characterized by a signatory displacement: "Signature is something that in a sign or concept marks and exceeds such sign or concept, referring it back to a certain field without leaving the semiotic to constitute a new meaning. . . . [S]ignatures move and displace concepts from one field to another, without redefining them semantically."[119] Signatures operate as pure historical elements precisely because they connect different fields and times.[120] A signature guides the interpretation of a sign or a concept in a specific direction, similarly to Benjamin's idea of "secret indices,"[121] where the past carries with it a secret index to be deciphered in the present when perceived.[122] In their historical work, signatures function "anachronistically" as they operate outside or against chronology. The signatures function on the basis of random interconnectedness, where one does not identifies a mythic origin but determines when signs first emerged on the horizon of perceptibility.[123] The signature has a (nonchronological) specific origin, a historical "moment of arising," and a large number of historical presentations, all of them paradigmatic.

Additionally, a system of reading signs is based on signatures where the relationship between them is not that of cause and effect but of resemblance and analogy. For Agamben, a signature is not a sign but the element that makes the sign intelligible; the meaning of a signature is not found in the sign or the semantic meaning but in the manner in which the signature allows things to be said or understood. The signature is a sign without a content and thus gives rise to a pure identity deprived of any meaning or signification.[124] The relation between the signature and the thing that it semiotically marks is analogical—this is why signatures, which (according to the theory of signs) should appear as signifiers, always already slide into the position of the signified: "*Signum* and *signatum* exchange roles and seem to enter into a zone of undecidability."[125]

[4]

We return now to our discussion of the image, its accompanying ephemeral signature, and the prospects of successful historiographic research, according to Agamben, as the result of the image's correct treatment.

The success of a historiographic research is determined not only by an effective tracing, reading, and deciphering of signatures but also by recognizing them as a means of understanding. How do signatures generate understanding? What form of epistemology do they contain that enables understanding?[126]

A similarity exists between Agamben's *signatures* and Benjamin's *dialectical images*. Both terms represent a constellation of moments beyond mere elements in a historical archive and function as "a potentially dynamic means of understanding—and changing—the present situation, one that acquires its potentiality only at specific, and fortuitous, points."[127] These points are crystallizations of historical experience in a moment of unprecedented relevance. This functionality of the dialectical image, as well as that of the signature, determines its possibility to appear at a certain moment, which is also (epistemology) related to language and meaning.

Before we observe the epistemological connection between the dialectical image/signature and language and meaning (at the unique moment of potentiality) let us briefly (moving on our axis in the opposite direction, that is, from the aesthetical to the philological) make a preliminary remark on the bond between the philological and the historical in Agamben. Because the dialectical image also concerns the historical dimension, we should keep it in mind as we move back and forth in the reading.

GLOSS XII—THE HISTORICAL AND THE PHILOLOGICAL

In his introductory notes to Agamben's book *Potentialities*, Daniel Heller-Roazen highlights the methodological principle according to which the Agambenian method thinks the historical and the philological as inseparable. Referring to Benjamin's concept of "redemption," and his prefatory notes to the "Theses on the Philosophy of History,"[128] the Agambenian historical method is always involved a moment, writes Heller-Roazen, "in which the practice of the 'historian' and the practice of the 'philologist,' the experience of tradition and the experience of language, cannot be told apart."[129] This observation is based on Agamben's idea that every communication between human beings must presuppose the fact *that there is language*:[130] without it, there is no transmission nor signification, and it is this fact that cannot be communicated in the form of statements since statements are possible only after speech has already begun. Thus the transmission of tradition, for Agamben, is conditioned by the transmission of language.

Since history and philology cannot be told apart, the past is saved not in its past form but in being transformed into something that never was, in being read as "what was never written." "What was never written" in all communication (linguistic and historical), according to Agamben, is the fact that there is language, and the fact that it was never written derives from the fact that it can enter into "writing" only in the form of a presupposition. Yet this fact can be "'read': exposed, it can be comprehended in its existence as potentiality."[131] "To read what was never written" means to bring back everything that has ever been said to the event of its taking place, to its pure potentiality. Language, in Benjamin's terms, is thus "redeemed"; though brought to its pure potentiality, speech has nothing to say.

Reduced to its speechless capacity for speech, the pure existence of language shows its own potentiality for expression, it shows its own existence, that there exists a medium in which communication takes place and that what is communicated in this medium is not one thing or another but communicability itself.[132] To examine the pure existence of language, free from any form of presupposition, is to consider a community inconceivable according to any representable condition of belonging, a "coming community" (to use another Agambenian phrase) without identity defined by its existence in language as irreducible, absolute potentiality.

In *Nymphs*, Agamben addresses the linguistic perspective of the functionality of the "dialectical image" and its epistemological implication. "Where meaning is suspended," he writes, "dialectical images appear. The dialectical image is, in other words, an unresolved oscillation between estrangement and a new event of meaning. . . . [T]he dialectical image holds its object suspended in a semiotic void."[133] The life of the image can thus be characterized by a pause highly charged with tension between the two poles. Not only dialectic is inseparable from the objects it negates "but also that the objects lose their identity and transform into the two poles of a single dialectical tension that reaches its highest manifestations in a state of immobility."[134] We see that the functionality of the dialectical image (and signature) results in a state of immobility and the suspension of meaning, which also causes the image to gain its fullness and legibility, to be unprecedentedly known. But how exactly does this epistemological process come about?

In chapter 1 of *The Signature of All Things*, Agamben examines dichotomy-based (particular-general) epistemological processes and the dialectics within them; that is, the processes of acquiring knowledge that is based on binary logic. By contrast, the epistemological model of the paradigm (that we previously looked at) is based on analogy and advances from singularity to singularity. The epistemological mechanism of the paradigm (as well as that of the dialectical image) is not logical (as in Hegel) but analogical and paradigmatic (as in Plato)—its formula, for whose explication Agamben credits Enzo Melandri, is "neither A nor B," and the opposition it implies is not dichotomous and substantial but bipolar and tensive. The two terms are neither removed nor recomposed in a unity but kept in an immobile coexistence charged with tension.[135] Each paradigmatic example becomes an exemplary case of a general law that could not have been stated a priori. Thus, the hermeneutic circle (which was previously discussed) is in fact a paradigmatic circle; there is no circularity between preunderstanding and interpretation, as meaning does not precede the phenomenon but stands, so to speak, beside it—the phenomenon shows the general, which is the paradigm.

This nondichotomous model or multipolar field of forces entails a methodological principle that prevails when dealing with dichotomies. That is, how exactly does one need to understand a dichotomy? How does a dichotomy form? What kind of relation keeps a dichotomy intact? And perhaps more importantly, is it possible to understand both elements not as relating, but connecting, touching one another? For when we think about two factions, elements or concepts, we create a relation between them; we create a representation of one in the other. We then tend to think that richer representation amounts to a stronger connection between them as a result of a greater degree of affinity, and the stronger the affinity, the closer they get. But contrary to common opinion, they will ultimately be articulated or joined together, they will be in real contact, only as a result of a complete *absence of representation*.[136] This is an opposite definition of infinite proximity to the one we usually give. As long as there is a degree of representation between both elements, as long as we do find a relation of one in the other, they are related but not yet unified. By absolutely unraveling all their connections, both factions disappear in and of themselves, making space for a third thing to emerge for the first time as a figure of their unification. This is the meaning of the verb "to coincide," from medieval Latin *coincidere*, meaning literally "to fall-upon-together."[137]

Moreover, Agamben's critique of deconstruction (although acknowledging its questioning of the primary precedence of origin and presence) maintains, at the same time, that deconstruction fails to question signification itself. Thus it never really escapes from the realm of representation, and "does not yet find a way beyond the implicit hold of representation."[138] In the context of the present discussion, that is, the understanding of how knowledge is generated through movement on the basis of the analogical model as opposed to the dichotomous particular/universal model ("littered with exceptions") that characterizes the realm of (deconstructionist) representation, Agamben puts forth the example as an opposite figure one can find in the model of the paradigm. An epistemological difference in thought models exists between the rule-based norm of representation or, in other words, the rule-based movement from the universal (norm) to the particular (application), and the paradigmatic example (through which others construct their own unique, always singular, identities), since the paradigm presents (not *re*-presents) neither the "original" nor the "copy" but its own point of origin. As Agamben writes: "A paradigm implies the total abandonment of the particular-general couple as the model of logical inference."[139]

As mentioned earlier, Agamben reminds us, on various occasions throughout his oeuvre, of the primacy of the cognitive paradigm in present Western culture, as well as of the fact that philosophy has become, after Kant, a doctrine of knowledge rather than one of anthropogenesis (that is, the becoming human of man). This claim challenges the epistemological threshold of the human sciences, and in this sense, by adopting the Benjaminian art of citing without quotation marks and the epistemology of the dialectical image/signature, Agamben is able to call into question "the automatic support of a tradition turned into a 'fortress of knowledge' and vindicates an anti-authoritarian experience of language which measures its truth value only against its own merits."[140]

[5]

Our discussion thus far of the epistemological dimension of the signature/image, their functioning as epistemological means of understanding, revolved around their relation to language. However, there is more to that: what do signatures (or Benjamin's "dialectical images") offer to Agamben, in terms of generating knowledge, that language cannot?

We can momentarily turn back to an earlier period in history (the Renaissance), where the connection between art and theory enables epistemology beyond discursive language. We will find, here as well, the relevance of the analogy-based model and its special epistemic functionality.

In *The Unspeakable Girl*, Agamben refers to Odo Casel's *Liturgy as Mystery Celebration* (1921), a manifesto for what will become the liturgical movement, which had an immense influence within the Catholic Church. Casel claimed that liturgy is not a doctrine but a mystery (thus having a generic relationship to the pagan mystery cults). Originally, mystery simply meant "gestures, acts and words through which divine action was effectively realized in time and in the world for the salvation of mankind."[141] Similarly, in Christian liturgy, the redemptive work of Christ is rendered present in and through the Church—what is rendered present in this mystery is not Christ as a historical individual but his "saving act," communicated through the sacrament. According to Casel, the force of liturgy lies in its "fullness of actuality of the saving action of Christ."[142]

The mystical experience is expressed through the verb "to see" (*opopen*), and "vision" (*epopteia*) is the term given to the supreme stage of initiation. *Epoptes* means both "initiate" and "spectator," and the mysteries these figures were contemplating "were 'living paintings' composed of gestures, words and the presentation of objects."[143] This constitutes, according to Agamben, the connection between the mystery cults and painting that was so active in Renaissance art. The philosophical tradition links supreme knowledge to mystery visions, knowledge that is experienced through seeing, touching, and naming, thus painting offered to this knowledge the most apt expression.

Agamben builds upon the work of Edgar Wind (in particular *Pagan Mysteries in the Renaissance*), according to which even though Renaissance culture (including the act of painting) regarded obscurity and mystery as necessary, there is another element that more than anything else defines "mystery" in this culture—that is, the relationship between form and content one can witness in different Renaissance artifacts. Renaissance allegories (like Eleusinian mysteries), for example, are not "mysterious" because of some concealed content but because in them form and content have become indistinguishable. The third element, neutralizing both form and content, is mysterious because it no longer conceals anything. Thus because there is nothing left to say on the discursive level, "thought and vision coincide." Form and content coincide not because the content is now exposed but because they "fall together" (as previously stated via the nondichotomous model), reduced and reconciled, and what we are then given to contemplate is pure appearance. For this reason, one cannot discursively present the knowledge depicted in such paintings but merely title them.

If the Renaissance allegories offer a richer expression of thought than contemporary philosophical treaties, then not only painting is returned to its true theoretical foundations but "the very nature of thought is illuminated." According to Wind, writes Agamben, the pagan mystical tradition exercised a decisive influence on German Idealism, particularly on how Hegel and Schelling conceived of the dialectical movement of thought (after the model of *coincidentia oppositorum*). The "profoundest mysteries of art," claimed Schelling, consist in conceiving at once the extreme discrepancy of opposed elements and their point of coincidence: "The third element, in which opposites meet, cannot be of the same nature as them and requires a different form of exposition, one in which the opposing elements are at once maintained and neutralized. It is the content but nothing contains it; it is form but it no longer forms anything—exposing, thereby, itself."[144]

This brings to mind Benjamin's idea of "image philosophy," that is, the "image of thought" or *Denkbild* that should not be taken as a metaphor but understood literally—like Renaissance allegory, writes Agamben, it is "a mystery wherein that which cannot be discursively presented shines for a moment out of the ruins of language."[145]

We will now attempt to unpack Benjamin's *Denkbild* for two reasons. First, it can be seen as exemplifying a clear equilibrium point on the philological-aesthetical axis, herein discussed, which advances a conception of history. Second, it can serve as a preliminary guideline for our forthcoming discussion (in the next chapter) of material-based methods (or artistic-hermeneutic techniques) of historiography.

As of 1923, Benjamin began to publish short narrative prose pieces, so-called *Denkbilder*, which bears a relation to the Baroque emblematic technique.[146] The Baroque emblem contains visual and verbal material in a tripartite form: *pictura* (icon or pictorial aspect), *inscriptio* (*motto*, written above and describes, somewhat enigmatically, the image), and *subscriptio* (epigram, written below the *pictura* as an explanatory poem or prose). The emblem aims to reveal a hidden meaning and significance (*res significans*) and, additionally, follows the two-fold intention of *Darstellen* (representation) and *Deuten* (interpretation).

Benjamin's *Denkbilder* work similarly. They generally have a three-part form consisting of a title, a narrated image, and a related thought and present an image as an integral albeit not immediately recognizable part of the thought. Neither is clear without the other, and their relation is subject to critical reflection of their interdependence. This interdependence of parts is characteristic of the Baroque emblem, and likewise in Benjamin's *Denkbilder* these parts are supposed to provide information about the hidden signatures of reality. The objects of the *Denkbilder* become signs for hidden, fabricated *human* meaning about the world (as opposed to *divine* meaning in the Baroque emblem). Because the emblematic structure is intimately bound to the concept of *res significans*, the author must believe in the possibility and necessity of uncovering a secret meaning in the world, whether religious (as for the Baroque writer) or materialist as for the modern artist. The reader is not presented with a clear meaning but is compelled to find the description of their own reflective process to be led into a careful contemplation of the world. Thus, *Denkbilder* relate to the hieroglyph—the tension between image and thought conveys polysemy. It is this polysemy that, once reflected upon prudently, may reveal the world's hidden meaning. This significance, however, may never be grasped fully, according to Benjamin; nevertheless, his *Denkbilder* are intended to illustrate that reality may be constructed in multiple ways.

The *Denkbilder* urge the reader to turn backward upon history, to recognize in itself "the past" as philosophical material that has yet to be represented "visually," wishing for the reader to discover it as a paradigm of (Benjamin's) experience of reality. Consider, for example, the following Benjaminian *Denkbild* titled *Heidelberg Castle*: "Ruins jutting into the sky can appear doubly beautiful on clear days when, in their windows or above their contours, the gaze meets passing clouds. Through the transient spectacle it opens in the sky, destruction reaffirms the eternity of these fallen stones."[147] The view through the castle ruin reveals the dependence of eternity on its contrast to transience—the ruins serve as an allegory for the lost past when it is identified by the observer as a permanent loss, also a loss that could be one's own. Simultaneously, the *Denkbild* of the castle ruin illustrates the multidirectional temporality of history, when the past is revealed (for a fleeting present moment) in its future revolutionary potentiality. The observer's perception of the ruins is revealed as the rubble of historical hegemony.[148] The aesthetic appreciation that was produced by the tension between eternity and transience turns into the understanding that the once-ruling historical protagonists have been overthrown and are permanently destroyed. Benjamin's *Denkbild* provides an insight into the tragically self-inflicted catastrophe of human history, a catastrophe stemming from a lack of understanding of the discontinuous relation of the present and the past. Benjamin, writing within the discourse of historical materialism, refers to this revelation as "profane illumination," which can occur only if the historian will recognize the reappearance of the past in the present; only then will past events gain their true significance. In this sense, according to Benjamin, history can be pictured as a kaleidoscope—infinite, ever-changing constellations of past and present moments (accordingly, for example, the calendar reveals itself as a document of historical time). From this perspective, the past does not progress linearly toward the present but (as the *Denkbild* demonstrates) rather endures in the present. As such, time is charged with a redemptive quality. Thus, the *Denkbild* gains importance as a historiographic narrative form.

It is important, however, to shed further light on the relationship Benjamin identifies between works/forms of art and history, or the manner in which one can extract a conception of history and historiography from art and what exactly is required for fulfilling that task.

In 1928, Benjamin seems to further develop his thinking of the functionality of the *Denkbilder*—he writes: "The function of artistic form is . . . to make historical content . . . into a philosophical truth."[149] This statement should not only be understood based on the five years (preceding 1928) during which Benjamin had experimented with the *Denkbilder* as (artistic) form but also based on what he wrote when this period began—and I specifically refer here to Benjamin's "Letter to Florens Christian Rang" (1923). Here Benjamin separates the line, perhaps taken for granted, connecting (works of) art and history, claiming that "art is in essence ahistorical" and even more radically that "there is no such thing as art history." Benjamin bases his claims on the lack of identifiable links between works of art once they are forcefully inserted into an artificial temporal dimension (links that do exist within human life or else life itself "would not really exist"), as well as the lack of new perspectives on their inner existence that we would supposedly expect to gain while they dwell in historical life. Nothing essentially links the works of art themselves to one another, as opposed to the events connecting human generations; thus, art history addresses the history of contents and forms for which works of art "provide merely examples or models." (This much resembles the "history" of philosophy, which is merely the history of dogmas or philosophers.) The historicity of works of art can thus be unlocked only by interpretations, according to Benjamin, rather than in "art history," since the process of interpretation reveals the (timeless) connection between those works—interpretation, then, temporalizes the world of art.

In the letter, Benjamin describes a metaphor in which ideas resemble stars that "in contrast to the sun of revelation" do not appear in the daylight of history but only in the night of nature (thus working in history only invisibly). As such, ideas are like works of art: both are "models of a nature," that is, ahistorical and lack the presence of mankind (in Benjamin's words: "the redeemed night").

The process of interpretation, however, entails the mortification of the works of art through their colonization by knowledge. Like Adam, who named nature in order to overcome it, so the process of interpretation overcomes works of art (and thus mortifies them, showing them as "nature returned" according to Benjamin). This explains the abovementioned quotation (1928) from Benjamin that eventually led him to claim that "all responsible human knowledge must take the form of interpretation and this form alone."[150]

GLOSS XIII—AESTHETICS AND EPISTEMOLOGY

The relationship between aesthetics and epistemology (and the relevancy of this relation to the fractured structure of Western culture at large) is analyzed by Agamben also in his relatively short but dense book, *Taste*.[151]

In the next chapter we will examine to what extent and by what means art works out the epistemology encapsulated within aesthetics at large to exert its supposed unique powers over the real. However, it may be the case that epistemological questions or discourses of knowledge have merely moderate significance for a research process intertwining theoretical and practical artistic tendencies, since the act of research alone (physical rummaging, working with materials, archive searching, etc.) creates a comprehensive diapason of acquaintances, comprising diverse degrees of relation of, by, and with its object; and this familiarity at least equally pertains to ontology and certainly no less to ethics. For the inquirer, one of the fundamental difficulties, whether in the conceptual or studio-based research phase, is that of communicating the insights thus accumulated to an interlocutor, most adequately and to the best of one's abilities. Also, the interpreter's act (as well as that of the reader or the listener), in and of itself, always remains partial and limited in its means to appropriate the knowledge generated and presented as if objectively, by and with the (art)work. A historical and epistemological dishomogeneity is constitutive of any attempt in art. Furthermore, even under the assumption that the process of sending and receiving knowledge is completed as fully as possible (after all, this is just an assumption, as well as a tentative process that might not necessarily include other possibilities of acquiring knowledge), knowledge formation is subjected to social conditions and restraints; in other words, as tirelessly repeated, knowledge is conditioned by the *episteme* and the operational power struggle that derives from it. Knowledge that is accepted as a norm, as a crystallized discourse, is forever liable to individuals' exchange of words, forever understood as "to the best of our knowledge," thus endangered in becoming outdated and nonstandard.

Somewhat ironically, in this sense, it was none other than Michel Foucault who marked that knowledge, as a field of historicity, as free of any constitutive activity, liberated from referring backward to an origin or forward to a historical or transcendental teleology. Knowledge, according to this definition, is a "series of denials"; it is not constitutive of anything, and thus is "epistemologically natural—*not value-free*, but saturated with *all* values . . . knowledge is . . . the possibility of everything we know."[152]

By means of contemplative concepts, philosophy—so it seems—does not constitute "substantive" knowledge but, as the word's etymology indicates, simply (not so simply) the love or passion for knowledge and wisdom (Socrates, we recall, never really defines the subject matter he interrogates but joyfully hovers over it; Aristotelian rhetoric uses enthymemes, etc.).

Art is likewise a manner of reflection but also simultaneously a (graduated) material attempt to actually intensify epistemological precariousness while standing in contrast to two reductive and opposite attempts to acquire knowledge of a thing: what it is made of and/or what it does. What is then the consequence of art epistemology?

Artistic research is a meadow for creating ideas. The research is not made in order to find facts and/or to present certain ideas but to generate them. Knowledge that was supposedly generated by artistic research cannot, in principle, be ultimately defined since any (artistic) knowledge always already carries with it the whole of Being, with its multiple and diverse knowledges thus accumulated prior to research.

[6]

We now come full circle back to the point where Benjamin's "citation without quotation marks" was discussed from an aesthetical perspective (as a "dialectical image"), where we leaned closer to the "aesthetical" pole of the philological-aesthetical axis.

Agamben's essay "The Melancholy Angel"[153] further elaborates Benjamin's concept of "citation without quotation marks," bringing it into the aesthetic domain. Quotations, according to Agamben, draw their power not from their ability to retrieve the past and enable the reader to relive it but from their capacity to expel from context while destroying the past in the course of happening.

Agamben points to Hannah Arendt's notes on this idea. According to Arendt, the transmission of the past relates to tradition and authority; "The break in tradition and the loss of authority"[154] that Benjamin identified in his own time, writes Arendt, were irreparable and thus required new ways of dealing with the past. Benjamin's solution, so to speak, was to replace the notion of the past's transmissibility with its citability, a solution that was born out of "despair of the present and the desire to destroy it," albeit with the hope "that something from this period [would] survive."[155]

Decontextualizing a fragment from the past makes it lose its character of authentic testimony while granting it an aggressive force, much like, according to Agamben, the artistic action of the ready-made in which an object loses its meaning (guaranteed by the authority of its daily use) and is charged "with an uncanny power to traumatize."[156] The radical break of this fragment from its past is linked to its hazardous state of alienation but also to the possibility of self-healing: "The past can only be fixed in the image that appears once and for all in the instant of its alienation, just as a memory appears suddenly, as in a flash, in a moment of danger."[157] The particular way of entering into a relation with the past resembles for Benjamin, according to Agamben, the figure of the collector who "quotes" objects outside of their context and destroys the order given to them by the internal order of their original disposition,[158] or of the figure of the revolutionary for whom the new can appear only through the destruction of the old.

As tirelessly repeated, the image of a man who has lost the link with his past and can no longer find himself in history is identified and described by Benjamin as the angel of history (*Angelus Novus*).[159] If Paul Klee's angel that Benjamin refers to is the angel of history, writes Agamben, then Albrecht Dürer's famous engraving depicting a melancholic angel is its analogy, the angel of art. Dürer's angel, however, "appears immersed in an atemporal dimension, as though something, interrupting the continuum of history, had frozen the surrounding reality in a kind of messianic arrest."[160] The past that becomes incomprehensible for the angel of history "reconstitutes its form in front of the angel of art; but this form is the alienated image in which the past finds its truth again only on condition of negating it, and knowledge of the new is possible only in the nontruth of the old."[161] Agamben thus grants aesthetics the role of the redeemer as it performs the same task that tradition performed before its interruption, resolving the conflict between old and new, and "opening for man a space between past and future in which he can find his action and his knowledge."[162]

The Man Without Content reserves a particular temporal status for the communicative, aesthetic gesture of the artist. If, in fact, the problem of art is to redeem the ever-possible conflict between past, present, and future, it is obvious that the work of the artist, the *poiesis* (being a lead to the presence, an unveiling independently of the will), must have access to "a more original temporal dimension."[163] All this is configured as a sort of messianic arrest of time, as a caesura that projects art into an "atemporal dimension" that is given, however, only in the transience (or lapse) of the work.[164] Agamben continues:

> The work of art . . . allows man to attain his original status in history and time in his encounter with it. This is why Aristotle can say in the fifth book of the Metaphysics[165]: "arts are also called 'beginning,' and of these especially the architectonic arts." That art is architectonic means, etymologically: art, *poiesis*, is pro-duction of origin, art is the gift of the original space of man, *architectonics* par excellence. . . . [I]n the work of art the *continuum* of linear time is broken, and man recovers, between past and future, his present space.[166]

It appears that, in the footsteps of Benjamin, Agamben grants aesthetics (or aesthetic operations) the role, however modest or limited, of the redeemer.

Aesthetics, as noted, opens for us a space (on the theological and epistemological horizon) between past and future as a messianic arrest of time, a gap between our conception of the present and our experience of it, which exhibits our inadequacy of being fully present "in-time" but also our ability to aesthetically work it out. The artist (or aesthetics), as a redeemer, must have access to an original temporal dimension—the messianic dimension that deactivates chronological time, as a caesura that transports a work of art into an atemporal existence. Messianic time resembles an underground alley—dug beneath history and enabling its redemption. Thus art, or *poiesis*, is a beginning, the "pro-duction" of origin, as it breaks the continuum of chronological time and can conceive of history as a blueprint for science fiction. But how is this done de facto?

Chapter Three

Ar[t]chaeology

A: Beauty That Falls

[1]

"Beauty That Falls," Giorgio Agamben's short text on the work of Cy Twombly, was originally published in 1998 and then again in 2002.[1] On the occasion of Twombly's 2006 German exhibition (*Cy Twombly in der Alten Pinakothek—Skulpturen*), an extended version of this text was published, now under the title "Falling Beauty."[2] In the text, Agamben meditates on the fallen movement of beauty as a special type of messianic spatiality in Twombly's artwork.

Merely by the text's title, one realizes its initial positioning at a theological-aesthetical crossroads, and since the text is published as part of an accompanying exhibition catalogue, one also notices its rubbing against the field of art criticism. In this sense, the text functions as a philosophical mediator (similar to other "perforated concepts" we previously encountered) or as a common locus where corresponding discourses are joined together under a central theme—in this case, falling beauty. "'What is falling beauty?' Or, put another way: 'How can we give form to broken and falling beauty?'"[3] Directed at the specific sculpture *Untitled* (Gaeta 1984), these questions are approached as the formal problem Twombly proposes in his sculpture, for which Agamben seems to suggest a confident response, if not a definite answer.

"Inscribed on a scroll on the sculpture's base," describes Agamben in preparation for his comparative analysis, is "the English translation of . . . the four verses concluding Rilke's Tenth Elegy, and thus the entire cycle of the *Duino Elegies*":

> And we, who think of happiness
> *ascending*, would feel the emotion
> that almost overwhelms us
> when a happy thing *falls*.

Rilke, in fact, introduces the vertical image of the fall in the preceding four verses:

> But if they were to awaken a symbol for us, the endlessly dead,
> see, perhaps they would point to the catkins of the empty
> hazels, the ones just hanging there, or
> the rain that falls upon the dark earth in Spring.

Here the idea of the fall is rendered in metric terms by a true split, signaled by an *enjambment* that interrupts the sense with a disjointed "or" (while the following four lines that Twombly transcribed on the base further underline the fracture, both metrically and semantically). What is the nature of this split that seems to condition the image of the fall in Rilke's poem?

Defined as a poetic phenomenon involving a certain measure of enjambment, a *caesura* (in poetry) is a pause or recess in a verse that is dictated by syntax and the natural rhythm of language. It interrupts a certain movement (through which it constitutes an image of beauty) that up to a certain point is pursued by "every great artist" (writes Agamben, perhaps too generally) as a continual ascent or upward movement; immediately afterward, it suddenly inverts and starts, visible vertically, falling downward. In the annotations on his translation of Sophocles's *Oedipus*, writes Agamben, Hölderlin develops a theory of the caesura.[4] There the caesura (which Agamben calls "anti-rhythmic interruption" or "anti-rhythmic suspension") is characterized as the epiphanic moment in tragedy when the drama suddenly comes to a complete halt and reveals its own nature as a tragic representation: when "the representation detaches itself from its production, or product, whether in image, word, gesture, deed, spectacle or sound, and lays bare the innermost nature of the representational process itself."[5] Accordingly, where the line is cut by the caesura, what the word reveals, what appears, is no longer what it says nor the alternation of representations (subject and sense) but the representation itself, the "pure word"; it is the vulnerable moment at the end of the poem where (following Dante) "the verses seem to fall hugging each other in the silence."[6]

Twombly's sculpture, according to Agamben, embodies the same movement that is conceived by Rilke's poem: just as the image of beauty that was pursued by the poet as a continual ascent suddenly inverts and starts falling directly downward, so too does the cracking wood in Twombly's sculpture reverse its upward movement and fall back to earth. As such, Twombly has succeeded in giving form to a caesura, displaying its sculptural equivalent. Just as the caesura displays the word itself, so does this sculptural equivalent display the work and the art themselves. Twombly's sculpture does not represent a caesura but is the caesura itself.

The caesura thus exposes the inactive core of every work, as though the movement of falling beauty has no weight. Every ascent is reversed and suspended, almost forming a caesura between an action and a nonaction: falling beauty. As Agamben concludes: "It is the point of de-creation, when the artist in his supreme way no longer creates, but de-creates, the messianic moment which has no possible title and in which art miraculously stands still, almost thunderstruck, fallen and risen at every moment."[7]

[2]

One of the better-known places where Agamben develops the philosophical basis for "Falling Beauty" is his discussion of the "End of the Poem" originally published in 1996,[8] where he attempts to define the end of the poem as a poetic institution.

Poetry, as it is claimed, lives only in the tension and difference between sound and sense between the semiotic and the semantic, in accordance with Paul Valéry's definition of a poem as "a prolonged hesitation between sound and sense." What is a hesitation in this context? Since enjambment makes evident the opposition of a metrical to syntactical limit, prosodic to semantic pause, metrical and semantic segmentation, it led some scholars to argue that the possibility of enjambment constitutes the only criterion for distinguishing poetry from prose. Poetry thus is the name given to the discourse where this opposition is made possible (and prose where this opposition is impossible). Or, as Nicolo Tibino's fourteenth-century definition of enjambment renders this notion more clearly: "It often happens that the rhyme ends, without the meaning of the sentence having been completed." This noncoincidence (in any poetic institution) between sound and sense is a schism, a disjunction between a semiotic and semantic event that is marked by the possibility of enjambment and is exemplified as (and by) a rhyme or caesura. Verse is the being that dwells in this schism and thus dwells in suspension; a poem is an organism grounded in the perception of limits and endings that define sonorous and semantic units.

If we follow this argument, then the end of the poem gains radical importance, as a verse that finds its crucial definition only at its end. This thought on limits and ends is quite characteristic of Agamben's thought in general; likewise, characteristic to Agamben's thought is the search for the word's philological root. *Verse*, he writes, relates to the Latin term *versure*, the point at which the plow turns around at the end of the furrow. At the end of the poem there can be no opposition between a metrical and semantic limit because there can be no enjambment in the final line of a poem. For if poetry is defined by the possibility of enjambment, it follows that the last line of a poem is not a line. Or does it mean that the last verse trespasses into prose? For poets, this end point represents a crisis in the poem, where the poem's very identity is at stake, where it is ruined, losing its breath, and interrupted with fragmentation. The disorder of the last verse points to the poem's structure and its (supposedly) impossibility of ending, since the end would imply a poetic impossibility, that is, the exact coincidence of sound and sense. At the point where sound is about to be ruined by sense, the poem (as if in seeking shelter) suspends its own end.

Building upon Dante's words that "the endings of the last verses are most beautiful if they fall into silence together with the rhymes,"[9] Agamben thus asks: What is this falling into silence of the poem? What is beauty that falls? And what is left of the poem after its (supposed) ruin? What happens at the end of the poem, which usually lives in the unsatisfied tension between the semiotic and the semantic, where this presumed opposition between them is no longer possible? Are sound and sense forever separated at this point (leaving an infinite empty space) or vice versa? According to Agamben's elegant argumentative progression, sound and sense in the poem are not two lines in parallel flight but one line that is simultaneously traversed by semiotic and semantic currents and in whose middle lies an interval maintained by poetic *mechanē*. In other words, sound and sense are not two substances (that together form a dichotomous structure where the disappearance of one necessarily entails the destruction of the other as well as the whole poetic *mechanē*) but two intensities of the same linguistic substance. But then we should further ask: how does Agamben maintain, in this view, the tension needed for the continuation of the poetic *mechanē*? What exactly is the relation between sound and sense under this (nondichotomous) framework? Unsurprisingly, here Agamben also holds a messianic stance maintaining the poem is like Paul's *katechon*: something that delays the advent of the Messiah, of He who would redefine the poetic machine by hurling it into silence. As Dante shows us, via Agamben, the most beautiful way to end a poem—at a place where verses fall in silence—reveals the poem's goal: that is, to let language finally communicate itself without remaining unsaid in what is said. The end of the poem, which at this point is supposed to be ruined by sense (to present a point of coincidence between sound and sense and thus the destruction of the poetic machine), dwells in silence as it is once again (in delaying the poetic ending perpetually) marking the tension between the semiotic and the semantic; the double intensity that animates language does not die away in a final comprehension—instead, it collapses into silence, so to speak, in an endless falling.

We should shed light on two important elements of this endless falling movement: the nature of it as collapsing and the auditory space in which it occurs. First, the nature of it as collapsing: as we previously saw in Melandri's nondichotomous epistemological mechanism of the paradigm, then in the issue of form and content in Renaissance allegories—and finally in the end of the poem—Agamben reaches the relational concept of "falling together" based on the philology of the medieval Latin *coincidere* and the idea of the collapsed binary opposition it stands for. Conceptualizing the relation in such a way is furthermore based on a certain form of relation one can find, as Agamben does, in Leibniz (and that we mention only at this point due to the pertinent auditory metaphor it includes). When Leibniz discusses (in his correspondence with Des Bosses that Agamben refers to) the unity of composite substances, he reaches the "acoustico-musical image" of echo to express the "peculiar nature" of the bond, and the curious intimacy between the monads it unites. Leibniz writes that the bond "demands [*exigit*] the monads, but does not essentially imply [*involvit*] them, because it can exist without the monads and vice versa . . . [The bond] is an echo of monads . . . with the result that once posited it demands monads, but does not depend on them."[10] The image of the echo, according to Agamben, expresses a curious intimacy between the monads, but (and this seems to be Agamben's essential critique of Leibniz) simultaneously an exteriority, since one cannot think an echo without the sounds that precede it. Additionally, it has to express exteriority because, if it does not, the Leibnizian echo would thus express a relation that collapses the opposition between supposedly dichotomous entities (monads) or terms, causing them to fall upon each other, to coincide.[11]

The abovementioned second element that characterizes the movement of endless falling is the auditory space in which it occurs, and that pertains to the Leibnizian echo: silence, as sound or as the "zero degree" of sound (if we are to use another of Agamben's terms), is conceived in such way as to prevent the destruction of the poetic *mechanē*. Furthermore, silence (conceived as such) thus radically opposes sense, as much as, in terms of language, a word reveals its maximal force exactly at the point when, out of the ruins of language, it is lacking. This conceptual view of silence, according to Agamben, is a consequence of a stubborn tradition that sees in absence the most extreme form of presence—a tradition that could be traced back to the pagan world of the Eleusinian mysteries where the initiates would experience something essentially silent: "A great awe in face of the gods silences the voice."[12] The power of silence has, in myth, the form of a privation of speech: the impossibility to speak.

Silence here plays a crucial role on a deeper level than that of the familiar sound-sense opposition and in the context of signifying language and poetry; it functions in a peculiar way with regard to another form of art, according to Agamben: painting.

In "Image and Silence," Agamben describes an idea by Simonides (via Plutarch) according to which painting is silent poetry, and poetry is painting that speaks—a generic opposition links the two arts that nonetheless have a common end. What is it? And more generally: what constitutes the tripartite relation between image, sound, and word? Painting mutes poetry, not because in painting poetry ceases to speak but because in painting the word and its silence are visible. How does painting display, in the form of an image, silence itself? Painting silences language, writes Agamben, "because it interrupts the signifying relation between name and thing, returning . . . the thing to itself," thus painting presents the thing in its pure "sayability," allowing it to appear in its "luminous, beatific sayability."[13] The thing returns to its anonymity, and the word (revealed in its nonreferring to the thing) recovers its silent status; and what shows itself in the threshold between them is, writes Agamben elsewhere, "the luminous spiral of the possible."[14] The common end of both painting and poetry is thus "a silence that has eliminated its unsayability, and which coincides with pure sayability."[15]

[3]

Part of what we have attempted thus far is to exemplify the manner in which Agamben thinks of poetry (and aesthetics more broadly) as that which is capable of manifesting its own means as such; in other words, poetry enables language by a prolonged suspended hesitation to "communicate itself." Poetry, for Agamben, is the messianic *désoeuvrement* of the communicative capabilities of language per se; therefore, once taking place, language reaches its own fulfillment, and consequently, its very end (supposedly).[16] This functioning, for Agamben, has further relevancy beyond poetry proper since he conceives of the poem as the comparable model for a certain type of operativity essential to human nature and its ontological dimension. This certain type of operativity is, in fact, inoperativity; and, in accordance with its poetic model, inoperativity is characterized not merely as aesthetical but also (and always in Agamben) as theological and philological.[17]

When Agamben thinks of language as communicating itself, he seems to conceive of the poem as the linguistic operation that renders language inoperative, as it deactivates its communicative and operative functions; it thus rests within itself, contemplating its own power to say and "in this way opens itself to a new possible use."[18]

The possibility of experience anew, beyond already-established norms and conventions, against existential passivity, and counter to an overwhelming technological-political-bureaucratic structure ("biopolitics"), is a leading motive behind Agamben's corpus. For him, overcoming the biopolitical machine becomes possible once again by the "appropriate" use of language—language that (communicating its own communication being) has the capacity, or *potency*, of not giving itself over to actuality; language that has the potentiality (*dynamis*) to say something but at the same time also the im-potentiality not to say it (the possibility not to). The reserve of potentiality is not a transcendental condition with respect to the empirical world but that which prevents the world from undergoing final reification.[19]

And, once again according to Agamben, one can find the most radical example for linguistic inoperativity in its entanglement with the theological sphere. In *The Kingdom and the Glory: For a Theological Genealogy of Economy and Government*, Agamben likewise discusses the hymn and Rilke's *Duino Elegies* and then concludes: "The hymn is the radical deactivation of signifying language, the word rendered completely inoperative and, nevertheless, retained as such in the form of liturgy."[20]

Still in the theological sphere (but beyond signifying language), the inoperativity and beatitude that "awaits the people of God," Agamben reminds us, is named by Paul "Sabbatism" (or the grandiose image of the Sabbath)—the most scared day (which exemplifies in Judaism the dimension most proper to God and man) "on which all work ceases."[21]

We ought to remember that inoperativity, and more precisely the concept of beatitude, although "awaiting" the people of God, carries more than a passive intonation to it, as it is situated somewhere between passivity and activity, between (to use Paul's own dichotomy) *dynamis* and *energeia*. Agamben treats this concept more broadly, however, outside the Jewish context per se, locating its concrete exemplification in the Gospels. In *What Is Philosophy?*, beatitude is discussed as the concept of *demand* in the context of the messianic—there, the possible does not necessarily demand to pass to the act, as we perhaps should expect, but somehow materializes itself in incorporeal messianic time: "The messianic presents itself as another world that demands to exist in this world . . . as if it were a—not always edifying—distortion of the world. . . . For this reason, demand has found a sublime expression in the Gospels' Beatitude, in the extreme tension that separates the Kingdom from the world."[22] In the Gospels' beatitude we find, once again, the unfolding of time in its present tense, since (as we previously saw) the messianic moment has already happened, it is already here and now in this world and needs no future factual realization. Thus, essentially, demand is beatitude. Beatitude/*demand* here relates more closely to the broader discussion of potentiality Agamben develops (thought in a Being that holds in itself all its possibilities, for eternity), and we should quote an entire paragraph if only for its beautiful rendering:

> Just as when we contemplate our beloved while she sleeps; she is there—but as if suspended from all her acts, involute, and wrapped around herself. Like an idea, she is there, and at the same time, she is not there. She lies before our eyes,

but in order for her to really be there we would have to wake her up, and, in doing so, we would lose her. The idea—and demands—is the sleep of the act, the dormition of life. All the possibilities are now gathered in a single complication, which life will gradually explicate—and has already in part explicated. But, hand in hand with the process of explication, the inexplicable idea goes always deeper and complicates itself. It is the demand that remains untainted in all its realizations, the sleep that knows no awakening.[23]

The concept of beatitude is further retraced by Agamben in the thought of Spinoza and, as its successor, Deleuze where it is connected to life and its immanent power to maintain the Being. When Spinoza develops a theory of "striving" (*conatus*) as the desire to persevere in one's own Being, he suggests an immanent movement that characterizes a Being who firmly remains in itself, who therefore desires its own desire, to constitute itself as desiring (in *conatus*, desire and Being perfectly coincide). Deleuze follows Spinoza in conceptualizing life as desire's variable field of immanence, offering, according to Agamben, a coincidence between the potentiality that constitutes life in the original sense and the desire to persevere in one's own Being. This is the Deleuzeian idea of "absolute immanence," and the reason he writes that life is "potentiality, complete beatitude." In Spinoza, writes Agamben,

> the idea of beatitude coincides with the experience of the self as an immanent cause, which he calls *acquiescentia in se ipso*, "being at rest in oneself," and defines precisely as *laetitia, concomitante idea sui tamquam causa*, "rejoicing accompanied by the idea of the self as cause." [. . .] The syntagma *acquiescentia in se ipso*, which names the highest beatitude attainable by human beings, [expresses] the apex of the movement of an immanent cause. It is precisely in this sense that Deleuze uses the term "beatitude" as the essential character of "a life. . ." *Beatitudo* is the movement of absolute immanence.[24]

Strictly from a spatial perspective (but not just), the concept of beatitude as "being at rest in oneself" equates here with the messianic moment in Twombly's sculpture when "art miraculously stands still, almost thunderstruck, fallen and risen at every moment." The Deleuzeian/Spinozan plane of immanence is always charged with "inactive" (regulative) potentialities that demand to materialize themselves, to use our previous formulation. It is a pleromatic self-sufficient plane of desires (to be actualized or deactualized) that therefore must be halted and contemplated on as occurs, for example, in the time of the Sabbath.

In Sabbatism, as the properly human praxis, the specific functions of the living are rendered inoperative and are thus opened up to unforeseen possibilities. This is the reason, writes Agamben, why Western philosophy has assigned such a central function to contemplative life and inoperativity, understood as the metaphysical operators of anthropogenesis that continuously produce new possibilities for man "by deactivating linguistic and corporeal, material and immaterial praxes."[25]

Only where there is contemplation of a potential is there (to use another term from the Agambenian vocabulary) "form-of-life," and although always about a certain work, "in contemplation, the work is deactivated and rendered inoperative, and in this way, restored to possibility, opened to a new possible use."[26] When crossed back to the aesthetical sphere, however, this turns out to be a constitutively difficult (if not impossible) task: *"The truth that contemporary art never manages to bring to expression is inoperativity, which it seeks at all costs to make into a work."*[27] The constitution of form-of-life, within artistic practice, is so difficult because in it there has been preserved the experience of a relation to something that exceeds work and operation and yet remains inseparable from it. Anyone (artists as well as thinkers) who practices a *poiesis* and an activity is not the sovereign subject of the creative process nor work but a living being who "by always rendering inoperative the works of language, of vision, of bodies, seek[s] to have an experience of themselves and to constitute their life as form-of-life."[28]

The lack of sovereignty over a creative process, and the utter independence of what conditions this process, is exemplified by Agamben (as one can expect) through yet another discussion of the creative use of language that is poetry. Agamben writes, in response to the question "to whom is poetry addressed?" that poetry's addressee is not a real person but an exigency. This exigency is essentially transcendental since it "coincides with none of the modal categories with which we are familiar" because its object is "neither necessary nor contingent, neither possible nor impossible . . . an exigency is, simply, beyond all necessity and all possibility." As an addressee that is positioned beyond subjectivity and formal logic, this exigency thus seems to acquire the status of a regulative idea, what one aspires to and actively works toward in spite of knowing it can never be reached. This apparent paradoxical characterization of the exigency is the reason why Agamben can further write that "a poem demands to be read, even if no one reads it [. . . and] insofar as it demands to be read, poetry must remain illegible. Properly speaking, there is no reader of poetry."[29] Poetry, by this thinking, is inherently granted an intensity, which animates it and renders it unattainable. The poem cannot have a reader since it is illegible, but for the same reason it cannot have a writer either; it does not acquire a space nor a subject but its own taking place in language, as intensity. Or, in Agamben's words, "the true addressee of poetry is the one who is not in a position to read it." The addressee (the illiterate) is not in a position to read poetry and will never be in such position—and this is equally true of the poet, who writes poetry with "an illiterate hand"; both subjects are illiterate subjects. Poetry here receives complete independence, or perhaps more accurately, is independent from time immemorial and as such a pure form of potentiality. Poetry, as a modus operandi, holds a vigilant potency capable of redeeming language, unleashing writing intensively, as constant volatility. Thus, Agamben can conclude, "Poetry is what gives all writing back to the illegible from which it comes and towards which it remains underway."[30]

That *poiesis* is incapable of expressing inoperativity as a form of truth is presented by Agamben somewhat ambivalently throughout his corpus—sometimes as a dogma but at other times in a less decisive manner. Whether contemporary art, as a material practice, is able to offer a path beyond language toward the constitution of a new conception of history is what we will try to examine next;[31] however, still within the boundaries of language, Agamben grants (as discussed above) poetry with a significant role in the effort to deliver truth and revive modern experience especially when, once again, it is entangled with the theological as its source.

Somewhat in accordance with what we have presented thus far, Colby Dickinson maintains that the poetic source of (human) potentiality is revealed and constructed, according to Agamben, in relation to its theological "mirror-image," that is, the abysmal source of God's creation. In Agamben's formulation of divine potentiality—God's power—God descends deeper and deeper into an "abyss," into its own source of (im)potentiality, in order to bring forth the forces of creation. This theme is expressed in numerous essays by Agamben. In "Bartleby, or On

Contingency," for example, he explicitly links this U-shaped advancement of divine potentiality to the poetic capacity of human creation:

> According to the mystics and Cabalists, by contrast, the obscure matter that creation presupposes is nothing other than divine potentiality. The act of creation is God's descent into an abyss that is simply his own potentiality and impotentiality, his capacity to and capacity not to. . . . As Jakob Böhme clearly states, it is the life of darkness in God, the divine root of Hell in which the Nothing is eternally produced. Only when we succeed in sinking into this Tartarus and experiencing our own impotentiality do we become capable of creating, truly becoming poets. And the hardest thing in this experience is not the Nothing or its darkness, in which many nevertheless remain imprisoned; the hardest thing is being capable of annihilating this Nothing and letting something, from Nothing, be.[32]

Dickinson terms the abovementioned linkage between the theological and the poetic as Agamben's "poetic atheology"—that which is united by a space of "pure potentiality," wherein "a regression of sorts takes place beyond the 'human being' typically constructed in the abyss between knowledge and experience. With an atheological poetry, there is a movement backwards into the potential which humanity holds, an almost indefinable experience of creative force beyond our normal cultural constructs."[33]

In this movement backward within and throughout that originary place "from which language (*logos*) arises and in which the name of God could be said to dwell,"[34] both God's divine utterance and, in its image, the poetic one made by Man confront (despite their unattainable and ungraspable character) the unsaid, beyond the said, in its locus within the abyss. What is truly revealed in this mythical and transcendent locus is "the unspeakable fact of our linguistic origins: that language exists in the first place but cannot be said as such in any 'pure' manner."[35]

Nonetheless, Agamben seems to insist on establishing poetry as a last refuge of meaning over and against the "destruction of experience" in the modern era; an insistence, according to Dickinson, that expresses Agamben's reformulation of the possibility for meaning to emerge beyond its inscription in language.

[4]

Before we end, it is necessary to conclude this subchapter with a minor reservation, put forward by Agamben in *Creation and Anarchy: The Work of Art and the Religion of Capitalism*, regarding art's (and artists') capacity to act in and upon the world. If it appears, somewhat justifiably, that Agamben ascribes art (or the aesthetic gesture of the artist) with unrealistic, grandiose power and potentiality, let us consider his suggestion that we "abandon the artistic machine to its fate."[36] What is the artistic machine?

In "Archaeology of the Work of Art" (the book's opening essay), Agamben raises the following question: what is the place of art in the present?[37] The essay tries to archaeologically analyze the problematic (in Agamben's perspective) position of the syntagma "the work of art," to determine which one (the work or the art) is the decisive element, if any, and whether their relationship is characterized better in terms of harmony or conflict. The decisive crisis in the notion of "work," as we experience it today according to Agamben, causes the work's disappearance from the sphere of artistic production—today art is more and more realized as an activity without a "work" because "the being-work of the work of art had remained unthought."[38] Agamben thus calls for a genealogy (in this short essay, though, he merely focuses on three key moments) of this fundamental ontological concept, by means of language analysis (since "philosophical problems are in the last analysis questions about the meaning of words"),[39] in order to resolve our contemporary problematic relationship with the "work of art."

In classical Greek, writes Agamben, artists are conceived as "technicians" who do not possess their own *telos*, their own end, because they produce a product that is exterior to them. Artists are constitutively incomplete beings (unlike the ones who contemplate or the visionaries, for example, who are philosophically superior to artists and hold within them their *energeia*, the being-in-act or being-at-work) since in unproductive activities such as thought (*theōria*), the subject perfectly possesses his end. Praxis, the action that has its end in itself, is superior to *poiēsis*, the activity whose end is in the work. Beginning from the Renaissance, Agamben writes, art becomes an action that no longer has its *energeia* in the exterior object but is slowly transformed into one of those activities (like knowing or praxis) that have their being-at-work in themselves. Art no longer resides in the work but in the mind of the artists, in their ideas, while they produce the work. This concept has its model (as discussed previously) in the theological idea of divine creation, according to which God created the world with a preexisting model in His "mind"; likewise, the artist already acquires the idea of the work of art before its realization. This is the theological vocabulary of creation in today's art writing according to Agamben. This process results in the modern status of the art object itself, as an unnecessary remainder with respect to the artist and its creative act. Thus, to quote Agamben, "*Ergon* and *energeia*, work and creative operation, are complementary yet incommunicable notions, which form, with the artist as their middle term, what I propose to call the 'artistic machine' of modernity. And it is not possible, . . . either to separate them or to make them coincide or, even less, to play one of against the other."[40]

Further into the essay, Agamben attempts to juxtapose, with regard to the present, the practice of the avant-garde and liturgy, based on (also previously mentioned) the writing of Odo Casel (the manifesto of the liturgical movement of the 1920s). Based on the idea that liturgy is not a "representation" or "commemoration" of the salvific event but is itself the event—and thus is carried out *ex opere operato* ("in that moment and in that place")—Agamben hypothesizes that a strong analogy exists between sacred action of the liturgy and the praxis of the artistic avant-garde and of the art called contemporary. These arts abandon, writes Agamben,

> the mimetic-representative paradigm in the name of a genuinely pragmatic claim. The artist's action is emancipated from its traditional productive or reproductive end and becomes an absolute "performance," a pure "liturgy" that coincides with its own celebration and is effective *ex opere operato* and not through the intellectual or moral qualities of the artist. . . . [L]iturgy and 'performance' insinuate a hybrid third, in which the action itself claims to present itself as a work.[41]

With the "invention" of the ready-made, Duchamp, according to Agamben's third and last genealogical moment, attempted to free art from what was blocking it, namely the "artistic machine." Duchamp attempted to deactivate this machine by forming a new place for the ready-made—"neither in the work nor in the artist, neither in the *ergon* not in the *energeia*, but only in the museum, which at this point acquires a decisive rank and value."⁴² Thus, in contemporary art there appears a historical conflict between art and work, *energeia* and *ergon*.

In conclusion, not only does Agamben suggest that we abandon the "artistic machine" but with it the idea that there is something like a supreme human activity that "by means of a subject, realizes itself in a work or in an *energeia* that draws from it its incomparable value."⁴³

B: Philosophical Archaeology as Artistic Modus Operandi

[1]

The second section of this chapter is meant to contextualize the archaeological orientation in contemporary art, as well as to generally examine how some artists have recently worked with archives or collections in their practice. The discussion does not intend to punctiliously demonstrate how philosophical archaeology works regarding our engagement with art but to picture, in general terms, how key elements of the methodology (that were presented thus far) are conceived within the discourse of contemporary art.⁴⁴ A connection is thus made between art's conception of the historical and the archaeological, between document and monument, in order to delineate a material conception of temporality. Consequently, the messianic conception of time (and its possible temporal realizations) is described in its relation to artistic, archaeological production.

What entails a material-based artwork, unfolding its inner most temporality in messianic terms, for a conception of history?

Let us offer two preparatory, guiding thoughts:

(1) In spite of the historical dimension in which it dwells, it also harbors the ahistorical. Its metaphor is that of the crystal, the artist's refractory tool, which reflects the very structure of living. "Reading" the crystal enables the artist to escape history altogether, since living and history are in opposition. The crystal "appears as the index of a certain aesthetic occurrence"⁴⁵ that represents reality in an ahistorical manner, as something primordial that happens before judgment or language. However, the index is materially produced, it sprouts from the depths of the ground, and in this sense the studio is for the artist what historiography is for the historian: "It is what says what can be said, how, and for whom."⁴⁶

(2) In the previous chapters we saw that the origin is not a factual event nor a mythical archetype but a vortex in the stream of becoming; it is that which emerges from the process of becoming and disappearance while it swallows the material involved in the process. As materiality, worldly things disrupt (in this process) the balance between the infinite and time—the infinite (the *apeiron*, according to Anaximander), although an *arché*, is crossed by time and cannot overrule it. Material things thus defy the infinite due to (their movement in) time but also defy time due to their inevitable return to the infinite.[47] As we saw, for Aristotle, the infinite is not a force of the cosmos but the intermediary between its elements; a mediatory field or space that is named "the middle (*meson*)." The infinite is a central space from which all elements are equally distanced due to the balance they are forced to maintain. Thus, as an *arché*, the infinite is not understood as a fixed point of origin and primary rule. The artistic *arché* is not a whole but a perforated concept—a characteristic that enables it to be a mediator; similarly, material time is formed as a porous structure.

GLOSS XIV—ART WRITING

How should one address, in writing, material art objects? According to Pedro Erber,[48] the critique of art objects tries out different approaches for sounding out an object, not in order to impose a specific, "correct" theory on it but rather as a process of negotiation through which its infinite potentiality of possible meanings is gradually revealed. The unsayable in an art object cannot be straightforwardly explained nor translated into a conceptual discourse or a form of narration. Nonetheless, the repeated attempt to do so is a fundamental task in art writing, which should be guided by the object and its potentiality to speak aesthetically. This working through resembles an idea by cultural theorist Mieke Bal, according to which an image is a dialogical partner rather than a case study subjected to the scholar's scalpel. Such a "speaking image" speaks back at its spectator, transforms the way the latter looks at art, and is termed by Bal (following French art historian Hubert Damisch) as a "theoretical object."[49] Theoretical objects, according to Bal, are not conceptual as opposed to material but are conceptual in their very materiality. This claim conceives of materiality as no longer dependent on visuality but, at the same time, as not in opposition to it either—thus, a theoretical object proposes a transformation of visuality into a participatory act, seducing the spectator into a relationship beyond contemplation. Art writing itself is a mode of "spectator participation," performed as a response to the object's seduction (yet resistance to translation). Conversely, the making of an art object can be seen as a material translation of something that resists conceptual expressivity. The British sculptor Antony Gormley speaks about material translation as the real challenge of sculpture, that is, how it is possible to connect with a viewer beyond ordinary language:

> How do you make something out there, material, separate from you, an object amongst other objects, somehow carry the feeling of being—for the viewer to somehow make a connection with it. . . . That idea that in some way there are things that cannot be articulated, that are unavailable for discourse, which can be conveyed in a material way, but can never be given a precise word equivalent for.[50]

Translation, in this sense, is no longer understood on the basis of correspondence between clearly defined and separate realms of significance; what's missing is correspondence itself as well as its conditions of possibility, that is, a clear division between the artistic and the theoretical, the material and the conceptual. Instead of corresponding, the kind of translation at stake here is more accurately conceived as *responding* to what demands (yet resists) translation. This translation, which adapts itself to its object, refers back to an "origin," in itself never completely exhausted in translation.

[2]

Recall, the term *philosophical archaeology* initially appears on the philosophical horizon, via Kant, at the end of the eighteenth century (in 1793, to be precise). Although discussed in the philosophical discourse, Kant's archaeological tendency or sensitivity can be conceived as being part of an overall (European) cultural desirability to the *arché*, which gains attention more or less at the same time. This social-historical orientation is manifested, in the art-informed context, with the increasing establishment of the grandiose European museums and art institutions: the Egyptian Museum Berlin in 1850, the British Museum in 1753, and finally (coinciding with the appearance of Kant's archaic formulation) the establishment of the Louvre in 1793.[51]

Likewise, in Germany, romanticist Goethe writes his essay "On Granite" (1784) marking a decisive desirability to the *arché*: "Here you stand upon ground which reaches right down into the deepest recesses of the Earth; no younger strata, no pile of debris comes between you and the firm foundation of the primal world."[52] Goethe crushes the world's foundation between his fingers, diminishing the geological distance, however colossal, by thought alone, lending himself to man's myths and enchanting historiography passed down from time immemorial. Is Goethe's desirability to the *arché* crystalized in an unprecedented historical moment, pertaining to the crisis of a present, or does it in fact reflect an untimely spiritual human psychic drive? How do we understand and experience this tension? What do we find, at the deepest recesses of the earth, once we dig up primordial soils and architypes? Do we pass through stratified matter in order to bridge our ongoing fragmentary existences? These familiar questions, we know, are deployed in time, all the time.

[3]

A key essay in the vigilant articulation of the archaeological orientation in contemporary art was published by curator Dieter Roelstraete in 2009, under the title "The Way of the Shovel: On the Archeological Imaginary in Art."[53] The essay's central argument concerns the identification of a "historiographic turn" in the art of the early twenty-first century, that is, a preoccupation with "looking back" among the generation of artists active at that time in the international art scene. Moreover, the essay questions whether this historiographic mode of artistic production and thinking might overemphasize the romantic notion that truth lies buried in history and thus distracts from more pressing issues of the present and the future.

Roelstraete's series of subsequent essays and curated exhibitions that he continued to develop on the subject matter culminated with the publication of *The Way of the Shovel*—a catalogue that accompanied an exhibition he curated at the MCA in Chicago under the same title (November 2013–March 2014). The catalogue contains, among others, Roelstraete's essay "Field Notes," which commences with a quote from an "archaeological" thinker who is perhaps the most appropriate to sound out a culture marked by fragments, shards, and traces—that is, Walter Benjamin: "He who seeks to approach his own buried past must conduct himself like a man digging."[54] The metaphor of digging, writes Roelstraete, seems to be an identifying (though ironic) feature of contemporary art: "that the one sector of culture most commonly associated with looking *forward* should appear so consumed by a passion for looking not just the proverbial other way but in the opposite direction—*backwards*."[55] Nonetheless, historical consciousness in the art world "appears to have reached a critical level, to have become something qualitatively *new*."[56]

A few of the exhibited works in *The Way of the Shovel* clearly illustrate the archaeological orientation in contemporary art that Roelstraete points to. One of them is *Plot* (2007) by Canadian artist Derek Brunen. It is a performance/video work that, in the course of six hours and twelve minutes, shows the artist literally digging his own grave, documenting his live performance in a solitary cemetery. This is a philosophically charged work that does not shy away from the big questions—life, death, fate, infinity—as it seeks answers to these questions that inevitably remain somewhat unanswered. This is the way of the shovel at its most literal sense, as earthly soil is dug out with a shovel in order to prepare for the artist's ultimate exiting. "In its appropriation of the endgame motif," Roelstraete writes, the artist proves "how the frustrated spectacle of the search for meaning can still engender an experience of the new."[57]

Another exhibited work that lucidly speaks to the manner in which contemporary artists construct their relation to history is *Message from Andrée* (2005) by Danish artist Joachim Koester. Drawing on both documentary and fiction, Joachim Koester's work reexamines and reactivates certain forms and traces from the past, with the intention of finding and translating the buried stories such marks might contain. While two prominent recurring concerns in his work are "how ideas and narratives take on a physical form" and "how stories and history materialize," equally important is the "dematerialized" question of the "tension between the apparent narrative, which the viewer immediately sees, and what remains invisible or illegible."[58]

Message from Andrée (usually presented as an installation of a 3:39 minute, 16mm film and two ink-jet prints) was inspired by a hot-air balloon expedition led by Swedish researcher Salomon August Andrée, who left Norway to journey across the North Pole in 1897. Thirty-three years later, the explorers' remains were found with a box of negatives that told the story of a crash and an ill-fated three-month trek across the ice. Koester photographed the negatives, which were covered in black stains, scratches, and streaks of light, and produced a film that just shows black dots of different sizes flicker over a field of white—those effects of film often ignored by historians. Koester writes: "Most historians studying the expedition ignored this layer of 'visual noise'. I, on the other hand, have made it my focus. If language defines our world, the black dots and light streaks on the photographs can be seen as bordering on the visible, or marking the edge of the unknown, pointing to the twilight zone of what can be told and what cannot be told, narratives and non-narratives, document and mistake."[59] While the viewer sees only inscrutable traces of something fluttering across the screen, the film evokes memories of the tragically optimistic explorers, the forces of time and severe weather conditions physically acting on the film, and the power of photography to reveal otherwise lost moments.

Message from Andrée, corresponding to a turning point for Koester, is his first work to include a film with a flicker effect and whose documentary dimension is a pretext for a perceptual experiment. From there, the artist concentrated more and more on a quest for "spirits." Koester's "ghost-hunting," which attempts to bring back forgotten people or places, often involves occultism or rituals that experiment with different types of perception. Spirits, for Koester, are all those things never fully realized in history. As Foster writes on Koester's work:

> Even as modernization obliterates history, it can also produce "points of suspensions" that expose its uneven development—or, perhaps better, its uneven devolution into so many ruins. Such are the "blind spots" that intrigue Koester. An oxymoron of sorts, the term suggests sites that, normally overlooked, might still provide insights; and, as Koester captures them, they are unsettled, an unusual mix of the banal and the uncanny, evocative of an everyday kind of historical unconscious.[60]

Foster's "points of suspension" is borrowed from Koester's (and Buckingham's) treatment and analysis of empty or indeterminate spaces and their relation to meaning embedded in material forms. They draw on the example of the Free City of Christiania, a twelve-hundred-person anarchistic squat located in Copenhagen, which since 1971 "exists as a police-free social experiment, self-governed under a direct-democratic process where all major decisions are made by unanimous vote. A sign posted at Christiania's main entrance declares: You are now leaving the European Union."[61] The representative flag comprises three yellow dots on a red background, a design that seemingly acts in opposition to "usual" symbols (that attempt to fix meaning against the flow of time) in the sense that it marks transience and fragmentation. "The three dots resemble an ellipsis, or 'points of suspension,' the typographical mark that indicates an omission, faltering speech, or an incomplete thought in a printed text."[62] The ellipsis marks the indeterminate but can also act as a connector of any two (or more) sentences and thus to form an infinite chain of possible thoughts. The three dots also form a broken horizon line, a limit that at the same time allows the mind spaces beyond the limit: "Empty spaces urging us onwards, reminding us that the vanishing point of history is always the present moment."[63]

A last example from *The Way of the Shovel* belongs to the artist that, as Roelstraete writes, "No survey of the archeological impulse in contemporary art would be complete without"[64]—Mark Dion. Dion's practice has become almost synonymous with the art of the archaeological dig, both as a metaphor and as a literal, physical act. In the exhibition, Dion presents a series of illustrations of mixed-media installations that he produced throughout his extensive artistic activities, as well as two crude and well-used shovels that have accompanied Dion on numerous digs. The emphasis of Dion's work, and in relation to the archaeological orientation in contemporary art, resides in its epistemological inquiry: "Dion's sprawling installations," writes Roelstraete, "regularly borrow from the aesthetic Lingua franca of nineteenth-century Victorian museum culture, consistently reversing the means and ends of scientific research and its 'objective' results or findings, to turn both the investigation and the locale—a desk, a lab coat, a tool kit—into a work of art."[65]

The new height of historical consciousness among contemporary artists, according to Roelstraete, is partly the result of the current knowledge economy that artists (as well as art critics, curators, and almost all art-world agents) are subject to; in other words, artists are part of a larger process of epistemological reorientation underway in society, a clearly identifiable process that (in the art world) is practiced through research done in the archive and library rather than in the studio, where such work (traditionally) used to take place.[66] In this quest for knowledge, artists aspire to recover long-forgotten artifacts but also (sometimes due to the impossibility of the mission of recovery) attempt to enhance our memory: to reconstruct, reenact, and repeat, as well as engage not only in practices of storytelling but of history telling: "Indeed, if the past truly *is* a foreign country . . . it is certainly one many artists feel called upon to rediscover from afar—the only terra incognita left to map, perhaps, in a world of total transparency in which everything is always immediately 'known.' "67

Moreover, in his attempt to answer the question "Why now?" of the historiographic turn, Roelstraete addresses the current crisis of history both as an intellectual discipline and as a fundament of contemporary culture more generally. Today's general state of postideological fatigue as well as the political evacuation of academia are signaled as the crisis's symptoms: "If 'progress,' " he writes, "in contemporary culture is predicated in part on accelerated oblivion, it is typically art's role to go against the grain of such dominant, homogenizing trends and slow down the spiral of forgetfulness, and even to occasionally turn back the clock."68

Another part of Roelstraete's answer to the question "Why now?" relates more directly to "the straightforward matter of chronology." The fall of the Berlin Wall in 1989 and the collapse of the Soviet Union in 1991 (being parts of a series of various political upheavals in [mostly] eastern Europe at the end of the twentieth century) mark the first clear milestones in this process according to Roelstraete; and the current generation of artists who grew up around that time are the ones who today attempt to, in some ways, preserve in memory the way of life on the "other" side (of the wall, the border, etc.) or to preserve what is no longer there. The other key event in this proposed chronology is the September 11, 2001, terror attack in New York, an event that signaled the end of the age of neoliberal complacency (following Francis Fukuyama's landmark essay "The End of History?" of 1989), an event that announced the dramatic *return* to History (with a capital H) and renewed calls upon art to take part in this process (as the present political worldwide climate is too miserable to handle): "The historiographic turn in contemporary art, then, was also a turning away from a present that art, as a whole, felt utterly powerless to change—or . . . uninterested in being a part of."69

Furthermore, the reason for art's recent attraction to the archaeological paradigm, according to Roelstraete, is related also to the discipline's truth claims—that is, "the rhetorical assumption that depth delivers truth, that the ground cannot lie."70 The archaeological, material-based quest or (re)search is an elaborated allegory of the artist's quest for the unknown and unknowable. In this quest, earthly soil plays a crucial role.71

[4]

If we accept the assumption that the ground cannot lie, and at the same time, recognize that archaeology is practiced (as a form of art) through engaging with its philosophical dimension, we can perhaps argue that philosophical archaeology in artistic practice confines this term to its proper meaning, that is, as potential truth.

In what he terms as "anteroom thought," Siegfried Kracauer advocates against the radical character of philosophical truths, due to their "generality and concomitant abstractness" as well as their favoring of "either-or decisions" and tendency for "freezing into dogma."[72] Resisting attempts at mediation, philosophical doctrines tend to leave no room for something to exist in the interstices between these truths. This threatens to overshadow potential truths that are not conceived as belonging to the "ultimate range of the general." Anteroom thought, on the contrary, requires the acknowledgment of philosophical truths and their claim to objective validity *alongside* the awareness of their limitations in terms of absoluteness and controlling power—"ambiguity is of the essence in this intermediary area."[73]

[5]

Art's current coupling of historical perspective and archaeological digging brings to mind a previous, similar coupling—between the document and the monument—described perhaps most elliptically by Foucault in this celebrated passage from *The Archaeology of Knowledge*: "In our time, history is that which transforms *document* into *monument*."[74] Foucault's critique, being a continuation of a historical tradition that started in France by the intellectuals of the *Annales* journal of the 1930s, emphasized a redefinition of the methodology involved in historical research. This critique of the document and history's fundamental relation to it, as well as the manner in which visual and textual materials were being used in historical research, highlight a more reflective use of the document that was exercised in academic circles but also (and perhaps more lucidly than in other fields) in artistic practices of the 1960s onward—using the document no longer as a site for interpretation but for construction. The document, Foucault maintained, is no longer for history an inert material: it actively manifests its potentiality in different ways if one just learns how to question it properly.[75] As opposed to the classic work of the historian, who investigates the document in order to uncover its supposed concealed truths, the artist is able to produce a document that is no longer part of a group of hidden evidence but rather constructed scenes of knowledge manufacture.[76]

The idea that, in the hands of artists, the document is no longer inert material (and that it has become a site for knowledge production) is reflected by multiple examples in recent contemporary art. Artists have continuously used archives and collections as a form of storytelling or history telling, in order to construct a desired narrative or to rewrite the historiography of a certain subject matter. To demonstrate that, and to further support the claim for the historiographic tendency in contemporary art, we can review a few prominent examples of the way artists have worked with and constituted archives or collections in the past, while shedding light on important sociopolitical consequences of it.

Mining the Museum (1992) was an exhibition curated and installed by artist Fred Wilson. Wilson was invited by the Contemporary (Baltimore) to create the exhibition using the archives and resources of the Maryland Historical Society. The society's collection is known for holding many objects from the "antebellum period." These items, along with their indexation, made the collection itself known for promoting an agenda of white supremacy. When Wilson culled objects from the permanent collection, he juxtaposed the products of slavery with fine art statuary, furniture, and silverware. It constituted an act of criticism directed at the institution itself, showing the gap between the society's own blind spots toward its past and the repressed history of the Black population in the United States today. For example, in one room titled "Cabinetmaking," he placed a set of antique armchairs in front of a whipping post (that was in use until 1938), as if to allow the audience to watch the white elite entertained by the abuse and humiliation of the Black population. In this room, as well as others, Wilson mimicked the usual methods of curatorial museum display (i.e., specially painted rooms, silkscreened wall texts, labels, audiovisual material, etc.) and through that mimicry radicalized a subgenre of conceptualism—the institutional critique.

Institutional critique became more entrenched in contemporary art from the time that artists were invited by the institutions themselves to act as critics within their own walls. An example from two years earlier was Joseph Kosuth's *The Play of the Unmentionable* (1990), which was exhibited in the Brooklyn Museum. Kosuth's project was part of a site-specific series of installations in the grand lobby of the museum, where artists were asked to further illuminate the debate "with an eye to history," as stated by Robert T. Buck, the director of the Brooklyn Museum. For this installation, Kosuth created a dialogue about what art is in its social and political context, and for that he chose approximately one hundred works from the museum's permanent collection "that were once considered acceptable in the cultures in which they were created, but now might be viewed by some as otherwise,"[77] as noted further in the museum press release.

Howard Halle notes in his essay "Mining the Museum" (1993) that most of the artists criticizing the institution of art represent minority groups, such as women (like Louise Lawler, Judith Barry, Silvia Kolbowski, and Andrea Fraser) or artists of color, like Wilson, as part of a struggle to redefine art history by erasing the demarcations of gender, race, and class. Claire Bishop (in her essay "Rescuing Collective Desires: Benjamin, History and Contemporary Art") agrees with Halle's comments on Wilson's project but notes that most exhibitions curated by artists are not trying to confront any element of art history but rather use the art collection as the extension of their own practice, in what should be considered "archival installation," as defined by Hal Foster. In "Archival Impulse" (2004), Foster argues that through the archival-like installation, artists collect and rearrange objects as part of an associative dialogue, jumping from one idea to the other, so that the installation acts only as a module of their taste. *Raid the Icebox 1 with Andy Warhol* (1969) is a good example of this. In early 1969 Andy Warhol was invited to select works for a traveling exhibition that intended to provide a fresh and less academic interpretation of the collections in the storerooms of the RISD Museum. This landmark exhibition was not only noteworthy for Warhol's idiosyncratic choice of objects—including shoes, parasols, chairs, hat boxes, Native American pottery and blankets, wallpaper, bundles of auction catalogues, even a ginkgo tree growing in the museum's courtyard—but for the radical way he chose to display the works: along with their storage cabinets, racks, and shelves, Warhol situated them just as they were stacked and grouped in storage when *he* first saw them.

The origins for both approaches to working with a collection, as Bishop notes, resides in two unfinished projects from the beginning of the twentieth century: Warburg's *Mnemosyne Atlas* (1924–29) and Benjamin's *Arcades Project* (1927–40). In the *Atlas* (conceived as a *Denkraum* [thought-space] or as a space of questions, a place to document problems),

Warburg used pictorial reproductions pinned on wooden panels to show the continuity of visual elements from the early pagan era to the renaissance of Christianity. By contrast, Benjamin's *Arcades Project* illuminates a process that locates the decisive shift to the modern age. Through a montage of quotations from, and reflections on, hundreds of published sources, arranged in thirty-six categories, Benjamin tells the history of nineteenth-century capitalism and what he calls the "commodification of things." From this research, he coined (as previously mentioned) the term "Dialectical Image," where past and present interact with one another as a method and subject of critical analysis. In other words, the juxtaposition of collected archival materials, as organized by Benjamin, can show how experience from the past can tell us something about present times and perhaps even something about the future. Artists working with collections in this way could create new readings of materials, retelling their stories and narratives: this could lead to new knowledge of the institution, its collection, and more generally of art history and beyond. But the detailed, repetitious, laborious act of uncovering buried "treasures," revealing the process of time's passage, etc.—approximate a "scientific" type of art—is needed before any new knowledge can be founded. In other words, this "new" knowledge has come to be increasingly dependent on the archaeology of the past, and therefore, the archaeological optic is one of the founding principles of modern museum culture (which in itself became a site to be explored) as well as the way contemporary artists work with and through archives or collections.

However, artists are not historians, and they should not attempt to be. They may create works that masquerade as documents and in doing so emphasize the extent to which documents are the products of conventions of knowledge production rather than vehicles for evidence. Their interest, in this case, lies less in uncovering than in unsettling historical truths and narratives. A great example is Walid Raad's Atlas Group (established in 1999), which researches and documents the contemporary history of Lebanon, in particular the years of the Lebanese Civil War (1975–91). Through the collection of the continuing effects of all the individual and collective experiences that constitutes history in the first place, the archive grows through not only found but also intentionally invented photographic, audiovisual, and written "documents" of everyday life in Lebanon. Raad aligns experience and memories of the past with "actual" photographs and documents from the time of the civil war; and by doing so, he asks an important question about the authenticity of documents:

why is a memory of the past less valid than a documentation of it? This important question is very much related to the world we live in today, where every experience seems to be photographed and uploaded immediately to humanity's largest archive—the internet.[78]

In her account of Walid Raad's work, Eva Respini emphasizes that "the Atlas Group presented itself as an organization founded to research and document the contemporary history of Lebanon, specifically the Lebanese Civil War, and as such as maintaining an archive of documents, films, notebooks, photographs, and objects."[79] Investigating how photographs, moving images, documents, and first-person narratives confer authenticity on official histories, be they histories of war or art, Raad's work weaves elements of the past, the present, and the future to build narratives that question how history, memory, and geopolitical relationships are constructed. Each Atlas Group document was attributed to a source, including the colorful historian Dr. Fadl Fakhouri who, however, was as fictional as the Atlas Group organization itself. For Raad, it seems, the opposition between fiction and nonfiction does not apply. A fact in his work incorporates fantasy and imagination while a fiction is grounded in real events, dates, and statistics: "Perhaps it is more productive to think of Raad's work in terms of its *imaginary* dimensions rather than its *fictive* ones."[80] In fact, it seems as if Raad's work's success hinges on our need to believe in official narratives. None of the "documents" produced by the Atlas Group is essentially faked: but when Raad re-photographs or scans them and mediates their presentation through story lines, literary titles, narrative wall texts, and engaging performances, they move into the imaginary realm. Raad's work turns to fiction in order to represent historical experience more adequately. He isn't concerned very much with "the fallaciousness of the material it presents,"[81] but in suggesting that only through fiction can an adequate image of reality be created.

[6]

This methodological research and understanding of history nonetheless transgress the proper discourse of art production. Media critic Knut Ebeling hypothesizes that in the twentieth century a new, archaeological thinking of the past appears next to its historical twin. This form of thinking is constituted via a few major, modern intellectual endeavors he terms "Wild Archeologies," that is, the dealing with archaeological projects outside archaeology proper. Such projects include, as he mentions, Freud's

"Archaeology of the Soul"; Benjamin's "Archaeology of Modernity"; and Foucault's "Archaeology of Knowledge." What all these projects share in common is that they are framed by Kant's "Archaeology of Philosophy" of 1793, as well as the fact that they experimented with a material reflection on temporality.

Thus, a shift occurs from nineteenth century's historical thinking to the twentieth century's archaeological thinking; intellectual history becomes archaeological, not historical. Ebeling writes that, nowadays, "Thinking temporality in the digital age requires a different line of thinking than historical discourse: not narrating, but counting; seeing rather than reading, not *historia* but *archaiologia*."[82]

"Wild Archeologies" present a certain suspicion toward history, in terms of historical facts, documentations, and records, and the "monopoly of scripture" that history once exclusively obtained. As opposed to history's constructs, to the printed word, and to the textbook version of the world, one finds the archaeological effort of uncovering that is systematically different—from simply "telling a story" to sounding out real debris, detritus, and the world of things, that is, from textual to material reflection of the past. Ebeling writes: "Archaeology does not represent the past; it materializes it. Archeologists work with the materiality of the past, whereas historians work with its written documents."[83] Thus, the difference is the one we have already mentioned: that of *document* versus *monument*, textuality versus visibility. Both archaeology and art secure remnants for visibility as opposed to history's telling of them.

Additionally, the encountered objects might tell something different than the wishful thinking of self-narration. This is the epistemic difference between *document* and *monument*. The archaeologists do not have a causal knowledge of the event or phenomenon; their knowledge of the contemporary is strictly material and needs to construct everything from a postcontemporary position, simultaneously, without sequencing semantics. This is the archaeological image, or as Benjamin called it, the *dialectical image*.

The second major difference between history and the archaeology is that of the language of inquiry—the historical account, whether written or oral, transforms everything into language, symbols, and digits, whereas the archaeological account first brings history and its object to light in order to consult the remnants themselves, not knowing in which language or logic to read and decipher them.

The third difference pivots around their conception of time as they sequence past contemporaneity[84] in different ways. Historical narration constructs time chronologically, linearly, and continuously, jumping back and forth on an immaterial axis of time—one always starts to narrate in the beginning. By contrast, material archaeology starts from the most recent, present moment (from the "contemporary ground," as Benjamin called it) and regresses backward in time, calculating back from the end, that is, the present.[85]

Thus, history and archaeology qualitatively differ in their temporalities, or as Agamben puts it (according to Ebeling), history explores the documented past that has already originated, whereas archaeology searches for the originating instead of the always already originated. The emergence of original temporalities is what interests the archaeologist. He calls it an "event": "the idea of an 'operation' whose effects are yet to come. . . . For the originating, effective past, or, more generally, for all effective operations—that lie in the past, but effect the present."[86]

Agamben, claims Ebeling, is somewhat less wild than the other "Wild Archeologists" previously mentioned, since his methodology "holds no materiality, it swallows and ignores the conflict between paper and stone, reading and seeing, text and technique," up to the point where it is "completely absorbed and assimilated by philosophy."[87] Is archaeology without materiality, asks Ebeling, still archaeology? To that I would suggest Agamben might reply with his proposition for a "minimal definition of thought" (in accordance with Aristotle's identification of the blank page as the pure potentiality of thought): "*To think means to recall the blank page while we write or read.* To think—but also to read—means to recall matter."[88] My suggestion emphasizes that even when the idea of "archaeology without materiality" is pushed to its extreme (i.e., becomes completely and merely "thinking"), the materiality of the blank page always lurks in the background—thoughts, in this sense, resemble readymades. Thus, my suggestion responds to Ebeling's question with a "yes."[89]

In his book on Agamben's work, David Kishik has an insight that can offer another pertinent angle in this regard. He writes:

> This attitude [i.e. the idea that philosophical prose must be "poeticized" or else it runs the risk of falling into banality] partly explains the mosaic-like nature of his work. The tesserae that make up his texts are fragments chiseled from larger

stones, or texts, written by others. It is a kind of historical materialism, not in the sense of a historical analysis directed at material processes but in the sense of a philosophical process that uses history as its material, indeed, as its capital, and thus wins over history itself by going against its grain. . . . A preliminary name for this method might be *détournement*: the cutting, pasting, and altering of found materials in the process of creating a new work.[90]

Materiality, according to Ebeling (as previously mentioned), is the common denominator of all "Wild Archeologies," which try, in varying ways, to construct archaeology outside archaeology proper. Materiality operates as *other*, as the other of history and historical knowledge.[91] "Wild Archeologies" of the modern period thus "transformed" the very idea of materiality—from immaterial idea to material understandings of it—which is, essentially, the base matter of archaeology.

The formulation of a new archaeological object (metaphysics in Kant; media in Kittler; souls in Freud; knowledge in Foucault, etc.), according to Ebeling, enables a culture to define and describe itself. The archaeological action can be interpreted as the art of constructing the missing link to the self.

[7]

In recent history, the art world (operating as a site of cultural discourse) has attempted to encounter, document, and interpret the past in various ways: the antiquarian endeavors of the eighteenth century (with its display technologies); the alignment of the advent of modern photography with archaeological pursuits of the nineteenth century; and the artistic responses to the formal aesthetics of archaeological artifacts of the early twentieth century are perhaps the most prominent constructions. In the second part of the twentieth century, according to curator and writer Ian Alden Russell, one witnesses a shift "from purely formal responses to archaeological aesthetics toward more reflective and critical treatments of the manifestations of traces of human agency in the world"[92]—a shift that was carried out by the works of a large and diverse group of artists (such as Henry Moore, Barbara Hepworth, Richard Long, Keith Arnatt, Cornelia Parker, Mark Dion, and perhaps most notably Robert Smithson), all contributing to the development of archaeological awareness as a mode of ecological sensitivity.

Moreover, Russell claims that in the latter half of the twentieth century, archaeology extends its metaphor to become an allegory, a historical development that refocuses critical engagement "from rhetoric of layers, depth, and progress (as in the twentieth century) to affect, performance, and meaning-making," so that the return to the past is not carried out primarily for the sake of inspiration, but "is a deployment of the past as a technique in itself—a search for liberation through the subaltern past as a means of resistance to and critique of the teleology of technological progress."[93] Thus, the first decade of the twenty-first century witnesses a strengthened relationship between archaeological and artistic practices and an ongoing effort toward a renewed conception of the past, so much so that an avant-gardist past, unconfined by various formal frameworks, one that is constituted as a creative process, might turn to be a new reality.

[8]

An avant-gardist, renewed conception of the past might be a different rehabilitation that Roelstraete seeks for the "tragic flaw of the historiographic turn in art," although not necessarily in the form of another "ism." Rethinking the past, or more generally, rethinking time as the medium in which the objects of historical research in art are taking part, is perhaps not an "ism" as such but is at least a radical shift that has equal value in our thinking and making and has the potential to open up renewed possibilities outside linear chronologies and against the blockage of the cultural imagination that art seemed to have reached.

In a feature for *Frieze* in late 2012 ("This Is So Contemporary!"), writer Amelia Groom surveys how a number of recent exhibitions have been integrating the past with the present, seeking to do away with correct chronological sequence and the confines of cultural context, in order to suggest that the time and place in which a thing was made should not shut it off from other times and places.

Groom offers heterogeneous examples: *The Russian Linesman* (2009) at London's Hayward Gallery, curated by Mark Wallinger, suggested surprising correspondences between vastly different objects spanning two millennia; *History of History* (toured between 2003 and 2009), organized by Japanese contemporary artist and collector Hiroshi Sugimoto, established intricate dialogues between new works and material culture from distant pasts; *Intolerance* (2010) by the Dutch artist Willem de Rooij, organized at the Neue Nationalgalerie in Berlin, presented a series of animal portraits from the Golden Age of Dutch painting alongside feathered ceremonial headdresses from eighteenth-century Hawaii, referred to the display as part of his ongoing work with "spatial collage"; *Never the Same River (Possible Futures, Probable Pasts)*, curated by Simon Starling at London's Camden Arts Centre in 2010–11, slipped between different histories in the present as the artist restaged works from Camden shows of the last half-century; *Shaped by Time* (2012) at the National Museum of Denmark, organized by artist Julie Sass and curator Milena Hoegsberg, positioned (in relation to the museum's prehistoric collection) fragmented pasts in dialogue with the present in order to consider the construct of history and reveal its fluidity; or when the Fifty-Fourth Venice Biennale (2011), curated by Bice Curiger, included paintings by Tintoretto in its line-up of new art.

These lines of thought, writes Groom, can be traced back to the art of the early 1960s (framed today as minimalism, conceptualism, and land art), which involve practices that were theoretically influenced by the Mesoamerican art historian George Kubler and his book *The Shape of Time: Remarks on the History of Things* (1962). Dismissing the rhetoric of progress in favor of more chaotic models of time, Kubler outlined how artistic innovation, replication, and mutation never unfold in a single unbroken direction. History's movements are turbulent, and art will always refuse to tell a fixed, unified story. *The Shape of Time* emphasized that the segmentation of the past is purely arbitrary and conventional and that an imposition of linear order on something that is infinitely more fluid and complex is problematic. Kubler further claimed that historic time is always at once progressive and regressive, in the same way that art modifies our conception of what went before it and what comes after it (for instance, one's knowledge of Auguste Rodin forever changes one's understanding of Michelangelo, according to Kubler).

Groom concludes:

> When we are presented with old art and new art together on equal terms, divisions become slippery and the past is made available for communicative interaction with the present. We form new associations, and possibly face up to contradictions we'd rather not acknowledge. The inclusion of things in displays of contemporary art that are neither strictly "contemporary" nor "art" is not, as some have suggested, a mere fleeting curatorial trend. It's part of a broader growing

awareness of the anachronism inherent in all time. After the failed productive-progressivism of modernity, we're dealing with the fact that then and now and later aren't proceeding along a flat line; they're synchronized and woven through each other.[94]

[9]

What entails a cultural condition that denies linear chronology and advancement along a flat line but nonetheless is considered and executed at the present time? What kind of (temporal) present does it present and represent?

In his meditation on the (cultural) contemporary, theorist Boris Groys addresses the present and its position within and in relation to chronology. Groys maintains that the present is no longer a chronological transition point between past and future but instead a site of the permanent rewriting of both. The artistic medium that best reflects this contemporary condition is, for Groys (and not without a touch of irony), time-based media:

> Because it thematizes the non-productive, wasted, excessive time—a suspended time . . . it captures and demonstrates activities that take place in time, but do not lead to the creation of any definite product. . . . But it is precisely because such a wasted, suspended, non-historical time cannot be accumulated and absorbed by its product that it can be repeated—impersonally and potentially infinitely. . . . Hence, practicing literal repetition can be seen as initiating a rupture in the continuity of life by creating a non-historical excess of time through art. And this is the point at which art can indeed become truly contemporary.[95]

Time-based art (as opposed to traditional artworks) is thus not based on a solid foundation of time, but rather documents time that is in danger of being lost as a result of its unproductive character.[96] This change in the relationship between art and time also changes the temporality of art itself—it ceases to be present, ceases to be "in the present" or "in time," and begins to document a repetitive present that can be prolonged into the indefinite future. The temporality of contemporary art, according to Groys, is thus "with time"—being contemporary, as the essay's title suggests, means being a "comrade of time."

For the most part nowadays, the actual conditions of spectatorship in time-based art (as it is often exhibited in art spaces) seem to support Groys's analysis. In modernity, the attitude of passive contemplation was discredited by celebrations of the potent movements of material forces. He writes: "While the vita contemplativa was for a very long time perceived as an ideal form of human existence, it came to be despised and rejected throughout the period of modernity as a manifestation of the weakness of life, a lack of energy."[97] Contemporary spectators, on the other hand, can no longer rely on having infinite time resources or perspectives ("the expectation that was constitutive for Platonic, Christian, or Buddhist traditions of contemplation"); contemporary vita contemplativa coincides with permanent active circulation. It is a repetitive gesture that leads to no result and to no established aesthetic judgment.[98]

The growing disbelief that characterizes the contemporary—the disbelief that cultural projects can realize their (past and future) promises in a way that reflects the disbelief of sociopolitical structures—causes Groys to speculate on a particular acute need of the contemporary: "The contemporary is actually constituted by doubt, hesitation, uncertainty, indecision—by the need for prolonged reflection, for a delay. . . . A prolonged, even potentially infinite period of delay."[99]

[10]

Ceal Floyer's video work "Drop" (2013)[100] is a clear example that seems to fulfill the contemporary's need (in Groys's perspective) for potentially infinite deferment that will allow for the messianic to "seep in."[101] The sublime emptiness of the present moment is manifested in her portrayal of the passing of time (and the present moment) in a material form—water drops accumulating very slowly until a breaking point occurs and gravity pulls it down, causing the drop to fall and shutter. The agonizing time of the viewer, who waits for the drop to disconnect, stretches out endlessly and becomes pure duration. The piece is not only a time-based work but also takes place *in* time—that is, it criticizes the metaphysics of presence in the sense that it shows the before and after of presence, of the present moment by stretching the past and the future to its extreme.[102] The actual moment of falling happens almost too quickly for the human eye to catch, the present withdraws and appears as if never took place. One is never contemporary with the present, as there is no now; the now is always deferred. What seems to undergo a profound change is not the water drop itself, as an essence or material entity in and of itself, but something in our understanding of it, in our appreciation of the drop perhaps like never before.

[11]

Let us attempt to offer a short summation of our current discussion before we part ways. In this chapter, the historiographic turn in contemporary art, characterized by the metaphor of the archaeological dig and the need to look backward, is depicted as contributing to artists' historical consciousness and in particular with regard to the societal knowledge economy. The constant artistic search for the unknown is exemplified, as an expanded metaphor, by the soil and buried past, that is now understood as the only terrain left for further explorations. History's traditional inert materials (documents, archives, etc.) are charged by artists with active forces and are archaeologically transformed into sites of knowledge construction. Various cultural archaeological projects reformulate a conception of time by materializing the past—examining and interpreting the material object, beyond the constrains of language, these archaeological projects constitute a porous, multidirectional conception of time and thus propel an epistemological difference between history and archaeology in regard to the object. In the hands of (some) contemporary artists, so it seems, the avant-gardist return to the past becomes a cultural production technique, capable of opening up new possibilities rather than being a merely romantic, inspirational caprice. This return is thus transformed into a deferred present where past and future are constantly rewritten, where (against the dematerialization of the ephemeral art object) the present moment is the only possible thing left to document. The artistic present requires a constant deferred reflection—messianic time. Living in messianic time means living in a potential without end, a purposefulness without purpose, which relates to Kant's aesthetics, a disinterested pleasure that we now call art. The messianic time of contemporary art, its "beatitude" as Agamben defines it, is conditioned by a caesura that shows the pure representation and the silent core that are constitutive to an authentic work of art. This is an image of beauty that is weightless and postponed, existing in a standstill between passivity and activity—a messianic moment of "de-creation." This beatitude is made possible due to the unforeseen, nonlinear flow of time: like Benjamin's kaleidoscopic conception of history, time is an ever-changing temporal constellation charged with a redemptive, messianic force.

[12]

The messianic world, in a return to Agamben, introduces a small displacement that does not affect the identity of the Absolute and our concrete world and does not concern the state of things but rather "their sense and their limits," as it takes place "in the space of ease between everything and itself."[103] In his *questio* about halos, Saint Thomas, writes Agamben, addresses this displacement by characterizing it as a "halo"—a surplus that makes the essential more brilliant, a supplement added to perfection, a vibration of that which is perfect, the incandescence at its margins (or, in Clarice Lispector's words, that which "comes from the splendour of the almost mathematical light emanating from people and things," a lucidity, characteristic of a state of grace, of "those who are no longer surmising: they simply know").[104] "This imperceptible trembling of the finite," writes Agamben, "that makes its limits indeterminate and allows it to blend, . . . is the tiny displacement that everything must accomplish in the messianic world. Its beatitude is that of a potentiality that comes only after the act, of matter that does not remain beneath the form, but surrounds it with a halo."[105]

Conclusion

"There will be no conclusion. I think, in fact, that in philosophy as in art, we cannot 'conclude' a work: we can only abandon it, as Giacometti said of his canvases."[1]

Notes

Prologue

1. Agamben, *The Signature of All Things*, 7–8. Feuerbach presents this idea (titled *Entwicklungsfähigkeit*) at the beginning of his 1837 monograph on Leibnitz. See Feuerbach, "Darstellung, Entwicklung und Kritik der Leibnizschen Philosophie."

2. Agamben is thus attributed to a tradition continued by different interlocutors such as, for example, French writer Alfred Jarry, which Agamben mentions in his books *What Is Philosophy?* and *Autoritratto nello studio*, among others.

3. Agamben conceives of practice, however, as preceding theory, as he writes: "Anyone familiar with research in the human sciences knows that, contrary to common opinion, a reflection on method usually follows practical application, rather than preceding it" (Agamben, *The Signature of All Things*, 7). This statement can be compared with Claude Lévi-Strauss's statement: "The truth of the matter is that *the principle underlying a classification can never be postulated in advance*. It can only be discovered *a posteriori* by ethnographic investigation, that is, by experience" (Lévi-Strauss, *The Savage Mind*, 58).

4. Agamben, *The Signature of All Things*, 7.

5. Quoted in Agamben, *What Is an Apparatus? and Other Essays*, 53. See also Agamben, *Creation and Anarchy*, 1. Elsewhere Agamben remarks: "I tend to work in crepuscular regions, at sunset, where the shadows are very long. For me they reach into the deepest past. There is no great theoretical difference between my work and Foucault's; it is merely a question of the length of the historical shadow." (Quoted in De La Durantaye, *Giorgio Agamben*, 246.)

6. Agamben, *The Signature of All Things*, 7.

7. Agamben, 7. For further references Agamben makes to this idea see Agamben, *I Luoghi della Vita*; and Agamben, *Intervista a Giorgio Agamben: dalla Teologia alla Teologia Economica*.

8. See Agamben, "Un Libro senza Patria," 45.

9. Agamben, *The Fire and the Tale*, 34.

10. For Agamben's pertinent definition of philosophy-as-intensity, see Agamben, "Philosophy as Interdisciplinary Intensity."

11. Considered from a historical perspective, the Agambenian methodology is in this sense part of a corpus of techniques of interpretation. This corpus, which can be dated back to the Greek grammarians, was somewhat in suspension throughout the seventeenth and eighteenth centuries and was not relaunched until the nineteenth century. As Foucault indicates in "Nietzsche, Freud, Marx," the corpus opened up once again the possibility of interpretation and hermeneutic. This new possibility, still relevant today, is characterized, according to Foucault, by the way these techniques of interpretation (including that of Agamben) were able to range signs "in a much more differentiated space, according to a dimension that could be called that of depth" (Foucault, "Nietzsche, Freud, Marx," 272). The interpreter is, for example, following Nietzsche, "the good excavator of the lower depths" (Foucault, 273) and thus the signifier "archaeology" (in philosophical archaeology) makes evident its belonging to this tradition. Another aspect that characterizes the techniques of interpretation, according to Foucault, emphasizes the idea that interpretation became an infinite task since signs are linked together in an inexhaustible network framed by an irreducible gaping and openness. This aspect of incompleteness of interpretation "is found once again . . . in the form of the refusal of beginning" (Foucault, 274). Agamben's methodology, as we shall see in due course, renounces the beginning much in the same way as Foucault's or Nietzsche's, but simultaneously renders it as categorically discoverable within, and at the end of, its archaeological dig.

12. Kishik, *The Power of Life*, 62–63.

Chapter One

1. Kant, "What Real Progress Has Metaphysics Made in Germany since the Time of Leibniz and Wolff?," 413–24.

2. Kant, "What Real Progress Has Metaphysics Made," 417. Quoted in Agamben, *The Signature of All Things: On Method*, 81. A philosophical history of philosophy, in this regard, is already discussed (albeit somewhat interchangeably or as a philosophical ruin) in the first edition of the *Critique of Pure Reason* (1781), where it is referred to as the "History of Pure Reason." By this, Kant means that reason is subjected to historical process, but once it reaches unity, reason overcomes its historicity and becomes a priori timeless truth or (philosophical) science. With the help of Kant's critical project/revolution, more broadly, philosophy is meant to undergo a complete transformation—from being a history-dependent doxa into timeless *episteme*.

3. Kant, "What Real Progress Has Metaphysics Made," 419. Thus, Kant's problem was not to formulate an a priori history but the developing pattern of reason as it takes place within empirical material; in other words, what "should have happened" must shine out of the ruins of "what did happen." The one who, at the end of this process (when, and only then, the architectonic of reason can be known), writes a philosophical history of philosophy, can understand past philosophical systems better than anyone else. The execution of this program, however, occurred historically only with Hegel.

4. Kant's ruinous archaeological terminology, which Agamben builds upon, extends beyond the particular manner in which philosophical archaeology (or pure reason at large) is formulated in the "Jottings." One can find its indexes, as said, already in the *Critique of Pure Reason* where, for example, with regard to a future task that is currently left open, Kant writes: "I will content myself with casting a cursory glance from a merely transcendental point of view, namely that of the nature of pure reason, on the whole of its labors hitherto, which presents to my view edifices, to be sure, but only in ruins." (Kant, *Critique of Pure Reason*, 702) Furthermore, a few pages earlier, he writes about the attempt to draw the architecture of all human knowledge, "which at the present time, since so much material has already been collected or can be taken from the ruins of collapsed older edifices, would not merely be possible but not even be very difficult. We shall content ourselves here with the completion of our task, namely, merely outlining the architectonic of all cognition from pure reason." (Kant, *Critique of Pure Reason*, 692–93).

5. Kant, "Conjectural Beginning of Human History (1786)," 163.

6. Kant, "Conjectural Beginning of Human History (1786)," 163. For a complementary discussion of the end of all things and phenomena (and therefore of history), see Kant, "The End of All Things (1794)" and Beck's edited volume *Kant: On History*.

Furthermore, in this context, Kant's thought on marginality/liminality is discussed in a chapter ("The History of Philosophy and Its Architectonic") from *Kant and the Philosophy of History* by Yirmiyahu Yovel where he identifies Kant as the first philosopher, prior to Hegel (and Marx), of the "end of philosophy." As opposed to philosophers before him who conceived their "final truths" as merely contingent and accidental in the context of the developing history of philosophy up to their time, Kant conceives his (by now renowned) philosophical revolution as the end of a necessary process of gradual explication of human reason; in other words, a conclusion to "the inevitable historization of reason." In the preface to the *Phenomenology of Spirit*, Hegel speaks about philosophy's need to drop the "philo" prefix in order to become actual knowledge ("sophia"), and this is what the Kantian *Critique* (a final revolution) was supposed to achieve according to Yovel—to bring out the true paradigm of reason that before Kant's work (i.e., the *history* of philosophy) contained flaws. Note that the major difference between Kant and Hegel, in terms of their theory of the history of philosophy, is as follows: Kant does not have a substantiated dialectical logic to make both poles (the empirical and the a priori) moments of a single developing whole. His theory of development, writes Yovel, "is only *declared*." Thus, this is also why "Kant cannot, in the last analysis, account for the importance of *time* as a medium for the development of reason . . . he cannot show that their temporal sequence is of major importance." There is another important difference, in this regard, between Kant and Hegel. With Kant's *Critique*, we are able to understand our history (what we did and what we ought to do), and there cannot be any more rational justification for latent action—henceforth, the primary of pure practical reason. In Hegel, social and political actions are subordinated "to the ultimate end of speculation" as he historicized the Aristotelian ideal of absolute knowledge, "making philosophical knowledge the supreme stage in the history of the world spirit." Self-knowledge is made possible only after the world had become rational in praxis as well. For Kant, on the contrary, "Self-knowledge is a prerequisite for rational action, not its result." Only after the history of philosophy is consumed does man understand for the first time the meaning of his own history and the future task still ahead of him: "to shape the world itself as a 'highest good.'"

In Kant, the history of philosophy takes a systematic form in and of itself but is likewise conceived "as a basic mode of the history of reason in general" since Kant includes the theory of the history of philosophy in the system of reason at large—even if the form of the history of philosophy remains concealed in the process of its development, it has the same form as the final system that it brings to light: "*the structure of the history of philosophy is inherently the same as that of the system of philosophy.*"

In terms of the problem Kant discusses—that is, the relation of philosophy to its history—he thus exhibits a proto-Hegelian view complemented with elements such as *opposition* and *revolution*. This view (an impossible concept of reason that supposedly includes contradictions) is not paradoxical, since we are dealing with the "development of reason" (or the *history* of philosophy), and thus it can be said to contain radical contradictions and not be continuous. Hence, according to Yovel, "The great controversies in the history of philosophy have their origin in the nature of pure reason." These historical controversies mean that reason, since it is fundamentally coherent, had yet to be satisfactorily explicated, and for now it is still a "field full of ruins." The various contradictions in the history of philosophy "are all governed by the architectonic of reason and gradually bring its harmony to light," thus Kant understands his *Critique* as opening the way to the most comprehensive systemization of the ends of reason. The system of reason is historicized, according to Kant, because of the finitude of human reason. That reason is finitude means that it is constituted as an organic whole, whereas each part/member in that whole "expound[s] the self-development of reason," and thus the whole system of human reason is historicized. All philosophical systems relate to one another and to a single unifying principle (of the pure reason); all are members of one organic totality governed by the pure architectonic of reason (Kant calls this underlying concept an idea or "original germ"). Since each philosophical system presents only part of the (whole) architectonic, the history of philosophy "must appear a concealed and distorted totality. . . . Thus, *the history of philosophy is the historicized form of the architectonic of reason.*"

7. Agamben, *The Fire and the Tale*, 84.

8. Perhaps the most outstanding example for that, in modern literature, is by another author closely related to Agamben's thought: Walter Benjamin. Vol. 4 of Benjamin's *Gesammelte Schriften* [Collected writings] presents a mass of preparatory notes, quotations, as well as photographic and bibliographic citations that were collected in preparation for his *Arcades Project* and were never assembled into coherent, finished narratives.

9. Both Christian and Jewish theological traditions identify this problem and contend with it. In the Christian tradition (having a Platonic origin and exerting its profound influence on the Renaissance conception of artistic creation) it is sometimes argued that God always had an "outline" of the ideas behind all created creatures and always possesses something that precedes creation, an immemorial "before" the work that was eventually accomplished in the biblical Hexameron. The Cabalistic tradition understands creation ex nihilo to mean that nothingness is the matter with which God made its creation and that the divine work is "literally made of nothing" (Agamben, *The Fire and the Tale*, 85).

10. This idea is described in Edgar Wind's essay "Critique of Connoisseurship" (Wind, *Art and Anarchy*, 30–46).

11. In accordance with Cézanne's formula that "one never finishes a painting, but simply abandons it" (Agamben, *The Fire and the Tale*, 89).

12. We will come back to this idea later on in the context of the philological meaning of the word *arché* and the manner in which it is understood as an "originary vortex."

13. Agamben, *The Fire and the Tale*, 93.

14. For a detailed discussion of how in the early centuries AD the roll was replaced as the vehicle for literature by the codex; see Roberts and Skeat, *The Birth of the Codex*. I return to the theme of forms of temporality in the next chapter.

15. Before we move on to broadly develop the idea of "essential dishomogeneity" and its relation to the *arché*, it is worth mentioning (still within the context of literature) the special (temporal) function dishomogeneity can articulate in the work of some authors.

For instance, an interview with writer Edmond Jabès (conducted by artist Bracha Ettinger Lichtenberg) opens the accompanying catalogue to the exhibition

Routes of Wandering: Nomadism, Journeys and Transitions in Contemporary Israeli Art (1991). In her preface to the interview, curator Sarit Shapira writes: "Jabès' texts are a succession of fragments that purport to be quotations from 'texts' from different times and places, which are printed at times with spaces between them that separate and fragment them; the sequence of the text is impaired also in the parts attributed to Jabès himself—because they are written in a technique that sabotages development of any kind, that mixes together different levels and kinds of language, and uses diversified generic formulas. . . . [I]n this way his writing concretely demonstrates the openness of the text—not only towards all prior texts, but also to the text that will be written out of it, in an act analogous to reading it. All active reading of this kind not only unites the foreign linguistic elements and fills the gaps in the text; all *reading* is also *tearing*, which echoes the breakage in the tablets of the covenant and the prolonged tearing that characterizes the history of the Jewish people. . . . [H]is view of the break as the source of all things and of the point as the minimal graph from which speech and writing grow, each time anew, brought Jabès close to the Kabbalah" (see Zalmona, *Routes of Wandering*, 255).

The complex relationship between the break (or "essential dishomogeneity"), the source (or the *arché*), and the point ("as the minimal graph") that Shapira refers to, and the fact that all three brought Jabès close to the Kabbalah, is exemplified further in the interview where Jabès claims the following: "I see my books as a cycle of gathering cycles, in which the last circle is a point. This is a reference to the Kabbalah, where it says that God, to manifest Himself, will reveal Himself as a point. I think this is marvellous, because the point in Semitic writing is the vowel. Hence, the point, which is at the end, is the center, is the vowel. . . . [the point is a vowel] because if you put three points under the consonant it'll be 'eh,' and if you put one point below it'll be 'ee'. In writing, it's the point. It's marvellous. The point is the meaning of the word. It's the very life of the word. Without vowels it's impossible. All the writing is only consonants, it's like the name of God, unpronounceable" (Zalmona, *Routes of Wandering*, 248).

In comparison, in "Hebrew Grammar," Spinoza writes about vowels only in passing: "Among the Hebrews vowels are called souls of letters, and letters without vowels are bodies without souls" (Spinoza, "Hebrew Grammar," 588).

16. Howard, "Archaeology and/or Genealogy: Agamben's Transformation of Foucauldian Method," 41.
17. Lawlor, *The Cambridge Foucault Lexicon*, 201.
18. Agamben, *The Signature of All Things*, 83.
19. Foucault, "Nietzsche, Genealogy, History," 369.
20. Foucault, "Nietzsche, Genealogy, History," 374. Although both Foucault's and Agamben's genealogies attempt to offer (among others and in this context) a critique of the present, it seems as if Foucault's critique is driven

more by social, political, and historical aspirations rather than by ontological or metaphysical ones (in the manner that Agamben seems to attempt, although he does share with Foucault a clear, critical aspiration for a political reform that results from a methodological, genealogical intention). However, both thinkers seem to disagree, or at least differ, on the importance of time (its structure and the role of its three traditional components of past, present, and future) to the process of genealogy, whether time (in fact, the past) "actively exists in" and "secretly animates" the present (according to Agamben, although as we will see later on, he does not consider this past a "usual" past) or functions otherwise (according to Foucault, and in accordance with his claims that the genealogist does not have much interest in restoring continuities or his wish to maintain the myriad events "in their proper dispersion").

Agamben will assert that Foucault never really questioned the implicit temporal structure of the "historical a priori" (Agamben, *The Signature of All Things*, 94), a claim that can further illuminate this difference between the two thinkers, at least from the perspective of Agamben's archaeology (on the basis, as will become evident later on, of its future anterior's movement in time).

One notices, however, that in his work *Introduction to Kant's Anthropology*, Foucault discusses (to some extent) the problem of temporality in relation to Kant's thought and specifically to the idea of the a priori. There Foucault ponders the account of time Kant proposes in the *Critique of Pure Reason*, "transforming it from a pure form of intuition—a transcendental condition of all possible experience that can be known a priori—to a dispersed framework that 'harbors and reveals' relationships that are both 'openings' and 'bond' " (Foucault, *Introduction to Kant's Anthropology*, 92). Assuming that the original form of the a priori is this dispersed temporality, then "it is reasonable to assume that Foucault found something like the historical a priori in his studies of temporality in Kant's *Anthropology*" (McQuillan, "Philosophical Archaeology and the Historical A Priori: From Kant to Foucault," 152). In other words, Foucault seems to defend the view that Kant's a priori is originally temporal, and that in its temporal form "the a priori disperses the synthetic activity of transcendental subjectivity" (McQuillan, "Philosophical Archaeology and the Historical A Priori," 156).

21. Foucault, "Nietzsche, Genealogy, History," 374.
22. Foucault, "Nietzsche, Genealogy, History," 373.
23. Foucault, "Nietzsche, Genealogy, History," 379.
24. Foucault, "Nietzsche, Genealogy, History," 380.
25. Lawlor, *The Cambridge Foucault Lexicon*, 165–74.
26. Lawlor, *The Cambridge Foucault Lexicon*, 170.
27. Foucault's methodological critique (and the relationship between his conceptions of archaeology and genealogy) is likewise referred to as follows: "Rather than transcendental, the criticism will be *archaeological* in its method and *genealogical* in purposes. The term 'genealogy,' clearly derives from Nietzsche,

becomes necessary to the completion of the 'excavation' carried out in the universalizing mechanisms of our knowledge in the search of what is contingent and empirical in them. . . . The conclusion will be, as we read in the introduction to *L'usage des plaisirs* (published in 1984, the year of Foucault's untimely death): finally 'free thought from what it silently thinks, and so enable it to think differently'" (Malinconico, "The Concept of Philosophical Archaeology in Kant and Foucault," 64–65).

28. Howard, "Archaeology and/or Genealogy: Agamben's Transformation of Foucauldian Method," 27–45.

29. Foucault, *Society Must Be Defended*, 10–11.

30. Agamben, as we will see, stresses the temporal issue and puts an emphasis on Foucault's discussion of emergence (*Entstehung*), citing Franz Overbeck as the source to Foucault's replacement of "origin" with "emergence." Prehistory, Agamben will claim, is "the history of the moment of arising" (*Entstehungsgeschichte*) (Agamben, *The Signature of All Things*, 85)—thus, Overbeck's idea of prehistory amounts to Foucault's historical a priori in terms of being that which conditions knowledge in a given historical epoch. The concept of prehistory, however, can be found before Overbeck—and in fact, within Kant and specifically in a text we already mentioned, however briefly: "Conjectural Beginning of Human History (1786)." There, Kant speaks about the prehistory of reason in the context of man's paradisical state in the Garden of Eden and man's process of humanization.

31. Howard, "Archaeology and/or Genealogy: Agamben's Transformation of Foucauldian Method," 35.

32. Howard, "Archaeology and/or Genealogy: Agamben's Transformation of Foucauldian Method," 41.

33. Agamben, *The Signature of All Things*, 84.

34. Agamben, *The Signature of All Things*, 90.

35. According to Agamben, however, it is impossible to gain a renewed access, beyond tradition, to the sources without putting into question the very historical subject who seeks access. Thus, the epistemological paradigm of inquiry itself is in question. Archaeology is a practice that eventually determines "the very status of the knowing subject" because the moment of arising is situated at a threshold of undecidability between object and subject, thus is both subjective and objective: "It is never the emergence of the fact without at the same time being the emergence of the knowing subject itself: the operation on the origin is at the same time an operation on the subject" (Agamben, *The Signature of All Things*, 89).

For a thorough discussion of subjectivity, in the context of philosophical archaeology, see de Libera, *Archéologie du sujet I: Naissance de sujet*; and Dolgopolski, "Who Thinks in the Talmud?," 7–11. For now, however, we can mention the following: As Alain de Libera's archaeological analysis (on the basis of Foucauldian concepts) portrays, the concept of a subject was conceived mutely and nonlinearly prior to Descartes, throughout the history of (Western) philosophy. He writes: "Descartes did not bring about a comprehensive concept unifying subjecthood, personality, identity, egoity, agency, and causality under the single word *subject*. Before being decentered, 'the' subject had to be centered. It had to become a 'centre' of perception, a 'centre' of acting and suffering. Such a concept had been delineated in the Middle Ages" (De Libera, "Subject (Re–/decentred)," 22; see also de Libera, "When Did the Modern Subject Emerge?," 185; 194–95; 202–3). Thus, the modern subject emerged through the combination, in late scholasticism, of two conflicting "models of subjectivity" inherited from late antiquity—the Aristotelian philosophical conception and the Augustinian theological conception—"enabling us to grasp the 'modern subject' as a 'bridging,' transdisciplinary entity." (De Libera, "Subject (Re–/decentred)," 22; see also de Libera, "When Did the Modern Subject Emerge?," 216). In this sense, with a nod to the later parts of this book, artistic practice involves a subject as a focal point of perception that also has an active, participatory role in the construction of the body of work. Allying itself with poststructuralist theory at large, and in contrast to a perspective rooted in the Renaissance, art historian Claire Bishop advocates for installation art's potential, however tentative, to elicit in the viewer/subject (after recognizing its fragmented and decentered subjectivity) a form of emancipation because the *activation* of the subject is analogous to the subject's engagement in the world. A tension prevails between the fragmented *model subject* of poststructuralist theory and a self-reflexive *viewing subject* capable of recognizing its own fragmentation, since installation art "insists upon the viewer's physical presence *precisely in order to subject it to an experience of decentering*" (Bishop, Installation Art, 133). What installation art offers, then, "is an experience of centering *and* decentering: work that insists on our centered presence in order then to subject us to an experience of decentering" (Bishop, *Installation Art*, 130).

36. Agamben, *The Signature of All Things*, 92. Agamben exemplifies in due course a few possible manifestations of this *arché*: "The archē is like the Indo-European words expressing a system of connections between historically accessible languages, or the child of psychoanalysis exerting an active force within the psychic life of the adult, or the big bang, which is supposed to have given rise to the universe but which continues to send towards us its fossil radiation" (110). These examples are already given in an earlier text from 2008 (originally in Italian, *Il sacramento del linguaggio: Archeologia del giuramento*): Agamben, *The Sacrament of Language: An Archaeology of the Oath*, 10.

37. Agamben further discusses Kojève's idea in Agamben, *Homo Sacer: Sovereign Power and Bare Life*, 60–62; and in Agamben, *Creation and Anarchy*, 1.

38. Agamben, *Potentialities*, 138–59.

39. Agamben, *Potentialities*, 155.

40. Quoted in Agamben, *Potentialities*, 156.

41. Goethe's morphology, which emanated from his research on nature (which is as important as his literary research or poetic work), is conceived via three domains: Botanics (*The Metamorphosis of Plants* of 1790); Osteology (*First Draft of a General Introduction to Comparative Anatomy* of 1795); and Theory of Colours (*Theory of Colours* of 1810). Common to all these domains is a particular way of seeing, a certain taming of the gaze exemplified by the following maxim (no. 1137): "The highest stage is seeing as identical what is different" (Goethe, *Maxims and Reflections*, 141). The form (the "morpheme") is not only a visible object but also the visible phenomenon and the ideal structure within it. It is the condition of possibility inherent to the phenomenon itself. This is the famous concept of *Urphänomen*—a theme that is visible only through its infinite variations. In the botanical realm, Goethe refers to the *Urphänomen* in Kantian terms, calling it a "transcendental leaf" (one cannot present a manifestation of a transcendental structure but can nevertheless recognize it in all botanic phenomena as the theme of their variations); in the osteological realm, the *Urphänomen* is the "original vertebra" whose transformation gives existence to all possible forms of bones, including the skull.

Goethe's morphological gaze exerted its influence also on the humanities at large, becoming a methodological model in the 1920s. A few examples include: Oswald Spengler's cultural morphology in *The Decline of the West*; Lucian Blaga's *Original Phenomenon*; Ernst Cassirer's *Philosophy of Symbolic Forms*; André Jolles's *Simple Forms*; Vladimir Propp's *Morphology of the Folktale*; and Ludwig Wittgenstein's anthropological *Remarks on Frazer's Golden Bough*. These studies share a common feature—a consideration of the relationship between the ideal and the phenomenal level, not as a mutual opposition but as mutual codetermination, a reciprocal relationship between idea and phenomenon or empirical level. See Minotti, "Origin vs Genesis: Warburg and Benjamin in the Footsteps of Goethe's Morphology."

42. In this theory, the exposition of the ideas and the salvation of the phenomena are simultaneous and merge in a single gesture. In philosophy, for Benjamin, the concept of Being (at issue in the Idea) is not satisfied by the phenomenon until it has consumed all its history, thus the phenomenon does not remain the same (as singularity) but becomes what it was not (totality). "To save phenomena in the Idea (to expose the Idea in phenomena)," writes Agamben, "is to show them in their historical consumption, as a fulfilled totality. To show this in the work of art is the task of criticism" (Agamben, *Potentialities*, 157).

43. See Convolute N2a, 4 in Benjamin, *The Arcades Project*, 462.

44. Agamben, *The Fire and the Tale*, 57–62.

45. Agamben, *The Fire and the Tale*, 58–59. Elsewhere Agamben adds: "Benjamin has written . . . that when one wants to grasp a phenomenon dialectically or monadologically outside the *continuum* of linear historical reckoning,

it is polarized and split according to its pre-history and its post-history, which does not mean simply past and present but designates two immanent forces in the field of tensions into which the phenomenon has thus been transformed (notes N7a, 1 and N10, 3 from the *Arcade Project*)" (Agamben, *The Kingdom and the Garden*, 151).

46. Agamben, *The Fire and the Tale*, 59–60. Likewise, relating (in a few pages earlier) to the becoming of man, or subjectivity, Agamben writes: "In an important book, Simondon wrote that man is, as it were, a two-phased being, which results from the dialectic between a non-individuated part and an individual and personal part. The pre-individual is not a chronological past that, at a certain point, is realized and resolved in the individual: it coexists with in and remains irreducible to it" (Agamben, *The Fire and the Tale*, 44).

47. A relation to the past can yield a characterization of the whole category of "Identity." Identity does not necessarily mean a substantial concept, just a temporal relation to the past, something that has to do merely with time. A relation to the past implies a certain temporal structure; a relation to one's past implies a certain movement in time, and only this movement is important (not the fact that time supposedly comprises three elements: past, present, and future). See Shlomo Pines, *La Liberté de Philosopher: De Maïmonide à Spinoza*. Pines's idea deprives the movement to the past from any substantiality (political, cultural, etc.), and just considers the simple movement in time (to the past) as being constitutive for man and the only essential element.

Jewish identity, according to Pines, should be regarded more as a problem rather than a fact, since identity is no longer a substance that one can define and limit but a complicated lace among cultures. In other words, Jewish identity is not a continuity but a lace that each time is woven among different cultures. This theory can be applied to any cultural identity, and nowadays in Europe the issue of continuity (as part of the identity of cultures) is a problem and should not be taken for granted. Cultural identity in present-day Europe is, as we witness, discontinuous and fragile.

48. Agamben writes: "The term *archè* in Greek means both 'origin' and 'command.' To this double meaning of the term there corresponds the fact that, in our philosophical and religious traditions alike, origin, what gives a beginning and brings into being, is not only a preamble, which disappears and ceases to act in that to which it has given life, but is also what commands and governs its growth, development, circulation, and transmission—in a word, its history" (Agamben, *The Use of Bodies*, 275). See also Agamben, *Creation and Anarchy*, 51–54.

In "On the Being and Conception of *Physis*," Heidegger writes that the Greeks usually hear two things in the word *arché*: "That from which something takes it egress and inception," and at the same time, "that which, as such egress and inception, at the same time reaches beyond whatever emerges from it, thereby dominating it" (Heidegger, "On the Being and Conception of *Physis*," 227). *Arché* thus means both inception and domination inseparably.

49. Schürmann, *Heidegger On Being and Acting: From Principles to Anarchy*, 97. In the domain of being, the *arché* is a substance that begins and commands everything; in the domain of becoming, the *archai* are the causes; and in the domain of knowledge, they are the premises on which cognition depends.

50. Schürmann, *Heidegger On Being and Acting*, 99.

51. The fragment reads: "Among those who say that the first principle [*archē*] is one and movable and infinite, is Anaximander of Miletus. . . . He said that the first principle [*archē*] and element of all things is infinite [*apeiron*], and he was the first to apply this word to the first principle; and he says that it is neither water nor any other one of the thing called elements, but the infinite is something of a different nature, from which came all the heavens and the worlds in them; and from which things are generated in their substance and to which they return of necessity when they degenerate; . . . for he says that they suffer retribution [*dikēn*] and give recourse [*tisin*] to one another for justice [*adikian*] according to the order of time . . . , putting it rather poetically" (Quoted in Gourgouris, "Archē," 9).

52. Gourgouris, "Archē," 9.

53. Gourgouris, "Archē," 10.

54. Gourgouris, "Archē," 10. Ground, writes Gourgouris, is merely metaphorical, for the *apeiron* rests on nothing and is abyssal and void.

55. Gourgouris, "Archē," 10.

56. Gourgouris, "Archē," 10.

57. "It is not death that signifies injustice, because this thought leads to the desire for an afterlife. It is life itself that signifies injustice because it interrupts the universal infinite fold. Finite creatures come into being and then this beautiful and perfect, even if incomplete, infinite is disrupted. Our death is retribution for the fact that we have come to be" (Gourgouris, "Archē," 14).

58. Gourgouris, "Archē," 11.

59. Vernant, *Myth and Thought among the Greeks*, 205.

60. Gourgouris, "Archē," 12.

61. Gourgouris, "Archē," 15.

62. Gourgouris, "Archē," 16–17.

63. In the context of Agamben's *Homo Sacer* project, this was evident in relation to politics, where "life is not in itself political—for this reason it must be excluded from the city—and yet it is precisely the *exceptio*, the exclusion-inclusion of this Impolitical, that founds the space of politics" (Agamben, *The Use of Bodies*, 263).

64. Agamben, *The Use of Bodies*, 264.

65. In Agamben, the mechanism of inclusive exclusion is constitutively connected to the event of language: the *ex-ceptio*, the inclusive exclusion of the

real from the logos and in the *logos*, is the originary structure of the event of language. Moreover, it is also the originary structure of society with its relation between nature and culture. In fact, according to Agamben, the mechanism of inclusive exclusion is the infrastructure of any relation, which is always political and ontological. Agamben narrates this relation in light of other structures of relation that were formulated in the course of the twentieth century mainly by structuralist and poststructuralist theories (according to which, put crudely, the meaning of a category is derived from and in relation to the meaning of its opposite category).

66. Agamben, *The Use of Bodies*, 265.

67. Colin McQuillan advances the claim that, according to Agamben, once one recognizes the structure of inclusion/exclusion that operates in our construction of the image of the past, one frees oneself from its supposedly tyrannical conditioning for the present moment, no longer understands it as an inheritance that must be carried into the future, thus archaeology presents the past "as a work of fiction" (McQuillan, "Philosophical Archaeology in Kant, Foucault, and Agamben," 43). McQuillan mentions the etymological origin of "fiction," that is, the Latin *fingere*, which means "to touch" but also "to shape" and "to form" (these being actions at the basis of any fiction). This recognition is the concrete meaning of redemption in Agamben, according to McQuillan, as it "unworks" the distinctions that organize our life and opens it to new possibilities.

68. Agamben, *The Use of Bodies*, 275. Agamben thinks the *archē*, in the anarchic context, also in relation to perhaps two of the most anarchic institutions ever to exist—Christianity and capitalism. The intimate connection Agamben draws between Christianity and capitalism (a parasitical one, in fact, on behalf of the latter, which he defines as "a religion in which faith—credit—has been substituted for God. Said differently, since the pure form of credit is money, it is a religion whose God is money" (Agamben, *Creation and Anarchy*, 70) is made to emphasize the an-archaic nature of both institutions. This connection, according to Agamben, reveals itself most clearly with respect to time and history. Attesting its religious character in any sphere of experience, "Capitalism has no *telos*; it is essentially infinite yet . . . always in the act of ending" (Agamben, *Creation and Anarchy*, 74). Thus, since it can never really end, "Capitalism also does not know a beginning; it is intimately an-archaic yet, precisely for this reason, always in the act of beginning again" (Agamben, *Creation and Anarchy*, 75). This is the an-archaic, anarchic essential characteristic of capitalism, "which is perhaps the most anarchic power ever to exist, in the literal sense that it can have no *archē*, no beginning or foundation" (Agamben, *Creation and Anarchy*, 75). And lastly, "Capitalism inherits, secularizes, and pushes to the extreme the anarchic character of Christology" (Agamben, *Creation and Anarchy*, 76).

69. In *Thinking Through French Philosophy*, Leonard Lawlor claims that French philosophy in the 1960s felt a need to rethink history without end and

without origin/*arché*. Perhaps for the first time in the history of philosophy, he writes, an entire system of thought was governed by a profound spatiality that came to be known as "transcendental topology," or, in other words, "archaeology" (Lawlor, *Thinking Through French Philosophy*, 24–31).

70. Philosophy of immanence is based on three propositions: (1) the world is all that exists, is the entirety of existence, and for us, this entirety is the only horizon that can be known; (2) existence is the only source for any moral decrees, legitimacy of political power, etc.; and (3) recognizing and assimilating the previous two propositions is the only available key to liberation that humans are capable of attaining. There exists a philosophy of immanence that we can name "dogmatic" (Spinoza, Hegel, or the pantheistic religions are just a few examples) and another that we can name "critical," which first and foremost recognizes human finitude and the incapability of our reason to reach the absolute, while recognizing that this immanence is finite rather than infinite. If we seriously consider the idea of finite immanence, we must also remain open to a dimension of transcendence that appears as a question rather than answer, an empty dimension of transcendence devoid of substances or ideas, whose sole function is to reflect back at us the sheer fact of the finitude of our existence. One does not address this dimension by speech but by silence, and this is where the primary distance between our French protagonists fundamentally manifests itself.

71. Foucault, *The Archaeology of Knowledge*, 203.

72. Freud elaborates on the archaeological metaphor to explain psychoanalysis in his essay "Constructions in Analysis": "[The Psychoanalyst's] work of construction, or, if it is preferred, of reconstruction, resembles to a great extent an archeologist's excavation of some dwelling place that has been destroyed and buried or of some ancient edifice. The two processes are in fact identical, except that the analyst works under better conditions and has more material at his command to assist him, since what he is dealing with is not something destroyed but something that is still alive. . . . But just as the archeologist builds up the walls of the building from the foundations that have remained standing, determines the number and position of the columns from depressions in the floor and reconstructs the mural decorations and paintings from the remains found in the debris, so does the analyst proceed when he draws his inferences from the fragments of memories, from the associations and from the behaviour of the subject of the analysis" (Freud, "Constructions in Analysis [1937]," 259).

73. Lawlor, *Thinking Through French Philosophy*, 29.

74. In his erudite book on Kant's methodology, Charles Bigger claims that although Kant destroyed traditional epistemology and metaphysics, he simultaneously offered a method for philosophy to advance in a new way he termed "archaeology." Archaeology stresses the role of the imagination in the constitution of the world, not in the sense of formulating the world from its

own constructs but rather that the imagination is founded in participation or dwelling. See Bigger, *Kant's Methodology*.

75. Lawlor, *Thinking Through French Philosophy*, 31.
76. See Foucault and Lotringer, *Foucault Live*, 39–40.
77. Foucault and Lotringer, *Foucault Live*, 13.
78. Lawlor, *The Cambridge Foucault Lexicon*, 13–19. It should be noted that "understood" might not be the most accurate choice of words here, since Foucault himself is very precise about one's conception of (or operation on) knowledge: "Knowledge [savoir], even under the banner of history, does not depend on 'rediscovery' . . . knowledge is not made for understanding; it is made for cutting" (Foucault, "Nietzsche, Genealogy, History," 380).
79. Foucault's definition to "Philosophical Archaeology" is the history of what makes necessary a certain form of thought ("L'historie de ce qui rend nécessaire une certaine forme de pensée") (Foucault, *Dits et écrits II*, 211).
80. Foucault defines the *Archive* as the ground rules that determine the appearance and disappearance of enunciations and its analysis as the conduction of archaeology. For further discussion, in this context, see Östman, "Philosophical Archaeology as Method in the Humanities. A Comment on Cultural Memory and the Problem of History," 81–84. Östman extracts, regarding Foucault's methodology, the following: (1) the *Archive* is not a form of storage which is given a priori; (2) archaeology is not the gathering of cultural traces; (3) archaeology examines language as lingual events in reality, that is, conditions of possibilities; (4) the *Archive* is similar to the paradigm—neither a priori nor a posteriori but contemporary; and (5) archaeology considers texts (or cultural artifacts at large) as *monuments* rather than *documents*; Agamben directly discusses Foucault's notion of the *Archive* in Agamben, *Remnants of Auschwitz*, 143–46.
81. "Foucault's account of knowledge . . . provides an alternative to the Cartesian assumptions of privileged subjectivity and fixed rationality. By situating knowledge in a setting of social practices, Foucault is able to provide a framework that makes discontinuity a possible fact and subjectivity a constituted item. It is this alternative conception of knowledge that is Foucault's true contribution to epistemic theory" (Wartenberg, "Foucault's Archeological Method," 357).
82. Lawlor, *The Cambridge Foucault Lexicon*, 16.
83. de Libera, "Subject (Re–/decentred)," 15; Foucault, *The Archaeology of Knowledge*, 12.
84. Ancient and medieval philosophy defined metaphysics according to its subject matter, thus interchangeably considered it as the science that investigates "being as such," "the first causes of things," and "things that do not change." The origin of the word "metaphysics" is uncertain but most probably was given by the editors of Aristotle's corpus to a series of fourteen books he wrote in order to distinguish them from his previous writings on physics (or nature); hence books

that come, and should be read, after (meta) those of physics that are characterized by the centrality of the concept of "change," the prime characteristic of nature. Thus, metaphysics for Aristotle deals with all things unchangeable, and he identified first philosophy with "being as such." In the seventeenth century, a shift occurred in the definition of metaphysics' subject matter, as subjects previously considered under "physics" were now considered as conceived under "metaphysics," such as mind-body relation or free will. Metaphysics becomes a general category for various exclusively unclassified philosophical problems. Roughly at the same time, in order to overcome the conceptual and categorical perplexity of classification, ontology becomes the science that particularly investigates "being as such."

85. Agamben, *The Use of Bodies*, 111.

86. Elsewhere, Agamben writes: "Being is the dimension opened to humans in the anthropogenetic event of language; . . . being is always, in Aristotle's words, something that 'is said'" (Agamben, *The Adventure*, 42).

87. Agamben, *The Use of Bodies*, 111.

88. Agamben, *The Use of Bodies*, 128. Why do we have the idea of historical a priori? Why does philosophy seem to need the historical a priori? And additionally, why is the historical a priori linked to language? In Agamben's thought, the connection between the two indicates a definition of what is at stake in philosophy. The connection exists because philosophy is not simply a set of conceptual statements (doctrine, cognitive formulation) but is constitutively linked with the anthropogenesis, with the becoming human of man, and this archi-event (anthropogenesis) is the historical a priori of philosophy. First philosophy (or metaphysics) has to do with the becoming speaking of the animal *homo*. Philosophy is a remembrance, each time, of the articulation between man and language and between language and the world. The word "remembrance" does not mean a memory in the common sense, but a repetition, a renewed experience, of the junction between language and man and between animal and man (between the inhuman and man; between becoming human and man). Anthropogenesis is the "archi" historical a priori since it is always in the process, we can never consider it as completed, we are always in the process of becoming human therefore we are always animals. Thinking (or philosophy) for Agamben means to experience anew the connection between becoming human and remaining inhuman (and therefore this connection is kept, in philosophy, in question). Thus, philosophical archaeology is immanent and constitutive to philosophy; it means going back (archaeologically) to the repetition and remembrance of this event.

89. Agamben, *The Use of Bodies*, 112. The term "historical *a priori*," which appears for the first time, in Foucault's *History of Madness* (1961) albeit as "concrete *a priori*," is used in *The Order of Things* to demonstrate that the prominent nineteenth-century discourses on life, labour, and language (biology,

Marxism, and linguistics, respectively) all emerge in the context of the same historical a priori: "the search for new practices of analysis in the wake of the epistemic breakdown of representation in the early modern period" (Lawlor, *The Cambridge Foucault Lexicon*, 201).

More generally, Foucault is consistent in his conception and use of the term "historical *a priori*," which is essentially used as part of Foucault's critique of our modern conception of history as a continuous, dialectical, and above all progressive process, otherwise referred to as the "philosophical myth of history" (Aldea and Allen, "History, Critique, and Freedom," 7).

90. Agamben, *The Use of Bodies*, 112. It can be argued that Foucault's conception of the historical a priori derives not only from new approaches to the history of science developed by Bachelard and Canguilhem and from Husserlian phenomenology but also (and essentially) from the historical turn that German philosophy took around the eighteenth and nineteenth centuries, beginning with Kant's idea of "philosophical history of philosophy" (which, as stated previously, was first explicated in the first edition to the *Critique of Pure Reason* [though by the wording "history of pure reason"] and later in his essay of the "Progress of Metaphysics") and subsequent developments by Karl Leonhard Reinhold and Hegel.

Foucault's archaeology is similar to the philosophical archaeology that Kant proposes in the sense that "instead of appealing to universal and necessary principles to explain the historical development of philosophy, Foucault reconstructs the order of scientific knowledge in different historical periods" (McQuillan, "Philosophical Archaeology and the Historical a Priori," 153). This Foucauldian archaeological approach can be traced back to a small set of principles and has resonance with Kant's essay on the "Progress of Metaphysics," which suggests some a priori principles that make certain ways of thinking necessary.

91. Agamben, *The Use of Bodies*, 112.

92. Philosophy is not usually conceived in terms of the "archi" historical a priori, with the becoming human of man, mainly due to the current primacy of the cognitive paradigm in Western culture. Especially since Kant, philosophy has become a doctrine of knowledge or condition of knowledge, as if what is at stake in philosophy is the definition of the possibility of knowledge. We can think of the historical a priori of individual philosophers. For example, Kant's historical a priori is the impossibility of metaphysics (or the impossibility of first philosophy). Kant starts from the impossibility of metaphysics and tries in some way to make it possible again, but in order to do so he has to confine metaphysics to the transcendental and exclude it from any empirical and historical reality. This is the idea of the "noumenon"—the space of metaphysics is a void space, a transcendental space. Thus, by trying to save metaphysics, he in a way eliminated it because philosophy after Kant was under the assumption that Kant had found a fortress in the transcendental, but this fortress eventually turned

out to be a trap (as post-Kantian philosophers remained trapped in this fortress). Trying to escape from conceiving metaphysics as a concrete empirical science, Kant transformed metaphysics into the transcendental but remained trapped in what he thought was a fortress. Philosophy, in the second half of the nineteenth century, until Heidegger, is an attempt to escape from the transcendental toward ontology (e.g., the work of Nietzsche, also with his attention to language, as well as consecutively, the linguistic turn as the historical a priori that substitutes for the transcendental).

In a way (as Agamben suggests us), our task today is to get rid of the transcendental and understand it in a different way. From a Kantian point of view, the experience of the transcendental is that of a void space that one cannot make any empirical statement about; on the contrary, we can say that the experience of language is an archaeology, a concrete investigation of language, etc. No longer is the metaphysical space a void space, but now archaeology can be considered a proper metaphysical field.

93. Agamben, *The Use of Bodies*, 112.

94. Agamben, *The Use of Bodies*, 113.

95. He writes: "The Aristotelian ontological apparatus, which has for almost two millennia guaranteed the life and politics of the West, can no longer functions as a historical a priori, to the extent to which anthropogenesis, which it sought to fix in terms of an articulation between language and being, is no longer reflected in it. Having arrived at the outermost point of its secularization, the projection of ontology (or theology) into history seems to have become impossible" (Agamben, *The Use of Bodies*, 133).

96. Agamben, *The Signature of All Things*, 93.

97. In *The Archaeology of Knowledge*, the "historical a priori" is described as a term that "does not elude historicity: it does not constitute, above events, and in an unmoving heaven, an atemporal structure: it is defined by the group of rules that characterize a discursive practice: but the rules are not imposed from the outside" (Lawlor, *The Cambridge Foucault Lexicon*, 203). The original text appears in Foucault, *The Archaeology of Knowledge*, 126–31.

98. Agamben, *The Signature of All Things*, 93.

99. Agamben, *The Signature of All Things*, 94. The historical a priori is thus a form of conceptual analysis but not in a timeless manner because concepts have their being in historical sites—as Ian Hacking writes of concepts: "The logical relations between them were formed in time, and they cannot be perceived correctly unless their temporal dimensions are kept in view" (Hacking, "Historical Ontology," 598).

100. Agamben, *The Signature of All Things*, 95. A further discussion of déjà-vu, in the context of the philosophy of history, appears in Virno, *Déjà Vu and the End of History*.

101. Agamben, *The Signature of All Things*, 95.

102. Agamben, *The Signature of All Things*; see Benjamin, *The Arcades Project*, 459.
103. Agamben, *The Signature of All Things*, 96.
104. Nietzsche, *Untimely Meditations*, 57–125.
105. Quoted in Agamben, *The Signature of All Things*, 97.
106. Agamben, *The Signature of All Things*, 98.
107. See Benjamin, "Theses on the Philosophy of History," 253–65.
108. Agamben, *The Signature of All Things*, 99.
109. Agamben, *What Is an Apparatus? and Other Essays*, 39–55.
110. Agamben, *The Mystery of Evil: Benedict XVI and the End of Days*, 16.
111. Agamben, *What Is an Apparatus? and Other Essays*, 50.
112. Agamben, *What Is an Apparatus? and Other Essays*, 50.
113. Agamben, *What Is an Apparatus? and Other Essays*, 51–52. "Philosophical Archaeology" is thus conceived by Agamben also as a temporal model, or as a "signature" (a concept to be discussed later) traversing his corpus, according to which the past is incomplete and includes its unlived moments as potential.
114. Agamben, *What Is an Apparatus? and Other Essays*, 52. Agamben, as we will see, identifies Paul's messianic time (the "time of the now," the being-contemporary with the Messiah) as the paradigm par excellence for this (chronologically indeterminate) encounter.
115. Agamben, *What Is an Apparatus? and Other Essays*, 53.
116. Agamben, *The Signature of All Things*, 101.
117. Agamben, *The Signature of All Things*, 103.
118. Cerella, "The Sacred and the Political," 225.
119. Agamben, *The Signature of All Things*, 106.
120. Agamben, *The Signature of All Things*, 108.

Chapter Two

1. For a related discussion, see Kracauer, *History: The Last Things Before the Last*, 139–63.
2. Agamben, *Infancy and History*, 92.
3. Agamben, *Infancy and History*, 93. The feature of the point (as a metaphysical-geometric concept) dominates Western thought in terms of the representation of time, and then is taken to be, as if in itself, the real time of experience. The concept of the instant as a "point" in time enables the opening through which the eternity of metaphysics insinuates itself into the human experience of time. Coming into conflict with this concept of the instant is the key to conceiving a new idea of time.
4. See also Kracauer, *History: The Last Things Before the Last*, 195–202.
5. Quoted in Agamben, *Infancy and History*, 94.

6. Agamben, *Infancy and History*, 94.

7. In the Jewish tradition, we already find two contradictory (but complementary) perspectives regarding the representation of time: the one, linear and teleological ("Know from where you came, where you are going, and before whom you are destined to give a judgment and accounting" [M. Avot 3:1]); the other, circular and endless ("That which hath been is that which shall be, and that which hath been done is that which shall be done; and there is nothing new under the sun" [Ecclesiastes 1:9]). The Jewish structure of time thus manifests a spiral form on the basis of this bipolar tension.

8. Quoted in Agamben, *Infancy and History*, 96–97.

9. "Historicism" refers to the study of the past on the past's terms; it seeks to understand the meaning and value of the past as it would have been understood at the time it happened. By contrast, "Presentism" (see Hartog, *Regimes of Historicity: Presentism and Experience of Time*) means to interpret and evaluate the past in terms of presently accepted values and understanding. Presentism holds that it is not possible to understand events in terms of their "historicity," while historicism holds that events can and should be understood in terms of their historicity. Historicity refers to the actuality and authenticity of events in the past. We can date an event in the past, but our understanding of its meaning will be bound to the present point of departure from which we seek to understand it.

10. Lévi-Strauss, for example, thus argued for an idea of the discontinuous nature of historiography, against any objective historical continuity. He rejected the equation of history and humanity. This does not mean the abandonment of history but rather the achievement of a more authentic concept of historicity.

11. Agamben, *Infancy and History*, 96–97.

12. Quoted in Agamben, *Infancy and History*, 98.

13. In Agamben's book *Language and Death*, the concept of negativity in Hegel's thought is articulated. In a manuscript of 1803–1804 and 1805–1806, writes Agamben, Hegel describes the reemergence of the spirit into light in the figure of consciousness. In the senses and in the imagination, consciousness has not yet come out into the light—it is still immersed in its "night." He writes: "Man is the night, this pure nothing that contains everything in its simplicity, a realm endlessly rich in representations and images. . . . In phantasmagoric representations he is surrounded by night; suddenly a bloody head juts forth here, there another white figure, and just as suddenly they disappear. One glimpses this night when one looks into the eyes of another human—into a night, which becomes frightening; here each of us is suspended confronting the night of the world" (Agamben, *Language and Death*, 41–42).

14. Agamben, *Infancy and History*, 99.

15. In the timeframe depicted by Agamben, there were substantial attempts to criticize and challenge the common, dominant conceptions of time (respectively

for each epoch), in particular the characterization of time as a "point" alongside its properties of "continuity" and "quantifiability." Agamben mentions just a few of these attempts, perhaps the ones most pertinent to his own thinking, and tries to formalize an adequate modern conception of time:

(1) In Gnosticism there appears an experience of time that is in radical opposition to both the Greek circular experience and the straight line of Christianity. It posits a concept whose spatial model can be represented by a broken line, thus striking against antiquity's unaltered duration, precise and continuous time.

Based on Gnosticism's (that is, as a religion) differentiation from both Greek cosmology and Christian redemption, the time of Gnosticism is an incoherent and inhomogeneous time: in an experience of interrupted time, when man (in a sudden act of consciousness) takes possession of its own condition of being resurrected, the Gnostic attitude is revolutionary as it "refuses the past valuing in it, through an exemplary sense of the present, precisely what was condemned as negative, . . . and expecting nothing from the future" (Agamben, *Infancy and History*, 101).

(2) In Stoicism, too, we find a different conception of time, one that refuses the astronomical time of Plato's *Timaeus*, an image of eternity, and the Aristotle's notion of the mathematical instant. Against a homogeneous, infinite, and quantified time that divides the present into discrete instants (thus producing an unreal time and an experience of deferral), the Stoics think of the experience of time as something neither objective nor removed from our control but derived from the actions of man. Its model is the *kairos*, the unexpected joining of times and occurrences where man grasps opportunity, and life is fulfilled in the present moment. Paul Chan portrays this concept clearly in his essay "A Time Apart." He writes that *cairós* (or *kairos*) is a "time charged with promise and significance . . . time that saturates time," as opposed to *chronos*, our familiar conception of time as measure, which is "a quantity of duration that changes in a uniform and serial order." It is an empty time in the sense of time "without content or meaning beyond its own linear progressing." *Kairos* designates the idea that time can be fulfilled and made anew through a rupture that crosses through it, radicalizing everything that happens thereafter. The relationship between *kairos* and *chronos* is not that of opposition, but "*chronos* is that in which there is *kairos*, and *kairos* is that in which there is little *chronos*." Thus *chronos* transforms into *kairos* by becoming a compressed form of itself: "In *kairos*, time is not kept: it is unleashed." *Kairos* also means the right time to act, an opportune moment, that becomes possible only "when time holds the most potential for change . . . when a crisis or rapture opens up and is catalysed with human will to create new potentialities." Time holds import, writes Chan, only when something ends, thus apprehending one's own end becomes a crucial task in the life of mortals. The fact that the end is ever near "charges every moment

with promise and significance," and propels the human "to find a shape of one's own, before it is too late."

(3) In Heidegger, the critique of time as continuous and quantified is subjected to a radical critique in terms of repetition-destruction, which invades Western metaphysics as a whole. The originality of *Sein und Zeit* is that of the foundation of historicity alongside a more authentic experience of time. At the core of this experience there is no longer the precise, fleeting *instant* throughout linear time "but the *moment* of the authentic decision in which the *Dasein* experiences its own finiteness . . . throwing itself forward in care . . . freely assum[ing] the destiny of its primordial historicity. Man does not fall into time, 'but exists as primordial temporalization'" (Agamben, *Infancy and History*, 103).

16. Agamben, *Infancy and History*, 104.

17. History for Agamben, as was previously indicated in relation to ontology and the anthropogenesis, is further (and always) thought through the prism of language. In this sense, history means the exposition of a fracture produced through the discontinuity between language and speech, the semiotic and the semantic (in Benveniste's terms), or sign system and discourse (in Foucault's terms). Only because of this discontinuity is man a historical being. A human becomes a historical subject by removing itself from its wordless experience; this speechless moment remains in discourse as its condition of possibility, as the passage that shows the "fall" from pure language to the babble of speech. The transition from pure language to discourse marks a limit, which is history. By entering history man exposes the discontinuity of language and time, thus history is not a linear progression but made of infinite gaps. Agamben's use of paradigms shows this—the paradigm is neither diachrony nor synchrony but a crossing of the two. Like Foucault's panopticon (which illustrates both the general functioning of panopticism and the threshold of modernity), Agamben's paradigms are analogical, moving from one singularity to the next. Their historicity resides in their immanent exposition as belonging to a group of historically specific singularities and, at the same time, their suspension of such belonging. History is a gathering, a relation that holds together individual images at an (ontological) zone of perfect equilibrium between generality and particularity. By grasping history's discontinuities, historical inquiry sutures the phenomena that unfold through time, transforming the present into an emergent structure with an intelligible relation to its past (Murray and Whyte, *The Agamben Dictionary*, 92–93).

18. Benjamin writes about history's dishomogeneity in other texts as well. See, for instance, convolutes N7, 7; N7a, 2; N9a, 6; N13, 2; and N15, 1 in *The Arcades Project*.

19. In this context it should be noted (even if taken for granted) that the messianic is not a person but an idea. The (Jewish) messianic concept means a defiance—it proclaims that the arbitrary historical circumstance that we find ourselves in is merely a coincidence and a temporary state. From creation to

salvation, the belief is that everything could turn out otherwise; even if the present experience is difficult, it is not the end. The hope, the future, and the open horizon of potentiality signify the messianic idea.

20. Romans 1:1 (New International Version). Agamben develops his ideas of messianic time in close relation to Heidegger's thinking on the topic as exemplified in his own reading of Paul's letters and other important works published around the 1920s, such as *The Phenomenology of Religious Life* (1920), *The Concept of Time* (1924), and *Being and Time* (1927).

21. Agamben, *The Time That Remains*, 4–5.

22. For Paul, as will become clear, the contraction of time (the "remaining" time) represents the messianic situation par excellence, the only real time.

23. Agamben, *The Time That Remains*, 10.

24. Agamben, *The Time That Remains*, 13.

25. Agamben, *The Time That Remains*, 16.

26. Agamben, *The Time That Remains*, 18.

27. Agamben, *The Time That Remains*, 23.

28. Agamben, *The Time That Remains*, 28. One of the important repercussions of vocation is that the voiding and transforming of every vocation frees it for a new usage. An ultimate experience (and experience of the last things) would entail experiencing penultimate things (which make up our everyday human and social condition) differently. Thus eschatology, as Agamben indicates elsewhere, "is nothing other than a transformation of the experience of the penultimate. . . . Paul expresses the messianic relation between final and penultimate things with the verb *katargein*, which does not mean 'destroy' but, instead, 'render inoperative'" (Agamben, *The Church and the Kingdom*, 19).

29. The Hebrew antecedent found in lexicons is *Shaliah*—a man who holds a mandate and is sent on his specific assignment (*Sheluhim*, in plural, are those who are sent to the diaspora). The term *Shaliah* is essentially a juridical notion that in Judaism acquires a religious meaning.

30. The legacy of the prophet (the *Navi*) in Judaism, and in general in antiquity, extends over the threshold of modernity and has never completely vanished. For instance, Aby Warburg marked both Nietzsche and Burckhardt as opposite kinds of *Navi*, the first toward the future and the latter toward the past; Foucault defines the prophet as one of the four figures of truth-tellers.

31. For comparison see Foucault, *The Courage of Truth*, 15.

32. In Judaism, prophecy is "something like a force or a tension that is in constant struggle with other forces that seek to limit it in its modalities, primarily in its time" (Agamben, *The Time That Remains*, 60). The first profound legitimate prophecy thus is time marked with the destruction of the Temple in 587 BCE.

33. See also Agamben, *The Church and the Kingdom*, 8.

34. Greek-speaking Jews distinguished between *aiones: ho aion touto* (this aeon) and *ho aion mellon* (the coming aeon); see Agamben, "The Time That Is Left," 2.

35. Agamben, *The Time That Remains*, 62.
36. Agamben, *The Church and the Kingdom*, 12.
37. "In Greek, *parousia* simply means presence (*par-ousia* literally signifies to be next to; in this way, being is besides itself in the present)" (Agamben, *The Time That Remains*, 70).
38. Agamben, *The Time That Remains*, 64.
39. Quoted in Agamben, *The Time That Remains*, 65.
40. Agamben, *The Time That Remains*, 65–66.
41. Agamben, "The Time That Is Left," 5.
42. Quoted in Guillaume, *Foundations for a Science of Language*, xiii.
43. Guillaume, *Foundations for a Science of Language*.
44. Guillaume, *Foundations for a Science of Language*.
45. Guillaume, *Foundations for a Science of Language*, xiv.
46. Guillaume, *Foundations for a Science of Language*, xvi.
47. Guillaume, *Foundations for a Science of Language*, 3.
48. Guillaume, *Foundations for a Science of Language*, 6. Guillaume will continue developing the concept of the spatialization of time in his work *L'architectonique du temps dans les langues classiques*.
49. Guillaume, *Foundations for a Science of Language*.
50. Messianic time, being the time it takes for a temporal representation to be accomplished, opposes secular time, which is a homogenous time comprising completed "time-images" or representations. Secular time contains within itself a second time that is required for the completion of the construction of representation, yet remains unaccounted for.
51. The disjointedness of messianic time indicates presence by marking our noncoincidence with it. Moreover, the gap that operational time measures further marks the noncoincidence also of thought with language, that is, the impossibility of an absolute sustained self-presence. Thus, messianic time is the measure of the disconnection of both oneself from one's image of time and subjective language (Doussan, "Time and Presence in Agamben's Critique of Deconstruction," 198).
52. Agamben, *The Time That Remains*, 67.
53. Agamben, *The Time That Remains*, 68. Elsewhere appears a slightly different translation of the Italian: "*the time which is left to us*" (Agamben, "The Time That Is Left," 5).
54. Paul twice uses the expression *ton kairon exagorazomenoi*, "buying up time," to convey the temporal condition of messianic time.
55. Agamben mentions Gershom Scholem's interpretation of messianic time according to which the messianic antinomy is defined as "a life lived in deferment" in which nothing can be achieved, that is, as if the messianic event is a transitional time that belongs to both eras and thus tends to be prolonged into infinity and renders unreachable the end that it supposedly produces (Agamben,

The Time That Remains, 70). Scholem's thesis (appearing in his essay "Towards an Understanding of the Messianic Idea of Judaism" of 1959) is also referred to by Agamben in "The Messiah and the Sovereign: Problem of Law in Walter Benjamin," where Agamben cites the following: "Messianism is animated by two opposed tensions: the first is restorative tendency aiming at *restitutio in integrum* [total reinstatement] of the origin; the second is a utopian impulse turned instead toward the future and renewal" (Agamben, *Potentialities*, 166). These opposed forces explain the antinomies of messianism and its essential character ("a life lived in deferral and delay") in which nothing can be brought to fulfillment and nothing accomplished once and for all; thus messianism possesses a tension that never finds true release.

56. *Kairos* and *chronos* are opposed to each other as they are qualitatively heterogeneous. The relation between them is characterized in the *Corpus Hippocraticum*: "*Chronos* is that in which there is *kairos*, and *kairos* is that in which there is little *chronos*" (Agamben, *The Time That Remains*, 68–69). *Kairos* (banally translated as "occasion") does not have another time at its disposal; when we seize *kairos* we do not have another time but a contracted and abridged *chronos*.

57. Agamben, *The Time That Remains*, 70–71. Likewise, in "The Messiah and the Sovereign: Problem of Law in Walter Benjamin," Agamben writes: "One of the paradoxes of the messianic kingdom is, indeed, that another world and another time must make themselves present in this world and time. This means that historical time cannot simply be canceled and that messianic time, moreover, cannot be perfectly homogenous with history: the two times must instead accompany each other according to modalities that cannot be reduced to a dual logic (this world / the other world). . . . Here we are confronted not with a compromise between two irreconcilable impulses but with an attempt to bring to light the hidden structure of historical time itself" (Agamben, *Potentialities*, 168).

Agamben's essay "The Messiah and the Sovereign: The Problem of Law in Walter Benjamin," alongside references it includes to Benjamin's text "Theological-Political Fragment" (see *Selected Writings*, Vol. 3; this text is considered as part of the core of Benjamin's conception of the philosophy of history), along with other pertinent ancient Jewish sources, attempts to comment on (among other ideas) Benjamin's conception of the relation between the profane and the kingdom.

The decisive problem that "Theological-Political Fragment" exposes is the relationship between the profane and the kingdom (history and messianic time). That the two are fundamentally heterogenic is exemplified in the text, first and foremost, as follows:

"Nothing historical can relate itself on its own account to anything Messianic." The profane and the kingdom are heterogenous but also related, and their relation is a result of their persistence in their own directions, which are opposite directions to one another, as Benjamin writes. The two orders are opposite, yet in their persistence in different directions, they in fact promote one another (a paradoxical relation). The important point in this fragment is that the profane order, according to Benjamin, cannot relate itself to anything messianic, the Kingdom of God cannot be set as a goal of the political sphere—only as an end term.

In a public lecture (see "On Walter Benjamin's Messianism"), Agamben maintains that this Benjaminian thesis contradicts our current representation of political action and obliges us to call into question our conception of politics. Thus, if we follow Benjamin's idea, any ideology (e.g., classless society in Marx) makes the major mistake of trying to flatten the messianic onto the historical (or trying to confuse one with the other), trying to realize in historical context these messianic ideas. These messianic ideas must be there but always kept heterogenous to the profane order and never to be conceived as a goal (or else they will lose their force and nature) but only as an end. The two heterogenous elements coexist but must not be confused or flattened together. This is perhaps, according to Agamben, why Marx, in his introduction to the *Critique of Hegel's Philosophy of Right*, says one cannot realize philosophy without immediately abolishing it and vice versa; if one tries to realize philosophy into politics one immediately abolishes philosophy. Thus, we should forget the idea of realizing something through politics—on the contrary, only if something remains unrealized or unachievable can it act on history.

The problem we thus have is to try and find a specific mode of being for each of the two orders. This means to think anew the problem of the relation between potentiality and actuality—*dynamis* and *energeia* (the two ontological categories, or the two experiences of Being to each corresponds a specific modality of existence) according to Aristotle—thus to think anew potentiality as something unreal that must be realized and fulfilled in an act. Possibility is real in itself. In terms of the Benjaminian context here discussed, this means not to think of potentiality as a goal of a certain praxis. This presence (of potentiality) breaks the historical continuum, according to Benjamin. Philosophy in itself already effects reality and is real in itself, as much as in the Benjaminian fragment the messianic kingdom acts on the historical order only if it remains unachievable, never conceived as a goal: only in this way can its essence of possibility be saved. The radical heterogeneity of the messianic does not allow the making of plans and calculations for its realization in a new historical order and thus must remain unachievable.

As will become clearer in due course, Benjamin's messianism is a notion of redemption that cannot be directly addressed in historical terms; the messianic kingdom cannot be conceived as the telos of human action. In his text on Benjamin's messianism, S. Khatib maintains that the messianic is a relation between the historical and the messianic—one can speak of an inaccessible messianic reference in the profane now (the messianic is an inaccessible relational concept). The messianic is a surplus of pressure, a "too muchness," within the historical itself. It is the index of a transcendent dimension situated in the innermost core of the profane. The relation of the historical and the messianic exists only in the absence of the messiah, yet its presence, however weak, is experienced in terms of the paradoxical relation between the historical and the messianic. Any human deeds, in this sense—politics, for example—are left only with the task of keeping free the empty place of the messianic within the profane. Thus, messianic politics is impossible. The messianic is a relation that connects and separates, at the same time, the historical and the messianic, a purely relational figure that expresses an inaccessible structure of referring, according to Khatib.

58. Of the concept of "figure" in relation to language, see Agamben, *The Coming Community*, 59.

59. Paul speaks about "for us, for whom the extremities of the times have met, are face to face" (quoted in Agamben, "The Time That Is Left," 9), that is, the two extremities of the *Olam hazzeh* and the *Olam habba* contact one another, "their face-to-face is messianic time" (Agamben, "The Time That Is Left," 9).

60. Agamben's idea of "inversion" is based upon Gershom Scholem's text (dedicated to Benjamin) where Scholem maintains that messianic time is the time of inverse *waw*. See Scholem, "95 Thesen über Judentum und Zionismus."

61. Agamben, *The Time That Remains*, 76.

62. Elsewhere, Agamben writes that messianic time, the being-contemporary with the Messiah, is the example par excellence for the term we encountered earlier, that is, "contemporariness," exemplified by the one who manages to use the fracture of time as a meeting place for times and generations: "Not only is this time [i.e., "the time of the now"] chronologically indeterminate (the parousia, the return of Christ that signals the end is certain and near, though not a calculable point), but it also has the singular capacity of putting every instant of the past in direct relationship with itself, of making every moment or episode of biblical history a prophecy or a prefiguration (Paul prefers the term typos, figure) of the present (thus Adam, through whom humanity received death and sin, is a 'type' or figure of the Messiah, who brings about redemption and life to human being)" (Agamben, *What Is an Apparatus? and Other Essays*, 53).

63. Quoted in Agamben, "The Time That Is Left," 9.

64. Agamben, "The Time That Is Left," 10.

65. Quoted in Agamben, *The Time That Remains*, 97.

66. Agamben originally begins to develop the concept of "inoperativity" (or "inoperativeness") in a discussion of sovereignty/law and Kojève's (historical) theme of *desœuvrement*; see Agamben, *Homo Sacer: Sovereign Power and Bare Life*, 61–62.

67. Agamben, *The Time That Remains*, 98.

68. Also see Agamben, *The Use of Bodies*, 273.

69. The messianic exigency reemerges in Hegel in the problem of the *plērōma* of times and the end of history—he thinks the *plērōma* not as each instant's relation to the Messiah (as Paul does, via the Torah) but as the final result of a global process. Both important interpreters of Hegel, Alexandre Koyré and Alexandre Kojève (who think the possibility of the Hegelian system in terms of the end of history), end up flattening out the messianic into the eschatological, mixing the problem of messianic time with the problem of posthistory (Kojève's concept of *désœuvrement*, a good translation of Pauline *katargein*, "inoperativity," appears in his definition of the posthistorical condition of man).

70. Furthermore, Benjamin relates Goethe's *Urphänomen* to another concept central to his work (soon to be discussed), that is, the *dialectical image*: "The dialectical image is that form of the historical object which satisfies Goethe's requirements for the object of analysis: to exhibit a genuine synthesis. It is the primal phenomenon of history" (Convolute N9a, 4 in Benjamin, *The Arcade Project*, 474).

71. Agamben, *The Time That Remains*, 139.

72. Benjamin, *Illuminations*, 254. The word is spaced in Benjamin's original (*Handexemplar*) manuscript in German, and merely italicized in the English translation.

73. *Typology* will become, in the Middle Ages, an interpretive system in Christian thought wherein people, events, and passages of the Old Testament are seen as prefigurations of New Testament (in order to prove that the New is a fulfillment of the Old).

74. Quoted in Agamben, *The Church and the Kingdom*, 5.

75. Benjamin, "Theses on the Philosophy of History," 264.

76. On the Jewish indebtedness to Benjamin, see, among others: Stéphane Mosès, *The Angel of History: Rosenzweig, Benjamin, Scholem* (trans. Barbara Harshar) (Stanford, CA: Stanford University Press, 2009); Eric Jacobson, *Metaphysics of the Profane: The Political Theology of Walter Benjamin and Gershom Scholem* (New York: Columbia University Press, 2003); and Susan A. Handelman, *Fragments of Redemption: Jewish Thought and Literary Theory in Benjamin, Scholem, and Levinas* (Bloomington: Indiana University Press, 1991.

77. The Greek term *Paroikousa* means the manner in which foreigners (and those in exile) dwell, as opposed to the Greek verb, *katoikein*, which designates how a citizen of the city dwells. *Paroikein* designates how a Christian ought to live in this world as well as his experience of time or messianic time. The experience of time proper to the Church is defined by the ecclesiastical tradition as "*ho chronos tē paroikias*" (Agamben, *The Church and the Kingdom*, 2), that is, parochial time (in the sense of sojourning like a foreigner). Sojourning here does not mean a fixed period of time nor is it to be understood in the sense of chronological time, but in the sense that the Church sojourns on earth

for a prolonged period without altering its messianic experience of time. This position preceded, according to Agamben, the Church's later position that took place on the background of the "delay of the parousia" (Agamben, *The Church and the Kingdom*, 4): "*Paroika* and *parousia*, the sojourn of the foreigner and the presence of the messiah, have the same structure, expressed in Greek through the preposition *pará*: a presence that distends time, an *already* that is also a *not yet*, a delay that does not put off until later but, instead, a disconnection within the present moment that allows us to grasp time" (Agamben, *The Church and the Kingdom*, 26). The initial Christian community expected the imminent arrival of the messiah (and thus the end of time) but was confronted with an inexplicable delay and thus had to reorganize its institutional and juridical organization, a repositioning resulting in the Christian community ceasing to *paroikein* (to sojourn as foreigners) so as to begin to *katoikein* (to live like a citizen), and as a result, lost its messianic experience of time. Also see Agamben, *The Kingdom and the Garden*, 146–52.

78. Quoted in Agamben, *The Time That Remains*, 145; Benjamin, *The Arcades Project*, 463.

79. The essay originally appeared in Italian, in the edited volume *Walter Benjamin: Tempo storia linguagio* (1983). English translations appeared as "Language and History in Benjamin" in the journal *Differentia* (1988); and a later version, albeit lacking a few final paragraphs, also appeared as "Language and History: Linguistic and Historical Categories in Benjamin's Thought" in the collection *Potentialities* (1999). A further treatment of this theme appears in *Potentialities* and also in "Walter Benjamin and the Demonic: Happiness and Historical Redemption," 138–59.

Additionally, Agamben also develops this theme in *Infancy and History*, in an attempt to develop a new experience of time and history that will be grounded, accordingly, in a new experience of language. There he picks up on Benjamin's essay "On the Program of the Coming Philosophy" (Benjamin, *Selected Writings*, 1:100–10) of 1918 where Benjamin calls for a reinvention of experience beyond the constrains of the Kantian model, a reinvention that by relating to the Kantian system would likewise be turned into knowledge. This would be a transformation of the concept of knowledge that begins to manifest itself in the acquisition of a new concept of experience, and at the center of this reinvention we find the question of language. Benjamin writes: "The great transformation and correction which must be performed upon the concept of experience, originated to one-sidedly along mathematical-mechanical lines, can be attained only be relating knowledge to language" (Benjamin, *Selected Writings*, 1:107–8) and, moreover, "a concept of knowledge gained from reflection on the linguistic nature of knowledge will create a corresponding concept of experience which will also encompass realms that Kant failed to truly systemized" (Benjamin, *Selected Writings*, 1:108).

80. Benjamin, *Gesammelte Schriften*, 1239. Quoted in Agamben, "Language and History in Benjamin," 169.

81. Isidore of Seville, *Etymologies*, 1:61. Quoted in Agamben, "Language and History in Benjamin," 170.

82. Augustine, *De Ordine*, 2, 12, 37. Quoted in Agamben, "Language and History in Benjamin," 170.

83. Agamben, "Language and History in Benjamin," 170.

84. Varro, *De Lingua Latina*, 5, 6. Quoted in Agamben, "Language and History in Benjamin," 171.

85. Agamben, "Language and History in Benjamin," 171–72. On the concept of "handing down" and/or "handing over" in the context of Christian theology, see Agamben, *Pilate and Jesus*, 26–29.

86. Agamben, "Language and History in Benjamin," 172.

87. Agamben, "Language and History in Benjamin," 173.

88. Agamben, "Language and History in Benjamin," 174.

89. Agamben will develop this theme in his later book *Infancy and History: On the Destruction of Experience*, where he deals with human linguistic infancy or how humans are expelled from language as such into a linguistic and metaphysical scission. Infancy refers to the interim state between our pure state of grace in language, echoing that of the animal and our acquisition of voice. Having language and the privation of voice are fundamental conditions of being human. "Animals are not in fact denied language . . . they are already inside it. Man, instead, by having an infancy . . . splits this single language and, in order to speak, has to constitute himself as the subject of language—he has to say I. . . . man's nature is split at its source, for infancy brings its discontinuity and the difference between language and discourse. The historicity of the human being has its basis in this difference and discontinuity" (Agamben, *Infancy and History*, 52). One can thus conclude that: (1) humans have no voice of their own; (2) as humans acquire their voice, a division is developed between speech and language; (3) this division and our awareness of it define *human* beings, as well as the way in which we come to have language (not the mere fact that we have one); and (4) we have language first as bifurcation (language-speech), then as subordination (speech over language), and then as negation (speech denies the experience of the nature of language as such). Yet because we have infancy we also have history, and because we have history we are human.

Moreover, infancy first names our coming away from being animal, then it indicates our ability to conceive of pure thinking not in terms of what cannot be said, but what can, and finally, it names the problem of human experience. The human experience of language, for Agamben, is always taken within language, but not entirely within language as if the division between language and speech never occurred. To undergo an experience within language is to undergo a new form of experience as testing ("experience" is related etymologically to "experiment" in Latin) or thinking, one that accepts the presence of language as such. Infancy is to be found in the human at all stages as both remnant of the animal and potential for the post-human (Watkin, *The Literary Agamben: Adventures in Logopoiesis*, 6–9).

90. Agamben, "Language and History in Benjamin," 175.

91. Also see Agamben, *The Kingdom and the Garden*, 148–49. It was Benjamin's break with a Marxist teleological reading of history that propelled his conception of a "weak messianic force" working through history in order to redeem those who were forgotten by history. Benjamin uses the notion of the messianic as a disruptive force working within the canonical representation of history; and just as the messianic is envisioned by Benjamin to be the redemptive figure of political liberation for the Jewish people, so he found a way to generate alternative meaning to history, through a messianic cessation, and against violently narrated ideological ends (Dickinson, "Canon as an Act of Creation," 137).

92. Agamben, "Language and History in Benjamin," 178–79.

93. The origin, with respect to language and names in particular, is elsewhere illustrated by Agamben via the metaphor of the vortex: "Names—and each name is a proper or a divine name—are the vortexes of the historical becoming of language, whirlpools in which the semantic and communicative tension of language clogs up into itself and becomes equal to zero. In a name, we no longer say—or do not yet say—anything; we only call. It is perhaps for this reason that, in the naive representation of the origin of language, we imagine that names come first, discrete and isolated as in a dictionary, and that we then combine them to form a discourse. Once again, this puerile imagination becomes perspicuous if we understand that the name is actually a vortex that perforates and interrupts the semantic flow of language, not simply in order to abolish it. In the vortex of nomination, the linguistic sign, by turning and sinking into itself, is intensified and exacerbated in the extreme; it then makes itself be sucked in at the point of infinite pressure, in which it disappears as a sign and re-emerges on the other side as a pure name" (Agamben, *The Fire and the Tale*, 61–62).

94. Agamben, "Language and History in Benjamin," 180.

95. Agamben, "Language and History in Benjamin," 180.

96. Agamben, "Language and History in Benjamin," 182. Benjamin's conception of this language seems to exceed a realization in a mere theoretical form. As if bodily experienced, it is grounded on actuality, closely tied to the *experience* of language, to the realization that *there is* language, and in the same manner as any other ontological substance, it is given in time and (from itself) involves a reflection on history.

97. See De La Durantaye, *Giorgio Agamben: A Critical Introduction*, 243–46. Furthermore, for Benjamin, the dialectical image in fact results from

the construction of countless quotations since "the place where one encounters [dialectical image] is language" (N2a, 3; Benjamin, *The Arcade Project*, 462).

98. Benjamin, *The Arcades Project*, 458. Furthermore: "Method of this project: literary montage. I needn't *say* anything. Merely show" (Benjamin, *The Arcade Project*, 460).

99. As indicated previously, and furthermore (in note N2, 6) where the principle of montage is carried over to history: "That is, to assemble large-scale constructions out of the smallest and most precisely cut components. Indeed, to discover in the analysis of the small individual moment the crystal of the total event" Benjamin, *The Arcades Project*, 461.

100. Agamben, "Difference and Repetition," 328.

101. Agamben, "Difference and Repetition," 329.

102. Quoted in Agamben, "Difference and Repetition," 330.

103. Agamben, "Difference and Repetition," 331.

104. Agamben, "Difference and Repetition," 332. We will further develop this trajectory in the next chapter.

105. Agamben, *What Is an Apparatus? and Other Essays*, 53–54.

106. De La Durantaye, *Giorgio Agamben: A Critical Introduction*, 244; Agamben, "Nymphae," 58.

107. Agamben, *The Signature of All Things*, 72.

108. See Watkin, 2014 (a and b).

109. For a discussion of the paradigm as a particular mode and function of a historical example see Agamben, *Infancy and History: On the Destruction of Experience*, 119–37. Additionally, Agamben dedicates the first chapter of *The Signature of All Things* to the question "What is a paradigm?" where he attempts to clarify a few misunderstandings or criticisms raised against him on the account of using facts as metaphors and vice versa, thus failing to act as a responsible historian. However, he insists on using concrete historical examples as paradigms that attempt to articulate a broader set of problems.

110. This relationship is also known in interpretive processes of knowledge as the hermeneutic circle—the idea that the part can be understood only by means of the whole and that every explanation of the part presupposes the understanding of the whole; or in other words, that knowledge of a single phenomenon presupposes knowledge of the whole (and vice versa), thus a paradox prevails and the epistemological procedure cannot begin. Agamben refers to the idea of the hermeneutic circle a few times throughout his oeuvre, often in an attempt to come to terms with its interpretive complexity, which adheres as a challenge to the human sciences at large.

In his essay on Aby Warburg's research methodology, "Aby Warburg and the Nameless Science," for example, he explains that philological and historical disciplines consider the hermeneutic circle to be the epistemological process that is proper to them and is the foundation of all hermeneutics. However, contrary to the common belief, this is not necessarily a vicious circle that sabotages processes of knowledge (it is, he claims, the rationality of the humanities) because if this science wants to remain faithful to its own law, it needs to "stay within it in the right way" (according to Heidegger). The passage from the part to the whole (and back) never returns to the same point; at every step it broadens its radius, discovering a higher perspective that opens a new circle: "The curve representing the hermeneutic circle is not a circumference . . . but a spiral that continually broadens its turns" (Agamben, *Potentialities*, 96).

In *The Signature of All Things* this theme is interrogated once again specifically in the context of the current discussion, that is, the paradigmatic method. Tracing the hermeneutic circle in the discourse of philology, from Georg Anton Friedrich Ast to Martin Heidegger, Agamben emphasizes the latter's crucial contribution to understanding the hermeneutic circle not as a vicious circle but as a virtuous one: "Grounding this hermeneutical circle in *Being and Time* on pre-understanding as *Dasein*'s anticipatory existential structure, Martin Heidegger helped the human sciences out of this difficulty and indeed guaranteed the 'more original' character of their knowledge" (Agamben, *The Signature of All Things*, 27). However, Agamben claims, if the interpreter's activity is always already anticipated by a preunderstanding that is elusive, it seems as if the inquirer must be able to recognize in phenomena the signature of a preunderstanding that depends on their own existential character, thus "the circle then seems to become even more 'vicious'" (Agamben, *The Signature of All Things*, 27). The *aporia*, according to Agamben, is resolved if we understand that the hermeneutic circle is, in fact, a paradigmatic circle: "There is no duality here between 'single phenomenon' and 'the whole' as there was in Ast and Schleiermacher: the whole only results from paradigmatic exposition of individual cases. And there is no circularity, as in Heidegger, between a 'before' and an 'after,' between pre-understanding and interpretation. In the paradigm, intelligibility does not precede the phenomenon; it stands, so to speak, 'besides' it (*para*). . . . The phenomenon, exposed in the medium of its knowability, shows the whole of which it is the paradigm. . . . With regard to phenomena . . . it stands neither in the past nor the present but in their exemplary constellation" (Agamben, *The Signature of All Things*, 27–28).

111. The metaphysical tradition presents any concept as a split structure (or as a bi-conceptual structure) between two heterogeneous elements: the common (unconditional power, founding element, signature) and the proper (singularity, a series of subsequent, dependent elements or paradigms, what's founded), which appears to actualize this original element.

Thus, research into a certain phenomenon reveals a multiplicity of paradigms that can be organized under a single overarching concept (signature) such as power, language, potentiality, poetry, life, etc.

This structure is illogical, paradoxical, and self-negating due to the common's self-founding fiction of presence. For example, what seems to be the founding element of the law is a product of the law itself. The common founds the realm of the proper, which itself invents the constant need for a fiction of foundation through the modes of its operation. Our ability to distinguish between the common and the proper becomes confused in a space that Agamben constitutes as a zone of indifference. There, we can no longer distinguish the common from the proper and which one is the founding element. At this place, the energy of this dialectical system is eliminated because it depends on oppositional difference. This could be said to be the case for any metaphysical concept of Western thought, since any concept is traditionally split, as we have previously stated, into two elements (common-proper). A system that depends on the common-proper distinction becomes inoperative once this distinction breaks down. Thus, for Agamben, this structure can become inoperative by (1) showing that its illogical; (2) demonstrating that every concept, being historically contingent, operates as a founding fiction of oppositional division (the signature is the act of presenting as necessary what is, in fact, an historical contingency), but nonetheless has an origin that can be revealed and thus will become inoperative; and (3) identifying the constant communication between the common and the proper (the identity-difference opposition), and the way to suspend the difference between them. Rendering this structure inoperative (in other words, rendering metaphysics indifferent)—and such escape from false necessities—is Agamben's aim.

In this sense, Agamben's methodology at large has a very precise and ambitious aim—to paradigmatically trace the *arches*, as identity-difference constructs (or signatures), in order to suspend them and thus to render historiography (as a mode of metaphysical signature) indifferent; or in other words, to render indifferent the two oppositional methods of Western epistemological thought: logical deduction and empirical induction. Agamben's methodology tries to go beyond the metaphysics of presence and difference through an archaeological excavation of paradigms; thus, through the exposition of paradigmatic order and its signatory distribution (through common-proper dialectics), it tries to render inoperative the conditioning, binary logic of Western thought. Moreover, Agamben's claim that all concepts (signatures) are historically contingent and not logically necessary also applies to the very concept of "difference." Thus the "common" and the "proper" are not existent ontological or transcendent states but a result of the philosophy of difference. Nonetheless, Agamben's attempt to free our intelligibility from our dependency on the structure of identity-difference does not necessitate the messianic future return to an ideal state of predivisive unity.

In contrast to the somewhat overly common interpretation of Agamben's aim, his work (in my view) does not offer merely a negative or nihilistic critique but wishes to constitute an epistemology that tries to allow us to see things differently than we are usually forced to. It seems as if the very concept of negativity in Agamben's work has unjustifiably earned an overly bad reputation, and it is mainly in his writings on art (as the next chapter will likewise attempt to show) where we can witness the "positive" sides of negativity in the form of *inoperativity* in art. For now, I will only point to a recent study of this topic by Malte Fabian Rauch, who claims that Agamben's writings on art offer a privileged perspective from which to approach the strand of negativity in his work. He already identifies in Agamben's first book, *The Man Without Content*, a certain ambivalence towards negativity, to which inoperativity (developed in Agamben's thought in parallel) can be seen as a response. Rauch writes: "The point . . . is to show how [the theory of inoperativity] transforms the very idea of negativity in art," and concludes that "[i]noperativity . . . is a form of privation that holds negation in suspense" (Rauch, "Archaeologies of Contemporary Art: Negativity, Inoperativity, Désœuvrement," 201–3).

112. Agamben, *The Coming Community*, 9.

113. Agamben, *The Coming Community*, 10.

114. Agamben further discusses the relation between an example and an exception in Agamben, *Homo Sacer: Sovereign Power and Bare Life*, 21–23.

115. See Aristotle, *Prior Analytics*, 69.

116. Paradigms do not constitute the transfer of meaning, but rather an analogical model. Analogy refers to the third order of relationality; metonymy is relation due to proximity (or contact); metaphor due to meaning transfer; while analogy is a deactivated relationality where it is neither proximate nor transferable, but a mix of both occupying a space of suspensive mediation. Analogical paradigm is the process by which identity and difference (or common and proper) is suspended in a state of indispensability.

117. Agamben, *The Signature of All Things*, 18.

118. De La Durantaye, *Giorgio Agamben: A Critical Introduction*, 350.

119. Agamben, *The Kingdom and the Glory*, 4. "Oikonimia," one of the book's themes, for example, is a signature whose meaning remains the same but whose location alters (domestic-theology-politics). More broadly, Foucault's archaeology, Nietzsche's genealogy, Derrida's deconstruction, and Benjamin's theory of dialectical images are all "sciences of signature."

120. On what claimed to be the Heideggerian precedent (*Spur*) to the Agambenian concept of signature, see Östman, "Philosophical Archaeology as Method in the Humanities. A comment on Cultural Memory and the Problem of History," 84–86.

121. Benjamin, "Theses on the Philosophy of History," 390.

122. Colilli, *Agamben and the Signature of Astrology*, xvi.

123. Colilli, *Agamben and the Signature of Astrology*, 24.

124. The idea that the signature is a pure, historical, and self-referential element brings to mind Pierre Nora's conception of "Lieu de mémoire" (Site of memory), according to which a site of memory does not have a reference in reality; in other words, it is the reference of itself, a sign that points merely to itself as a sign in its pure state. This does not mean, according to Nora, that a

site of memory lacks content, physical presence, or history, but what constitutes it as a site of memory is also the same thing that "de-historicizes" it as such. Thus, a site of memory is of a twofold character: a site of excess, sealed within itself, within its identity, folded around its name, and simultaneously attentive to reverberated space of its meaning (Nora, *Realms of Memory: Rethinking the French Past*).

125. Agamben, *The Signature of All Things*, 37.

126. Nevertheless, Agamben's epistemological discussion should be taken with a grain of salt since, following Heidegger, he seems to be under the impression that scholars are often busy with "sharpening knives" when there is nothing left to cut. Agamben mentions this metaphor in relation to criticism and its epistemological character, already in his early work *Stanzas: Word and Phantasm in Western Culture*: "What is now more and more frequently concealed by the endless sharpening of knives on behalf of a methodology with nothing left to cut—namely, the realization that the object to have been grasped has finally evaded knowledge—is instead reasserted by criticism as its own specific character" (Agamben, *Stanzas: Word and Phantasm in Western Culture*, xvi).

127. De La Durantaye, *Giorgio Agamben: A Critical Introduction*, 245. The signature/image is an impotentiality that permits potentiality to be altered through a movement to actuality (without actuality being a semiotic fullness). This movement brings two major Agambenian concepts together (which we will touch upon in due course): the logic of potentiality, which includes impotentiality, and the ontology of potential. (See also Colilli, *Agamben and the Signature of Astrology*, 8.)

128. "Historical method is a philological method, a method that has as its foundation the book of life. 'To read what was never written,' is what Hofmannsthal calls it. The reader referred to here is the true historian" (quoted in Agamben, *Potentialities*, 1). The quotation refers to Benjamin, *Gesammelte Schriften*, vol. 1, pt. 3, 1238.

129. Quoted in Agamben, *Potentialities*, 1. Note our previous discussion, in this context, of the anthropogenesis (Gloss VII).

130. This claim is echoed throughout Agamben's books *Infancy and History*, *Language and Death*, *The Sacrament of Language* and *What Is Philosophy?* as well as in his essays "The Idea of Language" and "Philosophy and Linguistics" (Agamben, *Potentialities*, 62–76) to name a few.

131. Quoted in Agamben, *Potentialities*, 22.

132. Philology, as Agamben states in *Infancy and History*, from the outset has the role of abolition between the thing to be transmitted and the act of transmission, "and since this abolition has always been regarded as the essential character of myth, philology can thereby be defined as a 'critical mythology'" (Agamben, *Infancy and History*, 146).

133. Agamben, *Nymphs*, 29–30.

134. Agamben, *Nymphs*, 31.
135. Melandri, *La Linea e Il Circolo: Studio Logico-Filosofico Sull'Analogia*, 798.
136. For a further explication of this idea, see Colli, *Filosofia dell'espressione*.
137. See also Agamben, *The Use of Bodies*, 164.
138. Dickinson, "Canon as an Act of Creation," 142.
139. Agamben, *The Signature of All Things*, 21.
140. Kotsko and Salzani, "Introduction: Agamben as a Reader," 8.
141. Agamben, "The Unspeakable Girl: The Myth and Mystery of Kore," 31. See also Agamben, *Creation and Anarchy*, 9–12.
142. Quoted in Agamben, "The Unspeakable Girl: The Myth and Mystery of Kore," 31. The "fullness of actuality" is what the theological tradition attached to the doctrine of the efficacy *ex opere operato* of the liturgical act, that is, to the idea that the saving power of the sacrament was unaffected in the case it was administered in an "impure" manner (because the effective power of the sacrament is not depend upon the celebrant but on Christ, the "mystical presence" who guarantees its efficacy through God). This irreducible liturgical operatively is, however, quite remote from what we find in the pagan mysteries, where salvation is described as "precarious" rather than as something of certainty.
143. Quoted in Agamben, "The Unspeakable Girl: The Myth and Mystery of Kore," 35.
144. Agamben, "The Unspeakable Girl: The Myth and Mystery of Kore," 38.
145. Agamben, "The Unspeakable Girl: The Myth and Mystery of Kore," 39. Benjamin's *Denkbilder*, however, follow, at least chronologically, the relatively lesser-known sonnets he published (lamenting the death of his close friend, the writer Christoph Friedrich Heinle) from 1914 to 1922, which likewise can be characterized as "images of thought."

On Benjamin's use of the tractatus form or method of scholasticism as a performative "method of indirection" and as a way to philosophize and to exhibit what cannot be represented in language, see Rotlevy, "Presentation as Indirection."

146. The following discussion of Benjamin's *Denkbilder* is based on Kirst, "Walter Benjamin's 'Denkbild': Emblematic Historiography of the Recent Past."
147. Benjamin, *One-Way Street and Other Writings*, 81.
148. The *Denkbild* demonstrates, in the context of the present discussion and as will become clearer through the broader discussion of art in the next chapter, how artistic forms can potentially develop forms of historiography, in accordance with the manner in which we identified, in chapter 1, philosophical archaeology as a form of historiography in terms of historical ruins ("ruinology" in the Agambenian vocabulary). We can thus further allude to a tradition of "ruinological art" or "destructive art" which generally constitutes itself as a form of material-based historiography. This tradition dates back chronologically to the beginning of the avant garde and includes various artworks, artists and

art movements: from Marinetti's *Manifesto of Futurism* (1909) and Duchamp's *Unhappy Readymade* (1919), to Haacke's *Germania* (1993) and beyond.

But what is revealed when we examine this tradition is not only its conceptual treatment of history through materiality but also (as its artworks exemplify) the very function and status of materiality itself within and during this process of historiography—it seems as if initially materiality is artistically used in order to help forming the representation of destruction, whereas later on materiality becomes a form of destruction in and of itself; in other words, materiality is dislocated, generally speaking, from the domain of the virtual to that of the actual.

This change also obviously influences art's conception of history and temporality—from putting an emphasis on the past and future, to illuminating the present moment. This is shown in the image of the fragment: the fragment (or ruin) in the artwork of the Renaissance or Romanticism expresses a desire for totality and unity (in keeping with its nonmaterial understanding in culture at large), for what will be achieved (with perfection) in the future, and thus is part of such temporality. In contemporary times, we witness a change in the function of the fragment, again in keeping with the idea that the world is constantly shifting, never finished, there is always another edition to retreat to or to add to. The fragment in the artworks of contemporary art no longer alludes to a whole but manifests the destruction itself and the various forces of segmentation in the present.

149. Benjamin, *The Origin of German Tragic Drama*, 182.

150. Benjamin, *Selected Writings, 1913–1926*, 1:387–90. Recall the discussion, in the prologue of this book, of Agamben's methodological principal regarding interpretation (which he attributes to Benjamin).

151. See Agamben, *Taste*. Taste, for Agamben, is an enigmatic "middle ground" between knowledge and pleasure, between knowledge that enjoys (itself) and enjoyment that knows (itself)—Taste is "this special form of knowledge that enjoys the beautiful object and the special form of pleasure that judges beauty" (Agamben, *Taste*, 5). The aesthetic judgment, according to Agamben, is based more on intuition than on pure reason.

152. Said, *Beginnings: Intention and Method*, 313.

153. Agamben, *The Man Without Content*, 104–15.

154. Arendt, *Men in Dark Times*, 193.

155. Arendt, *Men in Dark Times*, 193.

156. Agamben, *The Man Without Content*, 128n3.

157. Agamben, *The Man Without Content*, 104–5.

158. The other type of destruction performed by the collector is far more radical, according to Benjamin: "It is the deepest enchantment of the collector to enclose the particular item within a magic circle, where, as a last shudder

runs through it (the shudder of being acquired), it turns to stone" (Convolute H1a, 2 in Benjamin, *The Arcades Project*, 205).

159. Benjamin, "Theses on the Philosophy of History," 257–58; In "Walter Benjamin and the Demonic: Happiness and Historical Redemption" (Agamben, *Potentialities*, 138–59), Agamben attempts to show that Benjamin's reflection on the philosophy of history is shaded with a melancholic light as a result of Gershom Scholem's interpretation (Scholem, "Walter Benjamin and His Angel," 198–237) to Benjamin's angel as it is portrayed in Benjamin's prose titled "Agesilaus Santander" (Scholem, "Walter Benjamin and His Angel," 208). The angel (which has a redemptive role in Benjamin's conception of history), claims Scholem, hides the dark, demonic traits of "Angelus Satanas." Agamben's essay aims to open Benjamin's text to another possible interpretation and to trace Benjamin's lines of ethics. "Ethics" is referred to here in the sense of the use the Greeks had made of the word as "doctrine of happiness" as they linked the demonic to happiness. Benjamin's text also ties the figure of the angel to the idea of happiness. Since in the second thesis from the "Theses on the Philosophy of History" we find that happiness and redemption are inseparable, the presentation of Benjamin's theory of happiness, according to Agamben, must proceed only by clarification of his ideas on the philosophy of history, which have at their center the concept of redemption.

Scholem's reading of Benjamin's text is based on a hypothesis that the name "Agesilaus Santander" is in fact an anagram, a "secret name," for *der Angelus Satanas*. However, Scholem's formulation is preceded by a "disquieting shadow on the image of the angel" (Agamben, *Potentialities*, 139), which makes it hard to verify whether the hypothesis is necessary and whether it economically explains the text without leaving unresolved the most problematic aspects. Scholem thus anticipates the Luciferian reading of "Agesilaus Santander" without having demonstrated its validity, immersing Benjamin's text in a demonic light.

Scholem's interpretation is also based on iconographical elements of Satan, claiming that only Satan possesses claws and talons; however, this is not accurate, since in the European iconographic tradition, "There is only one figure that brings together purely angelic characteristics and the demonic traits of claws" (Agamben, *Potentialities*, 141)—this is not Satan but Eros, Love. A descriptive model, found for the first time in Plutarch, represents Eros as a winged (and often feminine) angelic figure with claws.

Thus, Benjamin's figure of the angel with claws and wings leads to the domain of Eros, that is, not to a demon in the Judeo-Christian sense but a *daimōn* in the Greek sense ("in Plato, Eros appears as the demon par excellence"). Additionally, Benjamin was aware of this specific iconographic type as he mentions it in his essay "The Origin of the German Tragic Drama" (which makes Agamben's claim more probable) as well as in his essay "Karl Kraus," where the angel is not considered a Satanic figure. Benjamin's portrayal of the claws of Angelus Novus does not have a Satanic meaning but instead characterizes the "destructive—and simultaneously liberating—power of the angel."

Thus, there is a correspondence between the clawed angel of "Agesilaus Santander" and the liberating angel who (at the end of the essay on Kraus) celebrates his victory over the demon "at the point where origin and destruction meet." This (Agamben's) reading nullifies Scholem's reading as the textual element that supports Scholem's reading (of the Luciferian nature of the angel) disappears. This does not mean that Scholem's reading is erroneous but, as Agamben writes, "that there is all the more reason to measure its validity only on the basis of its capacity to explain economically the most problematic aspects of Benjamin's text" (Agamben, *Potentialities*, 142). However, the Angelus appears only in passing in Benjamin's essay "Karl Kraus." Here the Angelus is mentioned in the context of the messenger in old engravings who announces anticipated disaster. Kraus, according to Benjamin, is described as someone who "stands on the threshold of the Last Judgment" (Benjamin, "Karl Kraus," 443) and thus resembles those saints in Baroque paintings who face, so to speak, an angelic flood. "Just as, in the most opulent examples of Baroque altar painting, saints hard-pressed against the frame extend defensive hands toward the breathtakingly foreshortened extremities of the angels, the blessed, and the damned floating before them, so the whole of world history presses in on Kraus in the extremities of a single item of local news, a single phrase, a single advertisement" (Benjamin, "Karl Kraus," 443). Benjamin refers here to the concept of citation, Kraus's basic polemical methodology, that further on becomes Benjamin's most adequate methodology reflecting (as we have just analyzed) the structure of his philosophy of history—the presentation of the whole through a cited part, or in other words, the attempt to capture most accurately the historical image through the revelation of its most trivial elements, its remainders or leftovers. The excavated fragment contains within itself the figure of the whole (Benjamin, as previously noted, was influenced in this regard by Goethe's *Urphänomen*).

160. Agamben, *The Man Without Content*, 109–10.

161. Agamben, *The Man Without Content*, 109–10.

162. Agamben, *The Man Without Content*, 110. Man's inability to recover his space in the tension between past and future history is exemplified most accurately, according to Agamben, in an image depicted by Kafka where train travelers entering into a tunnel are met with an accident, causing the train to halt and the travelers to lose a sense of spatiality, not knowing whether they are at the end or the beginning of the tunnel. Kafka, writes Agamben, "thus replaces the idea of a history infinitely unfolding along an empty, linear time with the paradoxical image of a *state of history* in which the fundamental event of the human condition is perpetually taking place; the continuum of linear time is interrupted, but does not create an opening beyond itself" (Agamben, *The Man Without Content*, 113). Thus, Kafka's image of a *state of history* is positioned side

by side with Benjamin's idea of "now-time" understood as a halt in happening. The creation of an opening beyond itself is likewise the theological horizon that the messianic opens up, working from within "given representations to de-stabilize them, as an eschatological horizon against which all particular identifications are rendered null and void" (Dickinson, "Canon as an Act of Creation," 158).

When does aesthetic redemption become possible? Is there a certain timeframe in which a metaphysical space, via aesthetics, opens up for man? What type of *poiesis* can, according to Agamben, initiate that? Can men overcome Kafka's *state of history* or is this a theological/messianic activity reserved exclusively for angels? As Agamben often works on the basis of, and in relation with, his Jewish interlocuters, we can mention a section from the Talmud where a description is given regarding the poetry of men and angels: "The Gemara raises an objection from the following *baraita*: The Jewish people are more dear to the Holy One, Blessed be He, than the ministering angels, as the Jewish people may recite a song of praise to God at any time, but ministering angels recite a song of praise only one time per day. And some say that the ministering angels recite a song of praise one time per week. And some say that they recite a song of praise one time per month. And some say that they recite a song of praise one time per year. And some say that they recite a song of praise one time in every seven years. And some say that they recite a song of praise one time per Jubilee. And some say that they recite a song of praise one time in the entire history of the world" (Chullin 91b, The William Davidson Talmud). The conflicting opinions regarding the frequency with which angels recite a song of praise contradict the common opinion according to which angels never stop reciting songs. This frequency likewise stands in relation to the idea according to which the life of angels tends toward infinity, as opposed to limited human life. Man can, theoretically at any given moment, spontaneously recite a song of praise or compose poetry, whereas angels are bound and subjected to certain temporal rules and even know, in advance, when will they recite songs. Man, on the other hand, does not know all that, which is equally true in regard to any human artistic activity; the artist cannot know in advance when the poetic moment will arrive, but can only sense, internally, that this time has come.

163. Agamben, *The Man Without Content*, 101.

164. See Agamben, "Un Libro senza Patria," 43–46. One recalls that in *The Time That Remains*, Agamben retakes the problem of time, and more accurately, the problem of the caesura of messianic time. Messianic time seems to be an underground alley, dug under the internal history of the West, in order to access salvation through the suspension or deactivation of chronological time and the works that are contained in it. I return to Agamben's idea of the caesura as art's atemporal dimension in the next chapter.

165. Aristotle, *Metaphysics V*, 1013a.

166. Agamben, *The Man Without Content*, 101–2.

Chapter Three

1. In *Cy Twombly: Eight Sculptures* (Rome: American Academy); and in *Writings on Cy Twombly*, edited by Nicola Del Roscio (Munich: Schrimer/Mosel), respectively.

2. Giorgio Agamben, "Falling Beauty," in *CY Twombly, Sculptures 1992–2005* (Munich: Alte Pinakothek München and Schirmer/Mosel, 2006), 13–15.

3. Agamben, "Falling Beauty," 14.

4. Hölderlin's work is one of only a few modern attempts to formulate a philosophy of meter, according to Agamben. The other attempts include works by Hegel, Mallarmé, and Max Kommerell. See Agamben, *The End of the Poem*, 34.

Benjamin writes about Hölderlin's caesura in his account of Hölderlin's discussion of tragedy in "Goethe's Elective Affinities." See Benjamin, *Selected Writings, 1913–1926*, 340–41.

5. Astrachan, *Naming the Gods: Cy Twombly's Passionate Poiesis*, 5.

6. Agamben, *Writings on Cy Twombly*, 283.

7. Agamben, *Cy Twombly, Sculptures 1992–2005*, 15. Note the entanglement between the aesthetical and the theological dimensions Agamben extrapolates from Twombly's multifaceted artwork—as if, in this entanglement, Agamben finds a material reflection to his theoretical chewing of the cud.

Furthermore, one can sense in this case as well our previous discussion of the *dialectical image* and Benjamin's overall influence on Agamben's thought. Benjamin identifies the arrest of thought's movement as a *caesura* (he uses the descriptor "the expressionless" to name the moment of arrest): "To thinking belongs the movement as well as the arrest of thoughts. Where thinking comes to a standstill in a constellation saturated with tensions—there the dialectical image appears. It is the caesura in the movement of thought. Its position is naturally not an arbitrary one. It is to be found, in a word, where the tension between dialectical opposites is greatest" (Benjamin, *The Arcade Project*, 475; N10a, 3).

Thus, for Agamben the idea of cessation of (art)work is placed at the root of his thinking at large, as if theory is already a form of action even when nothing much seems to be going on when we are just reading, thinking, or experiencing a work of art.

8. See the bibliography: Agamben, *Categorie italiane: Studi di poetica*; in English, Agamben, *The End of the Poem: Studies in Poetics* (109–115 and also 34–37).

9. *De Vulgari eloquentia*, Book II, XIII, 7–8, quoted in Agamben, *The End of the Poem*, 113.

10. Quoted in Agamben, *The Use of Bodies*, 149.

11. Further on this subject, in reference to Agamben, see Waltham-Smith 2020.

12. Agamben, *Image and Silence*, 95.

13. Agamben, *Image and Silence*, 97.
14. Agamben, *Potentialities*, 257.
15. Agamben, *Potentialities*, 257. Also see Agamben, "On the Impossibility of Saying 'I': Epistemological paradigms and poetic paradigms in the work of Furio Jesi," 1053.
16. See Agamben, *The End of Thinking*.
17. The constitutive inoperativity of humanity as such is described, writes Agamben, by Aristotle in the *Nicomachean Ethics* (1097b), where he proposes that "the function of man" might be, in its essence, a possible inoperativity of all human species. For Aristotle, any human activity that has a certain function (*ergon*) or activity (*praxis*)—artists included—has its value in its function, whereas the function of man as such is identified "*with that particular 'operativity' (energeia) that is life according to the* logos" (Agamben, *The Kingdom and the Glory*, 246; also see Agamben, "The Work of Man," 1–10).
18. Agamben, *The Kingdom and the Glory*, 252. The full quotation reads as follows: "What is poetry if not an operation in language that deactivates and renders inoperative its communicative and informative functions in order to open them to a new possible use? . . . [W]hat poetry accomplishes for the potentiality to say, politics and philosophy must accomplish for the potentiality to act. Rendering inoperative economic and social operations, they show what the human body is capable of; they open it to a new possible use" (Agamben, *The Fire and the Tale*, 55; and Agamben, *Creation and Anarchy*, 27–28).
19. See Bernstein, *The Paradoxical Transmission of Tradition and Agamben's Potential Reading of the Rishonim*, 227–30.
20. Agamben, *The Kingdom and the Glory*, 237. Let us recall that in *The Time That Remains*, Agamben describes Paul who uses the verb *Katargeō* to mean "inoperative, not-at-work (*a-ergos*), inactive," thus saying "I make inoperative, I deactivate, I suspend the efficacy." (We find the verb *argeō*, before Paul, in the Septuagint translation of the Hebrew word that signifies rest on Saturday or the sabbatical suspension of work.) *Katargeō* thus signals a taking out of *energeia*. When Paul uses the Greek opposition *dynamis/energeia*, potentiality/act, the messianic enacts as an inversion, that is, the moment when potentiality passes over into actuality and meets up with its telos. This is done not by force but by *astheneia* ("weakness"), not by annihilation or destruction but by deactivation or rendering inoperative and ineffectiveness, and not by wearing itself out but by remaining powerful (in the thing worked on) in the form of weakness, restoring it to the state of potentiality (Also see Agamben, *The Church and the Kingdom*, 19).

Furthermore, the special quality of life in messianic time (*ho nym kairos*, the time-of-now) is marked by a special indicator of inoperativity: the *hōs mē*, the "as not"; it maintains, and at the same time, deactivates all conditions and behaviors of the members of the messianic community but not as mere inertia or rest but, on the contrary, as what enables them to open up new life possibilities, "the messianic operation par excellence" (Agamben, *The Kingdom and the Glory*, 249).

21. Agamben, *The Kingdom and the Glory*, 239. In the Book of Exodus (Parashah Vayakhel-Pekudei), the commandment of the Sabbath is linked to the construction of the tabernacle (the Tent of the Congregation). Hazal sought to define activities prohibited during Sabbath—thus, due to this linkage, ruled that any activity (Melakhah) that was carried out in the tabernacle would be prohibited during Sabbath. Therefore, we have the idea of the thirty-nine Melachot—the types of work prohibited in Sabbath according to the Jewish law, and the basis for the Halakha of Sabbath.

In Leviticus, the people of Israel are asked to sanctify themselves ("For I am the LORD your God; sanctify yourselves therefore, and be ye holy") (11:44), thus the priests (Kohanim) are required to teach the people the rules of sanctity (laws, commandments, prohibitions, etc.); and since a large part of the laws is hard to memorize, there was a need to write them down. In order to have a written format, authors and writers were needed—they would appear as soon as a segment of the population was exempted from the burden of working the land in favor of free time, free time in the sense of *Schola* (σχολη in Ancient Greek), that is, free time for studying and exemption from work. Thus, the Kohanim and the Levites were chosen out of all of the twelve tribes of Israel, and only a single tribe (Levi) had no land appropriation ("The priests the Levites, even all the tribe of Levi, shall have no portion nor inheritance with Israel") (Deuteronomy, 18:1) in order to pursue Liturgy. They made sacrificial offerings during two or three weeks of the year and in the remaining forty-nine or fifty weeks taught the Israelites the rules of sanctity. The priesthood was divided into twenty-four shifts whereas the tribe of Levi thus constitutes the yearly cycle of time. Each shift lasts a week; therefore, in each year, every shift served twice, and four shifts would serve three times: in total, fifty-two weeks. When each of the twenty-four shifts had served thirteen times, they reached the *Shmita* (the sabbatical year, the seventh year, during which all agricultural activity is forbidden and the land left to lie fallow); when each shift had serviced ninety-one times, they had reached the *Jubilee*—that is how the cycle of time and sanctity were kept. Each seven days, Sabbath; each seven years, *Shmita*; each seven cycles of *Shmita*, *Jubilee*; and the first seven months of the year, the seven Jewish holidays (*Mikrae Kodesh*: "The appointed seasons of the LORD, which ye shall proclaim to be holy convocations, even these are My appointed seasons.") (Leviticus 23:2)

In Hebrew, the word "seven" ("Sheva") and the word "oath" ("Shvuah") share a common philological root. The Kohanim pass on their knowledge to the whole of Israel throughout seventy *Mikrae Kodesh* (fifty-two Sabbaths plus eighteen holy days) during which all are free from labor in order to read the holy scriptures.

The Sabbath ("on the seventh day is a sabbath of solemn rest, a holy convocation; ye shall do no manner of work") (Leviticus 23:3) is the basis for Jewish time since it is a time *heard*, not seen, dependent on divine commandment and on counting and oath; it does not appear in the cycle of natural seasons nor in relation to a new moon but exists only auditorily. The Sabbath came to be only once it was written as a commandment that testifies on memory and covenant, and only once a continuous counting of days is kept by a group of believers who remembers its holy days and its Sabbaths. The essence of slavery and freedom relates to sovereignty over time. A slave does not master their time, and vice versa. Jewish time grants one day of freedom each week, and seventy days of freedom from work each year. Sanctity and sacredness relate in the Torah first and foremost to time rather than to place, to the cycle of Sabbaths and holy days rather than to land, to the abstract memory of freedom rather than to concrete reality that is always subjected to the danger of subjugation. Time is sanctified for the sake of the freedom of the general public and is at the core of Jewish thought.

22. Agamben, *What Is Philosophy?*, 33–34.

23. Agamben, *What Is Philosophy?*, 33–34. Note the following verse from the Old Testament: "I sleep, but my heart waketh" (Song of Sg. 5:2).

24. Agamben, *Potentialities*, 237–38. Also see Agamben, *The Use of Bodies*, 62–65.

25. Agamben, *The Kingdom and the Glory*, 251. See also Agamben, *The Use of Bodies*, 277–78. For philosophy's future role in the continuous process of anthropogenesis, and its function of inoperativity in terms of technological developments, see Agamben, "Sulla tecnica e l'arte."

The degree to which Agamben is accurate here should be examined carefully; whether, in the West, inoperativity is conceived as opening up a new possibility in an act of radical human freedom. For example, as Cornelius Castoriadis reminds us: "There's a marvellous phrase from Thucydides: 'it is necessary to choose: rest or be free.' I think it's Pericles who says this to the Athenians: 'if you want to be free, you have to work.' You cannot rest" (Castoriadis, *Postscripts on Insignificance*, 17).

26. Agamben, *The Use of Bodies*, 247.

27. Agamben, *The Use of Bodies*, 247.

28. Agamben, *The Use of Bodies*, 247. For a recent, thorough elaboration on Agamben's notion of form-of-life in relation to a broader discussion of inoperativity, see Bonacci, 2020.

29. Agamben, "To Whom Is Poetry Addressed?," 11.

30. Agamben, "To Whom Is Poetry Addressed?," 11.

31. It seems as if the current condition of life, that is, life under the state of exception, has become messianically paralyzing (on a global scale) in terms of our possible conception of time and therefore of history, since Western societies

had lost their capacity to imagine political alternatives beyond the present state of affairs, beyond the present as such. Our experience of time is, so it seems, is futureless, and all that is left for us is simply to wait—an endless waiting for an end. Is there, at present time, a practice that one can use in order to address the future directly? Agamben, it seems, thinks there is no such practice. Art (it will become clearer) enables the "tearing" of time by its capacity to fragmentize time and work toward surfacing unforeseen potentialities; likewise, it has the capacity to deprive time of its power to continuously form illusions of singular worldview or perspective. The messianic in art, as art, conceptualizes (at least theoretically) alternative histories.

32. Agamben, *Potentialities*, 253; and also, in "On Potentiality," 182–83.
33. Dickinson, "The Poetic Atheology of Giorgio Agamben," 212.
34. Dickinson, "The Poetic Atheology of Giorgio Agamben," 208.
35. Dickinson, "The Poetic Atheology of Giorgio Agamben," 209.
36. Agamben, *Creation and Anarchy*, 13.
37. Agamben, *Creation and Anarchy*, 2. Agamben mentions Giovani Urbani, the late Italian art critic, as the first perhaps to pose this question in a coherent way and to whom Agamben's book *The Man Without Content* is dedicated (and where he claims that "the crisis of art in our time is, in reality, a crisis of poetry, of poiēsis") (Agamben, *The Man Without Content*, 59).
38. Agamben, *The Man Without Content*, 3.
39. See also Agamben, *Potentialities*, 177.
40. Agamben, *Potentialities*, 8–9.
41. Agamben, *Potentialities*, 11.
42. Agamben, *Potentialities*, 12.
43. Agamben, *Potentialities*, 13.
44. For an overarching discussion of the *archaeological turn* (or the archaeological form of thought) in the humanities more broadly, see Boelhower 2005. Boelhower defines the archaeological turn "not as an object in and of itself so much as a set of procedures implying a general heuristic."
45. Whyte, "Studio as History," 1.
46. Whyte, "Studio as History," 2.
47. On medieval materiality as resisting time, see Shalem 2018.
48. See Erber, "Theory Materialized."
49. Erber, "Theory Materialized," 4; Bal, *Louise Bourgeois' Spider: The Architecture of Art-Writing*, 5.
50. Hutchinson et al., *Antony Gormley*, 12.
51. Five years later, on July 1, 1798, Napoleon will land for the first time in Egypt, one of the pinnacles of the ancient world and the plundered source of Europe's archaeological desire.
52. Goethe, "On Granite," 913.

53. For the reverse orientation, in other words, for the recent influence of the visual arts on the discipline of archaeology, see Renfrew, Gosden, and DeMarrais, *Substance, Memory, Display: Archaeology and Art*. For their mutual influence, in general, see Renfrew, *Figuring It Out*. One of the important claims in these texts is that both art and archaeology involve making subtle modifications in the landscape, explore natural materials and processes of change, as well as ask profound questions about the nature of the human condition. The difference between them relates to the fact that archaeologists explore their field in the form of objective knowledge, attempt to formulate statements about their findings that "go beyond one's own personal experiences and subjective beliefs" (Renfrew, Gosden, and DeMarrais, *Substance, Memory, Display: Archaeology and Art*, 166). Artists, on the other hand, have no such constraints and are expected to indulge in self-expression. The need to figure out what one is looking at when facing a monument in the field or an artwork in the gallery is common to both disciplines, but the difference between them is that this need is an obligation for the archaeologist whereas for the artist is rather a meadow for further explorations.

54. Benjamin, "Excavation and Memory," 576; Roelstraete, "Field Notes," 14.

55. Roelstraete, "Field Notes," 15–16.

56. Roelstraete, "Field Notes," 19.

57. Roelstraete, *The Way of the Shovel*, 65. For another film that shows an artist digging his own grave, see *The Hole* (1972–74). The film was a part of a two-year project, culminating in the film itself. Shot under the influence of LSD and bathed in eerie, hazy light, this short film shows the artist Jacques Katmor staging his own burial while drawing Cabalistic and Jewish symbols on the ground and with the movements of the camera.

58. Koester, *Message from the Unseen*, 40.

59. Caron, *Joachim Koester: Of Spirits and Empty Spaces*, 178.

60. Foster, "Blind Spots: Hal Foster on the Art of Joachim Koester," 216.

61. Koester and Buckingham, *Points of Suspension*, 56.

62. Koester and Buckingham, *Points of Suspension*, 60.

63. Koester and Buckingham, *Points of Suspension*, 62.

64. Roelstraete, *The Way of the Shovel*, 100.

65. Roelstraete, *The Way of the Shovel*, 100.

66. In order to support this claim, Roelstraete mentions two previous important texts written on the phenomenon: Godfrey's "The Artist as Historian" (2007) and Foster's "An Archival Impulse" (2004).

67. Roelstraete, "Field Notes," 25. This artistic inclination toward researching and presenting alternative histories, according to Roelstraete, is also a result of current technological and political burdens.

68. Roelstraete, "Field Notes," 33.

69. Roelstraete, "Field Notes," 39. The one tragic flaw of the "historiographic turn" in art, writes Roelstraete, is "its inability to grasp or even look at the present, much less to *excavate* the future" (Roelstraete, "The Way of the Shovel," 6). In a follow-up essay, Roelstraete offers a fix to this flaw, maintaining the need to view the art world as a historical whole, "to finally be able again to capture art in a handful of isms" (Roelstraete, "After the Historiographic Turn: Current Findings," 7). Specifically, after the financial crisis (in the art market) of 2008, a true historical thinking on the grand scale of "isms" is required (as we often expect or witness after a "natural" breed of realisms crises). We hardly have any realism in art and culture now, according to Roelstraete, because there "have not been real crises," and "there simply has not been terribly much engagement with something akin to a 'real' world in recent times" (Roelstraete, "After the Historiographic Turn: Current Findings," 9).

70. Roelstraete, "Field Notes," 43. However, even if one believes the assumptions that "depth deliver[s] truth, that the ground cannot lie," this belief does not necessarily entail its grasping. Isaiah Berlin writes, with regard to the division between "surface" and "depths," the following: "There is a vision, or at least a glimpse, a moment of revelation which in some sense explains and reconciles, a theodicy, a justification of what exists and happens, as well as its elucidation. What does it consist in? . . . [W]e are here plainly intended to see that these 'heroes' of the novel—the 'good' people—have now, after the storms and agonies of ten years and more, achieved a kind of peace, based on some degree of understanding: understanding of what? Of the need to submit: to what? . . . To the permanent relationship of things, and the universal texture of human life, wherein alone truth and justice are to be found by a kind of 'natural'—somewhat Aristotelian—knowledge. . . . How can this be known? . . . By an awareness, not necessarily explicit or conscious, of certain general characteristics of human life and experience. And the most important and the most pervasive of these is the crucial line that divides the 'surface' from the 'depth'—on the one hand the world of perceptible, describable, analyzable data . . . [a]nd, on the other hand, the order which, as it were, 'contains' and determines the structure of experience . . . [W]e are in art living in a world the constituents of which we can discover. . . . [B]ut in part, we are immersed and submerged in a medium that, precisely to the degree to which we inevitably take it for granted as part of ourselves, we do not and cannot observe as if from the outside . . . cannot even be wholly aware of, inasmuch as it enters too intimately into all our experience, is itself too closely interwoven with all that we are and do to be lifted out of the flow (it is the flow) and observed with scientific detachment, as an object. It—the medium in which we are—determines our most permanent categories. . . . [It is] the ultimate framework, the basic presuppositions wherewith we function. . . . Yet some human beings are better aware—although they cannot

describe it—of the texture . . . [I]t is . . . a special sensitiveness to the contours of the circumstances in which we happen to be placed . . . [T]his inexpressible sense of cosmic orientation is the 'sense of reality,' the 'knowledge' of how to live" (Berlin, "The Hedgehog and the Fox," 487–89).

71. In this sense, Roelstraete mentions Georges Bataille's idea of "Base Materialism" according to which both art and archaeology are forms of work that involve our bodily engagement "*in* the world," diminishing the distance from the material and the work itself, forcing us to touch and scratch it, "intensifying out bodily bondage."

72. Kracauer, *History: The Last Things Before the Last*, 214.

73. Kracauer, *History: The Last Things Before the Last*, 214. Siegfried Kracauer's "anteroom thought" can perhaps be realized in the context of post-structuralism, and especially its relation to language. In *Experiencing the Past*, Michael Shanks clearly explains this multilayered connection. Metaphysical judgments, he writes, are judgments about what really exists, that is, ontology. The object of study is the origin. The past, present in its traces, is the beginning and end of archaeology. The word itself—archaeology—contains all that exists in its project: (arché) meaning origin and beginning, power and sovereignty; (logos) meaning account, reason, explanation, expression, discourse. Whether these elements have presence and meaning in themselves is to be questioned in a poststructuralist account, especially ideas of identity, origin, and meaning.

It is argued that the past has no determinate meaning, but it constantly slips from our conceptual hold. The reason for this is because it depends on foregrounding language and its structure. Language is argued as central to human experience, and language is primarily signification—communication in and through signs. Saussure's structural linguistics, as is well known, established a fundamental *split* within the sign: between the (differential, sensible) *signifier*, that is, a sound or image that acts as a vehicle; and the (formal, intelligible) *signified*, that is, a concept referred to. Signifiers have no necessary meaning in themselves but hold potential. This potential comes from signifiers being located in a structure of signifiers that differ from each other. A word on its own means nothing; rather, its meaning comes from its difference from other words—this structure of difference enables the signifier to be tied to the signified (both components of the sign, differs from the actual object in reality, which is called the referent).

We relate the word and its associations with others. The result is a texture; each word is formed on the basis of traces within it of other words. Nothing is ever simply present or absent, and there is no end to this differing. We are always delayed in reaching meaning. Meaning is constantly deferred, divided from itself. There are only webs of signifiers. This entails meaning always being absent, in a way—it is not present in the sign. Thus, if our "hold" on reality is primarily through language, then identity and meaning are elusive.

When one holds an object in one's hands, various attributes (decorations, markings, colours, styles, etc.) are associated with the object that seem to give it its identity. These attributes are not present *within* the object but are constantly shifting; the object is becoming and not being. It does not have identity and being so much as difference and becoming. The meaning of the object is here and elsewhere. The signifier is subverted; the (object's) past is not the origin of meaning.

In conclusion, Shanks claims that poststructuralist argument does not question truth to replace it with a free play of signifiers, but the truth of the past is material and institutional, social and personal; and archaeologists write in the space between past and present.

74. Foucault, *The Archaeology of Knowledge*, 7.

75. Foucault builds upon the work of the French historian Marc Bloch, who writes: "For even those texts or archeological documents which seem the clearest and the most accommodating will speak only when they are properly questioned. . . . [E]very historical research supposes that the inquiry has a direction at the very first step. In the beginning, there must be the guiding spirit" (Bloch, *The Historian's Craft*, 64–65). If we adhere to the idea that any document is fraught with ideological overtones, we should also approach any monument in the same way. The historian Jacques Le Goff, a follower of Marc Bloch, adds that a document is made a monument through historical societies' efforts to impose—voluntarily or involuntarily—a certain image of themselves into the future. He writes: "There is no truthful document. Every document is a lie. It is the task of the historian to deconstruct, to demolish this montage, to re-structure this construction, and to analyze the conditions of production of these documents-monuments" (Le Goff, "Documento/Monumento," 455).

The other assumption, according to Bloch, that permits the historian its research is the conception of time as "a multiple operator . . . as the source of the heterogeneous multiplicity and polysemy of reality." In characterizing time as both continuous and changing, Bloch conceives of time as causing "history to be experienced in a multiplicity of ways and within a multiplicity of meanings. . . . Time becomes a locus of distribution of multiple meanings" (Calcagno, "Abolishing Time and History," 21).

76. For a discussion of art epistemology, see Govrin, "Art Epistemology (Project for a Review)."

77. Brooklyn Museum, "The Brooklyn Museum Collection: The Play of the Unmentionable (Joseph Kosuth)." Brooklyn Museum (press release), September 1, 1990. https://www.brooklynmuseum.org/opencollection/exhibitions/819

78. For another recent project that addresses the intersections between photography and archaeology, see *The Ar(t)chaeology Project: Intersections of Photography and Archaeology*.

79. Respini, Flood, and Raad, *Walid Raad*, 29.

80. Respini, Flood, and Raad, *Walid Raad*, 29.
81. Godfrey, "The Artist as Historian," 145.
82. Ebeling, "The Art of Searching," 7. Ebeling's idea corresponds and supports Roelstraete's claim regarding artists' current enthusiasm for narration and (story and history) telling strategies, as well as their archaeological, material conception of the past.
83. Ebeling, "The Art of Searching," 9.
84. For a germane discussion of this term, and in the context of art production, see Osborne, *The Postconceptual Condition*, 3–58.
85. This also entails a spatial difference between history and archaeology. Archaeology shows spatially what once was, while history narrates something chronologically in time. History chooses from chronological time while archaeology preserves it all for display in the archaic regime of visibility (from transcendental model of historical time to strata of time, in other words, material time, the deep time of the layer). Archaeology renders time sensible.
86. Ebeling, "The Art of Searching," 11.
87. Ebeling, "The Art of Searching," 14.
88. Agamben, *The Fire and the Tale*, 108.
89. This suggestion is based on a broader definition of "archaeology," conceiving it also as a metaphor or allegory.
90. Kishik, *The Power of Life*, 61. The method of *détournement* might propel a reference to artists working with language in a similarly materialistic ways; one example, out of many, is Robert Smithson's essay "Language to be looked at and/or things to be read" (1967) in relation to his drawing/work "A Heap of Language" (1966). See Smithson, *The Collected Writings*, 61.

In this sense, *Détournement*, as the artistic technique developed by the Letterist/Situationist International, propels another reference to the influence Guy Debord has had on Agamben's work.

91. On the relation between "Otherness" and material debris, see Bell, "Rag-Picking."
92. Russell, "The Art of the Past: Before and After Archaeology," 308.
93. Russell, "The Art of the Past: Before and After Archaeology," 311–12. Russell further brings various recently curated international exhibitions (organized around 2010) and scholarly publications as examples to the growing allegorical appropriation of archaeology.
94. Groom, "This Is So Contemporary!"
95. Groys, "Comrades of Time," 6.
96. For the suggestion that, from the perspective of production, time-based media promotes an understanding of the plasticity of time, see Birnbaum, *Chronology*.
97. Groys, "Comrades of Time," 8. This claim is supported, for example, by Hannah Arendt's writing on Thomas Aquinas's concept of *Stillness*. In *The*

Human Condition, Arendt emphasizes Aquinas's accentuation of the stillness of the soul and the life of *vita activa*, which both exhaust and "[quieten] interior passions" (quoted in Summa theologica ii. 2. 182. 3), and therefore prepare man for contemplation of the eternity (and as such): "The primacy of contemplation over activity rests on the conviction that no work of human hands can equal in beauty and truth the physical *kosmos*, which swings in itself in changeless eternity without any interference or assistance from outside, from man or god. This eternity discloses itself to mortal eyes only when all human movements and activities are at perfect rest" (Arendt, *The Human Condition*, 15).

98. This claim corresponds with Peter Osborne's argument according to which "the mode of attention appropriate to the conditions of contemporary art is best conceived in terms of a *historical dialectic of boredom and distraction*, rather than the strictly transcendental timelessness of the model of 'contemplative immersion' historically associated with the exhibition-value of modern art" (Osborne, *Anywhere or Not at All*, 176).

99. Groys, "Comrades of Time," 3.

100. HD video, silent, 11:18 min, loop, https://www.303gallery.com/artists/ceal-floyer/video-slideshow/undefined?view=slider#2 (and a Hi-Res version at: http://www.contemporaryartdaily.com/2016/04/ceal-floyer-at-aargauer-kunsthaus/). As far as my research was able to reveal, this work was shown for the first time at *Museion* (Bolzano, Italy) in 2014 and later on at *Aargauer Kunsthaus* (Aarau, Switzerland) in 2016, and at *Kindl* (Berlin, Germany) in 2016–17.

101. Paul, as we recall, used the expression *ton kairon exagorazomenoi*, "buying up time," to convey the temporal condition of messianic time against the representation of chronological time that separates us from ourselves as impotent spectators.

102. Ebeling, "Debris Field: An Archaeology of Contemporaneity."

103. Agamben, *The Coming Community*, 53.

104. Lispector, *Selected Crônicas*, 24–25.

105. Agamben, *The Coming Community*, 55.

Conclusion

1. Agamben, *Creation and Anarchy*, 76.

Bibliography

Agamben, Giorgio. *Autoritratto nello studio*. Milan: Nottetempo, 2017.
———. *Categorie italiane: Studi di poetica*. Venice: Marsilio, 1996.
———. *Creation and Anarchy: The Work of Art and the Religion of Capitalism*. Translated by Adam Kotsko. Stanford, CA: Stanford University Press, 2019.
———. "Difference and Repetition: On Guy Debord's Films." In *Art and The Moving Image: A Critical Reader*, edited by Tanya Leighton. 328–33. London: Tate, 2008.
———. "Falling Beauty." In *CY Twombly: Sculptures 1992–2005*. Munich: Alte Pinakothek, 2006.
———. *Homo Sacer: Sovereign Power and Bare Life*. Translated by Daniel Heller-Roazen. Stanford, CA: Stanford University Press, 1998.
———. *I Luoghi della Vita*. By Roberto Andreotti and Federico De Melis. RAI Radio Tre, February 8, 2004.
———. "Image and Silence." Translated by Leland de la Durantaye. *Diacritics* 40, no. 2, (Summer 2012): 94–98.
———. *Infancy and History: The Destruction of Experience*. Translated by Liz Heron. London: Verso, 1993.
———. *Intervista a Giorgio Agamben: dalla Teologia alla Teologia Economica*. By Gianluca Sacco. Roma, March 8, 2004. Transcript (in Italian) available at http://www.lavocedifiore.org/SPIP/article.php3?id_article=1209.
———. *La fine del pensiero*. Paris: Le Nouveau Commerce, 1982.
———. *Language and Death: The Place of Negativity*. Translated by Karen E. Pinkus (with Michael Hardt). Minneapolis: University of Minnesota Press, 2006.
———. "Language and History in Benjamin." *Differentia: Review of Italian Thought*: Vol. 2, Article 13 (Spring 1988): 169–83.
———. "Lingua e storia. Categorie linguistiche e categorie storiche nel pensiero di Benjamin" In *Walter Benjamin. Tempo storia linguaggio*. A cura di Lucio Belloi e Lorenzina Lotti. Rome: Editori Riuniti, 1983.
———. *Nudities*. Translated by David Kishik and Stefan Pedatella. Stanford, CA: Stanford University Press, 2010.

———. "Nymphae." *Aut aut*, 14, 15, (July 2004): 53–67.
———. *Nymphs*. Translated by Amanda Minervini. London: Seagull Books, 2013.
———. "On the Impossibility of Saying 'I': Epistemological paradigms and poetic paradigms in the work of Furio Jesi." Translated by Kevin Attell. *Theory and Event* 22, no. 4, (October 2019): 1047–57.
———. "On Walter Benjamin's Messianism." Public lecture at Freie Universität Berlin, Germany, June 14, 2019.
———. *Opus Dei: An Archaeology of Duty*. Translated by Adam Kotsko. Stanford, CA: Stanford University Press, 2013.
———. *Pilate and Jesus*. Translated by Adam Kotsko. Stanford, CA: Stanford University Press, 2015.
———. "Philosophy as Interdisciplinary Intensity," interview by Antonio Gnoli, translated by Ido Govrin. *Religious Theory*, February 6, 2017. http://jcrt.org/religioustheory/2017/02/06/philosophy-as-interdisciplinary-intensity-an-interview-with-giorgio-agamben-antonio-gnolioido-govrin/
———. *Potentialities: Collected Essays in Philosophy*. Translated by Daniel Heller-Roazen. Stanford, CA: Stanford University Press, 2000.
———. *Remnants of Auschwitz: The Witness and the Archive*. Translated by Daniel Heller-Roazen. New York: Zone Books, 1999.
———. *Stanzas: Word and Phantasm in Western Culture*. Translated by Roland L. Martinez. Minneapolis: University of Minnesota Press, 1992.
———. "Sulla tecnica e l'arte." *Laboratorio Archeologia Filosofica* (Marzo 23, 2020). https://www.archeologiafilosofica.it/sulla-tecnica-e-larte/
———. *Taste*. Translated by Cooper Francis. Calcutta: Seagull Books, 2017.
———. *The Adventure*. Translated by Lorenzo Chiesa. Cambridge, MA: MIT Press, 2018.
———. *The Church and The Kingdom*. Translated by Leland De La Durantaye. Chicago: University of Chicago Press, 2012.
———. *The Coming Community*. Translated by Michael Hardt. Minneapolis: University of Minnesota Press, 1993.
———. *The End of the Poem: Studies in Poetics*. Translated by Daniel Heller-Roazen. Stanford, CA: Stanford University Press, 1999.
———. "The End of Thinking." Translated by Peter Carravetta. *Differentia: Review of Italian Thought* 1, no. 9 (1986): 57–58.
———. *The Fire and the Tale*. Translated by Lorenzo Chiesa. Stanford, CA: Stanford University Press, 2017.
———. *The Highest Poverty: Monastic Rules and Form-of-Life*. Translated by Adam Kotsko. Stanford, CA: Stanford University Press, 2013.
———. "The Idea of Language: Some Difficulties in Speaking about Language." *Graduate Faculty Philosophy Journal* 10, no. 1 (Spring 1984): 141–49.
———. *The Kingdom and the Garden*. Translated by Adam Kotsko. London: Seagull Books, 2020.

———. *The Kingdom and the Glory: for a Theological Genealogy of Economy and Government*. Translated by Lorenzo Chiesa (with Matteo Mandarini). Stanford, CA: Stanford University Press, 2011.
———. *The Man Without Content*. Translated by Georgia Albert. Stanford, CA: Stanford University Press, 1999.
———. *The Mystery of Evil: Benedict XVI and the End of Days*. Translated by Adam Kotsko. Stanford, CA: Stanford University Press, 2017.
———. *The Omnibus Homo Sacer*. Stanford, CA: Stanford University Press, 2017.
———. *The Open: Man and Animal*. Translated by Kevin Attell. Stanford, CA: Stanford University Press, 2003.
———. "The Power of Thought." *Critical Inquiry* 40, no. 2 (trans. Kalpana Seshadri) (Winter 2014): 480–91.
———. *The Sacrament of Language: An Archaeology of the Oath*. Translated by Adam Kotsko. Stanford, CA: Stanford University Press, 2011.
———. "The Thing Itself." *Substance*, no. 53, translated by Juliana Schiesari, (1987): 18–28.
———. *The Signature of All Things: On Method*. Translated by Luca Di Santo and Kevin Attell. New York: Zone Books, 2009.
———. "The Time that Is Left." *Epoché* 7 (Fall 2002): 1–14.
———. *The Time That Remains: A Commentary on the Letter to the Romans*. Translated by Patricia Dailey. Stanford, CA: Stanford University Press, 2005.
———. "The Unspeakable Girl: The Myth and Mystery of Kore." In *The Unspeakable Girl*. Translated by Leland De La Durantaye. Calcutta: Seagull Books, 2014.
———. *The Use of Bodies*. Translated by Adam Kotsko. Stanford, CA: Stanford University Press, 2016.
———. "The Vocabulary and the Voice." Foreword to *Dictionary of Indo-European Concepts and Society*. By Émile Benveniste, ix–xx. Chicago: HAU, 2016.
———. "The Work of Man." In *Giorgio Agamben: Sovereignty and Life*, edited by Matthew Calcarco and Steven DeCaroli, 1–10. Stanford, CA: Stanford University Press, 2007.
———. "To Whom Is Poetry Addressed?" *New Observations* 130 (2014): 10–11.
———. "Un Libro senza Patria: Giorgio Agamben intervista di Federico Ferrari." *Eutropia*, I (2001): 44–46.
———. *What Is an Apparatus? and Other Essays*. Translated by David Kishik and Stefan Pedatella. Stanford, CA: Stanford University Press, 2009.
———. *What Is Philosophy?* Translated by Lorenzo Chiesa. Stanford, CA: Stanford University Press, 2017.
Aldea, Andreea Smaranda, and Allen, Amy. "History, Critique, and Freedom: The Historical a priori in Husserl and Foucault." *Continental Philosophy Review* 49, no. 1 (2016): 1–11. http://doi.org/10.1007/s11007-015-9359-8.
Arendt, Hannah. *Men in Dark Times*. New York: Harcourt, 1968.

———. *The Human Condition*. Chicago: University of Chicago Press, 1958.
Aristotle. *Metaphysics*. Translated by W. D. Ross. Scotts Valley: CreateSpace, 2012.
———. *Prior Analytics*. Translated by Robin Smith. Indianapolis: Hackett, 1989.
Bal, Mieke. *Louise Bourgeois' Spider: The Architecture of Art-Writing*. Chicago: University of Chicago Press, 2001.
Beck, Lewis White, ed. *Kant: On History*. New York: Prentice Hall, 1963.
Bell, Kirsty. "Rag-Picking." *Frieze*. March 27, 2016. https://frieze.com/article/rag-picking.
Benjamin, Walter. *Gesammelte Schriften*. Vol. 1. Edited by Rolf Tiedemann and Hermann Schweppenhäuser. Frankfurt am Main: Suhrkamp, 1974–89.
———. "Karl Kraus." In *Selected Writings, Volume 2: 1927–1934*, edited by Michael W. Jennings, Howard Eiland, and Gary Smith. 433–58. Cambridge, MA: Harvard University Press, 1999.
———. "Excavation and Memory." In *Selected Writings, Volume 2: 1927–1934*, edited by Michael W. Jennings, Howard Eiland, and Gary Smith. 576–77. Cambridge, MA: Harvard University Press, 1999.
———. *One-Way Street and Other Writings*. Translated by Edmund Jephcott and Kingsley Shorter. London: NLB, 1978.
———. *Selected Writings, Vol. 1: 1913–1926*, edited by Marcus Bullock and Michael W. Jennings. Cambridge, MA: Harvard University Press, 1996.
———. *Selected Writings, Vol. 3: 1935–1938*, edited by Howard Eiland and Michael W. Jennings. Cambridge, MA: Harvard University Press, 2006.
———. *Selected Writings, Vol. 4: 1938–1940*, edited by Howard Eiland and Michael W. Jennings. Cambridge, MA: Harvard University Press, 2006.
———. *The Arcades Project*. Translated by Howard Eiland and Kevin McLaughlin. Cambridge, MA: Harvard University Press, 1999.
———. *The Origin of German Tragic Drama*. Translated by John Osborne. London: Verso, 1998.
———. "Theses on The Philosophy of History." In *Illuminations*, edited by Hannah Arendt, 253–65. New York: Schocken Books, 1968.
Bergson, Henri. *L'Énergie Spirituelle*. Paris: PUF, 1919. (English translation: *Mind-Energy*. Translated by H. Wilson Carr. New York: Palgrave Macmillan, 2007.)
Berlin, Isaiah. "The Hedgehog and the Fox." In *The Proper Study of Mankind: An Anthology of Essays*, eds. Henry Hardy and Roger Hausheer, 436–98. New York: Farrar, Straus and Giroux, 1997.
Bigger, Charles P. *Kant's Methodology: An Essay in Philosophical Archeology*. Athens: Ohio University Press, 1996.
Birnbaum, Daniel. *Chronology*. Berlin: Sternberg Press, 2004.
Bishop, Claire. *Installation Art: A Critical History*. New York: Routledge, 2005.
———. "Rescuing Collective Desires: Benjamin, History and Contemporary Art." In *Walter Benjamin: Exile Archive*, edited by Noam Segal and Raphael Zagury-Orly, 77–86. Tel-Aviv: Tel-Aviv Museum of Art, 2016.

Bloch, Marc. *The Historian's Craft*. Translated by Joseph R. Strayer. New York: Vintage, 1953.
Boelhower, William. "Mnemohistory: The Archaeological Turn in the Humanities from Winckelmann to Calvino." *Symbiosis* (2005): 3–23.
Bonacci, Valeria. "Form-of-Life and Use in Homo Sacer." *Journal of Italian Philosophy* 3 (2020): 217–45.
Calcagno, Antonio. "Abolishing Time and History: Lazarus and the Possibility of Thinking Political Events Outside Time." *Journal of French Philosophy*, 17, no. 2 (2007): 13–36.
Caron, Thomas. *Joachim Koester: Of Spirits and Empty Spaces*. Milan: Mousse, 2014.
Caruth, Cathy. *Unclaimed Experience. Trauma, Narrative, and History*. Baltimore: Johns Hopkins University Press, 1996.
Castoriadis, Cornelius. *Postscripts on Insignificance*, edited by Gabriel Rockhill, translated by Gabriel Rockhill and John V. Garner. London: Continuum, 2011.
Cerella, Antonio. "The Myth of Origin: Archaeology and History in the Work of Agamben and Girard." In *The Sacred and the Political: Exploration on Mimesis, Violence, and Religion*. London: Bloomsbury, 2016.
Chan, Paul. "A Time Apart." In *Greater New York*, ed. Klaus Biesenbach, 53–55. New York: MoMA PS1, 2010.
Colli, Giorgio. *Filosofia dell'espressione*. Milan: Adelphi, 1969.
Colilli, Paul. *Agamben and the Signature of Astrology: Spheres of Potentiality*. New York: Lexington Books, 2015.
De La Durantaye, Leland. *Giorgio Agamben: A Critical Introduction*. Stanford, CA: Stanford University Press, 2009.
Dickinson, Colby. "Canon as an Act of Creation: Giorgio Agamben and the Extended Logic of the Messianic." *Bijdragen*, 71, no. 2 (2010): 132–58. http://doi.org/10.2143/BIJ.71.2.2051601.
———. "The Poetic Atheology of Giorgio Agamben: Defining the Scission Between Poetry and Philosophy." *Mosaic* 45, no. 1 (March 2012): 203–17.
Doussan, Jenny. "Time and Presence in Agamben's Critique of Deconstruction." *Cosmos and History: The Journal of Natural and Social Philosophy* 9, no. 1 (2013): 183–202.
Dolgopolski, Sergey. "Who Thinks the Talmud?" *Journal of Jewish Thought and Philosophy* 20, no. 1 (2012): 1–34.
Ebeling, Knut. "Debris Field: An Archaeology of Contemporaneity." June 17, 2017, at the Contemporary Condition, Aarhus University, Aarhus, Denmark, video, 1:01:04, https://vimeo.com/229639415.
———. "The Art of Searching: On Wild Archeologies from Kant to Kittler." *The Nordic Journal of Aesthetics*, no. 51 (2016): 7–18.
Erber, Pedro. "Theory Materialized: Conceptual Art and Its Others." *Diacritics* 36, no. 1 (2006): 1–10.

Feuerbach, Ludwig. "Darstellung, Entwicklung und Kritik der Leibnizschen Philosophie." In *Gesammelte Werke*, edited by Herausgegeben von Werner Schuffenhauer. Berlin: Akademie-Verlag, 1984.

Foster, Hal. "An Archival Impulse." *October*, no. 110 (2004): 3–22.

———. "Blind Spots: Hal Foster on the Art of Joachim Koester." *Artforum* 44 (April 2006): https://www.artforum.com/print/200604/blind-spots-the-art-of-joachim-koester-10615.

Foucault, Michel. *Dits et écrits* II (1976–1988). Paris: Gallimard, 2001.

———. *Introduction to Kant's Anthropology*. Translated by Roberto Nigro and Kate Briggs. Los Angeles: Semiotext(e), 2008.

———. "Nietzsche, Freud, Marx." In *Aesthetics, Method, and Epistemology*, ed. James D. Faubion, 269–78. New York: New Press, 1998.

———. *Society Must Be Defended: Lectures at the Collège de France 1975–1976*. Translated by David Macey. New York: Picador, 2003.

———. *The Archaeology of Knowledge and The Discourse on Language*. Translated by A. M. Sheridan Smith. New York: Pantheon, 1972.

———. *The Courage of Truth*. Translated by Graham Burchell. London: Palgrave, 2011.

———. *The Order of Things: An Archaeology of the Human Sciences*. New York: Vintage, 1973.

Foucault, Michel. and Sylvère Lotringer, eds. *Foucault Live: Collected Interviews, 1961–1984*. Translated by Lysa Hochroth and John Johnston. New York: Semiotext(e), 1996.

Freud, Sigmund. "Constructions in Analysis [1937]." In Vol. 23 of *The Standard Edition of the Complete Psychological Works of Sigmund Freud*, edited by J. Strachey, 257–69. London: Hogarth, 1964.

Godfrey, Mark. "The Artist as Historian." *October*, no. 120 (2007): 140–72.

Goethe, Johann Wolfgang von. *Maxims and Reflections*. Translated by Elisabeth Stopp. London: Penguin, 1998.

———. "On Granite." In *The Essential Goethe*, edited by Matthew Bell, 913–16. Princeton, NJ: Princeton University Press, 2016.

Gourgouris, Stathis. "Archē." In *Political Concepts: A Critical Lexicon*, edited by J. M. Benrstein, Adi Ophir, and Ann Laura Stoler, 5–24. New York: Fordham University Press, 2018.

Govrin, Ido. "Art Epistemology (Project for a Review)." *Journal for Artistic Research Online* (January 18, 2019). https://doi.org/10.22501/jarnet.0016.

Groom, Amelia. "This Is So Contemporary!" *Frieze*. October 1, 2012. https://frieze.com/article/so-contemporary.

Groys, Boris. "Comrades of Time." *e-flux*, no. 11 (December 2009): 1–11. https://www.e-flux.com/journal/11/61345/comrades-of-time

Guillaume, Gustave. *Foundations for a Science of Language*. Translated by Walter Hirtle and John Hewson. Amsterdam: John Benjamin, 1984.

———. *Temps et verbe. Théorie des aspects, des modes, et des temps.* Paris: Librarie Honoré Champion, 1968.
Hacking, Ian. "Historical Ontology." In Vol. 2 of *In the Scope of Logic, Methodology and Philosophy of Science*, edited by P. Gärdenfors, J. Wolenski and K. Kijania-Placek, 583–600. Boston: Kluwer Academic, 2002.
Hartog, Francois. *Regimes of Historicity: Presentism and Experiences of Time.* Translated by Saskia Brown. New York: Columbia University Press, 2015.
Hutchinson, John, E. H. Gombrich, Lela B. Njatin, and W. J. T. Mitchell. *Antony Gormley.* London: Phaidon, 2000.
Heidegger, Martin. "On the Being and Conception of Physis in Aristotle's Physics B, 1." Translated by Thomas J. Sheehan. *Man and World* 9 (1976): 219–79.
Howard, Stephen. "Archaeology and/or Genealogy: Agamben's Transformation of Foucauldian Method." *Journal of Italian Philosophy* 1 (2018): 27–45.
Kant, Immanuel. "Conjectural Beginning of Human History (1786)." In *Anthropology, History, and Education*, edited by Günter Zöller and Robert B. Louden, 160–75. Cambridge: Cambridge University Press, 2007.
———. *Critique of Pure Reason.* Translated by Paul Guyer and Allen W. Wood. Cambridge: Cambridge University Press, 1998.
———. "The End of All Things (1794)." In *Religion and Rational Theology*, edited by Allen W. Wood and George Di Giovanni, 217–32. Cambridge: Cambridge University Press, 1996.
———. "What Real Progress Has Metaphysics Made in Germany since the Time of Leibniz and Wolff?" In *Theoretical Philosophy after 1781*, edited by Paul Guyer and Allen W. Wood, 337–424. Cambridge: Cambridge University Press, 2007.
Katmor. Jacques, dir. *The Hole* (1972–74). Tel-Aviv: The Third Eye, 1974.
Khatib, Sami R. "A Non-Nullified Nothingness: Walter Benjamin and the Messianic." *Stasis* 1 (2013): 82–108.
Kirst, Karoline. "Walter Benjamin's 'Denkbild': Emblematic Historiography and the Recent Past." *Monatshefte* 86, no. 4 (1994): 514–24.
Kishik, David. *The Power of Life: Agamben and the Coming Politics.* Stanford, CA: Stanford University Press, 2012.
Koester, Joachim. *Message from Andrée.* Berlin: Sternberg, 2009.
———. *Message from the Unseen.* Rotterdam: Veenman, 2006.
Koester, Joachim, and Matthew Buckingham. "Points of Suspension." *October* 100 (2002): 55–63.
Kojève, Alexnader. *Introduction to the Reading of Hegel: Lectures on the Phenomenology of Spirit.* Translated by James H. Nicholas Jr. Ithaca, NY: Cornell University Press, 1969.
Kotsko, Adam, and Carlo Salzani. "Introduction: Agamben as a Reader." In *Agamben's Philosophical Lineage*, edited by Adam Kotsko and Carlo Salzani, 1–12. Edinburgh: Edinburgh University Press, 2017.

Kracauer, Siegfried. *History: The Last Things Before the Last*. New York: Oxford University Press, 1969.
Kubler, George. *The Shape of Time: Remarks on the History of Things*. New Haven, CT: Yale University Press, 1973.
Lawlor, Leonard. *Thinking Through French Philosophy: The Being of the Question*. Bloomington, IN: Indiana University Press, 2003.
———. and Nale John, ed. *The Cambridge Foucault Lexicon*. New York: Cambridge University Press, 2014.
Le Goff, Jacques. "Documento/Monumento." In *Enciclopedia*, ed. Romano Ruggiero. Torino: G. Einaudi, 1977.
Lévi-Strauss, Claude. *The Savage Mind*. Translated by John Weightman and Doreen Weightman. Chicago: Chicago University Press, 1966.
Libera, Alain de. *Archéologie du sujet: Naissance de sujet*. Paris: Vrin, 2007.
———. "Subject (Re-/decentred)." *Radical Philosophy* 167 (May/June 2011): 15–23.
———. "When Did the Modern Subject Emerge?" *American Catholic Philosophical Quarterly*, Vol. 82, No. 2 (2008): 181–220.
Lispector, Clarice. *Selected Crônicas*. Translated by Giovanni Pontiero. New York: New Directions, 1996.
Malinconico, Dario. "The Concept of Philosophical Archaeology in Kant and Foucault." *Metalogicon* XXV, 1 (2012): 51–66.
Mauss, Marcel. *A General Theory of Magic*. Translated by Robert Brain. New York: Routledge, 1972.
McQuillan, J. Colin. "Philosophical Archaeology and the Historical A Priori: From Kant to Foucault." *Symposium* 20, no. 2 (Fall 2016): 142–159.
———. "Philosophical Archaeology in Kant, Foucault, and Agamben." *Parrhesia* 10, (2010): 39–49.
Melandri, Enzo. *La Linea e Il Circolo. Studio Logico-Filosofico Sull'Analogia*. Bologna: Il mulino, 1968.
Minotti, Andrea. "Origin vs Genesis: Warburg and Benjamin in the Footsteps of Goethe's Morphology," 15 June 2012 at The Warburg Institute, London, UK, video, 30:38, https://www.youtube.com/watch?v=_4xPHiHQQsE.
Murray, Alex, and Jessica Whyte, eds. *The Agamben Dictionary*. Edinburgh: Edinburgh University Press, 2011.
Nietzsche, Friedrich Wilhelm. "On the Uses and Disadvantages of History for Life." In *Untimely Meditations*, edited by Daniel Breazeale, 57–125. Cambridge: Cambridge University Press, 1977.
Nora, Pierre. *Realms of Memory: Rethinking the French Past*. Translated by Arthur Goldhammer. New York: Columbia University Press, 1996.
Osborne, Peter. *Anywhere or Not At All: Philosophy of Contemporary Art*. London: Verso, 2013.
———. *The Postconceptual Condition*. London: Verso, 2018.

Östman, Lars. "Philosophical Archaeology as Method in the Humanities. A Comment on Cultural Memory and the Problem of History." *Danish Yearbook of Philosophy* 46 (2011): 81–103.
Pines, Shlomo. *La Liberté de Philosopher: De Maïmonide à Spinoza*. Ed. Rémi Brague. Paris: Desclée de Brouwer, 1997.
Rauch, Matle Fabian. "Archaeologies of Contemporary Art: Negativity, Inoperativity, Désœuvrement." *Journal of Italian Philosophy* 3 (2020): 191–215.
Renfrew, Colin. *Figuring It Out: What are we? Where do we come from? The parallel visions of artists and archeologists*. London: Thames & Hudson, 2003.
———. Chris Gosden, and Elizabeth DeMarris, eds. *Substance, Memory, Display: Archaeology and Art*. Cambridge: McDonald Institute for Archeological Research, 2004.
Respini, Eva, Finbarr Barry Flood, and Walid Raad. *Walid Raad*. New York: Museum of Modern Art, 2015.
Roberts, Colin H. And T. C. Skeat. *The Birth of the Codex*. Oxford: Oxford University Press, 1983.
Roelstraete, Dieter. "After the Historiographic Turn: Current Findings." *e-flux journal* 6 (May 2009).
———. "Field Notes." In *The Way of the Shovel: On the Archaeological Imaginary in Art*. Chicago: Museum of Contemporary Art in association with the University of Chicago Press, 2013.
———. "The Way of the Shovel: On the Archaeological Imaginary in Art." *e-flux journal* 4 (March 2009).
Roelstraete, Dieter, ed. *The Way of the Shovel: On the Archaeological Imaginary in Art*. Chicago: Museum of Contemporary Art in association with the University of Chicago Press, 2013.
Rotlevy, Ori. "Presentation as indirection, indirection as schooling: The two aspects of Benjamin's scholastic method." *Continental Philosophy Review* 50 (4), (2017): 1–24.
Russell, Ian Alden. "The Art of the Past: Before and After Archaeology," in *The Way of the Shovel: On the Archaeological Imaginary in Art*. Chicago: Museum of Contemporary Art in association with the University of Chicago Press, 2013.
Scholem, Gershom. "95 Thesen über Judentum und Zionismus." In *Tagebücher*. 300–306. Vol. 2. Frankfurt: Jüdischer Verlag, 2000.
———. "Walter Benjamin and His Angel." In *On Jews and Judaism in Crisis: Selected Essays*, ed. Werner J. Dannhauser, 198–237. New York: Schocken Books, 1976.
Schürmann, Reiner. *Heidegger on Being and Acting: From Principles to Anarchy*. Bloomington: Indiana University Press, 1987.
Shalem, Avinoam. "Resisting Time: On How Temporality Shaped Medieval Choice of Materials." In *Time in the History of Art: Temporality, Chronol-*

ogy, and Anachrony, ed. Dan Karlholm and Keith Moxey, 184–204. New York: Routledge, 2018.
Shanks, Michael. *Experiencing the Past: On the Character of Archaeology*. London: Routledge, 1992.
Smithson, Robert. *The Collected Writings*. Edited by Jack Flam. Berkeley: University of California Press, 1996.
Spinoza, Baruch. "Hebrew Grammar." In *Complete Works*, edited by Michael L. Morgan, 584–676. Indianapolis: Hackett, 2002.
Styllanous, Elena, Artemis Eleftheriadou, and Yiannis Toumazis, eds. *The Ar(t)chaeology Project: Intersections of Photography and Archaeology*. 2 vols. Nicosia: IAPT Press, 2008.
Vernant, Jean-Pierre. *Myth and Thought among the Greeks*. London: Routledge, 1983.
Virno, Paolo. *Déjà Vu and the End of History*. Translated by David Broder. London: Verso, 2015.
———. "Déjà Vu and the End of History." *e-flux journal* 62 (February 2015).
Waltham-Smith, Naomi. "The Use of Ears: Agamben, Overhearing Derrida Overhearing Heidegger." *Parrhesia* 33 (2020): 113–49.
Wartenberg, Thomas E. "Foucault's archeological method: A Response to Hacking and Rorty." *The Philosophical Forum* 15, no. 4 (Summer 1984): 345–64.
Watkin, William. (a) *Agamben and Indifference: A Critical Overview*. London: Rowman and Littlefield, 2014.
———. *The Literary Agamben: Adventures in Logopoiesis*. London: Continuum, 2010.
———. (b) "The Signature of All Things: Agamben's Philosophical Archaeology." *Mln* 129, no. 1 (2014): 139–61.
Whyte, Ryan. *Studio as History*. Elmwood, CT: Potes & Poets Press, 1998.
Wind, Edgar. *Art and Anarchy*. Evanston: Northwestern University Press, 1985.
Yovel, Yirmiahu. *Kant and the Philosophy of History*. Princeton, NJ: Princeton University Press, 1980.
Zalmona, Yigal, ed. *Routes of Wandering: Nomadism, Journeys and Transitions in Contemporary Israeli Art*. Jerusalem: Israel Museum, 1991.

Index

Agamben, Giorgio, works of:
Autoritratto nello Studio, 121n2;
Creation and Anarchy, 95, 121n5,
129n37, 131n48, 133n68, 157n141,
163n18, 172n1; *Difference and
Repetition*, 152nn100–104; *Falling
Beauty*, 83; *Homo Sacer*, 129n37,
147n66, 155n114; *I Luoghi della
Vita*, 121n7; *Image and Silence*, 88,
162nn12–13; *Infancy and History*,
39, 59, 139nn2–3, 139nn5–6,
140n8, 140nn11–12, 141nn15–16,
149n79, 150n89, 152n109,
156n130, 156n132; *Intervista a
Giorgio Agamben*, 121n7; *Language
and Death*, 140n13, 156n130;
Language and History in Benjamin,
150nn80–88, 151n90, 151n92,
151nn94–96; *Lingua e storia*, 60;
Nymphae, 152n106; *Nymphs*, 70;
On the Impossibility of Saying 'I',
163n15; *Pilate and Jesus*, 150n85;
*Philosophy as Interdisciplinary
Intensity*, 122n10; *Potentialities*, 69,
129nn38–40, 130n42, 145n55,
145n57, 149n79, 153n110,
159n159, 163nn14–15, 165n24,
166n32, 166nn39–43; *Remnants
of Auschwitz*, 135n80; *Stanzas*,
156n126; *State of Exception*, 18;
Sulla tecnica e l'arte, 165n25;
Taste, 77; *The Adventure*, 136n86;
The Church and the Kingdom, 59,
143n28, 143n33, 144n36, 148n74,
148n77, 163n20; *The Coming
Community*, 147n58, 155nn112–13,
172n103; *The End of the Poem*,
85, 162n4, 162n9; *The End of
Thinking*, 163n16; *The Fire and
the Tale*, 3, 121n9, 130nn44–46,
151n93, 163n18, 171n88; *The
Highest Poverty*, 9; *The Kingdom
and the Garden*, 131n45, 149n77,
151n91; *The Kingdom and
the Glory*, 18, 90, 155n119,
163nn17–18, 164nn20–21,
165n25; *The Man Without Content*,
155n111, 158n153, 158nn156–57,
160nn160–63, 166n37; *The
Mystery of Evil*, 139n110; *The
Open*, 18, 25; *The Sacrament of
Language*, 129n36, 156n130; *The
Signature of All Things*, xi, 1, 8–10,
29, 66, 71, 121nn3–4, 121nn6–7,
122n2, 126n18, 127n20, 128n30,
128nn33–36, 138nn96–103,
139nn105–6, 139n108, 139nn116–
17, 139nn119–120, 152nn109–10,
155n117, 156n125, 157n139; *The
Time That Is Left*, 143n34, 144n41,

Agamben, Giorgio, works of *(continued)* 144n53, 147n59, 147nn63–64; *The Time That Remains*, 44, 57, 59, 143n21, 143nn23–28, 143n32, 144n35, 144nn37–40, 144nn52–53, 144n55, 145nn56–57, 147n61, 147n65, 147n67, 148n71, 149n78, 161n164, 163n20; *The Unspeakable Girl*, 73; *The Use of Bodies*, 18, 25, 162n10, 131n48, 136nn87–91, 138nn93–95, 148n68, 157n137, 165nn24–28; *The Work of Man*, 163n17; *To Whom Is Poetry Addressed?*, 92; *Un Libro senza Patria*, 121n8, 161n164; *What Is an Apparatus?*, 121n5, 139nn111–15, 147n62, 152n105; *What Is Philosophy?*, 90, 121n2; *What Is the Contemporary?*, 32
Anaximander, 16–17, 98
angel, 31, 64, 79–80, 161n162
anthropogenesis, xiv, 25–27, 72, 92, 138n95, 142n17, 156n129
apeiron, 16–18, 98
arché, xi, xiv, 2–3, 5, 10, 12–13, 15–19, 33, 36–37, 57, 98–100, 125n12, 133n68, 154n111, 169n73
archive, xvii, 23, 69, 77, 97, 103, 106–9, 117
Arendt, Hannah, 79, 172n97
Aristotle, 4, 15–16, 18, 26, 40, 42–43, 45, 50, 67, 78, 80, 98, 111, 124n6, 129n35, 135n84, 136n86, 138n95, 141n15, 146n57, 163n17, 168n70
artistic research, 78–79
aufheben, 56
Augustine of Hippo, Saint, 4, 60–61, 129n35

Bataille, Georges, 169n71
beatitude, xvi, 90–91, 117–18

Benjamin, Walter, xiii, xv–xvi, xviii, xix, 9–10, 13–15, 18–19, 27, 30–31, 38, 44, 53, 57–66, 68–70, 72–77, 79–81, 100, 107–8, 110–11, 118, 125n8, 130n42, 130n45, 145n57, 147n60, 149n79, 155n119, 156n128, 162n4, 162n7
Benedict XVI (pope), 33
Benveniste, Émile, 27, 142n17
Bergson, Henri, 29, 35
Berlin, Isaiah, 168n70
Bishop, Claire, 107, 129n35
Bloch, Marc, 170n75
Böhme, Jakob, 94
brachylogy, xix
Burckhardt, Jacob, 143n30

caesura, xvi, 4, 33–34, 49, 54, 65, 80–81, 84–86, 117, 161n164
cairós. See *kairos*
Caruth, Cathy, 34
Castoriadis, Cornelius, 165n25
citation without quotation marks, xv, 58, 64, 72, 79
Colli, Giorgio, 157n136

Dante (Durante degli Alighieri), 85–87
Debord, Guy, 64–65, 171n90
Deleuze, Gilles, 91
de Libera, Alain, 24–25, 128n35
denkbild, 74–76
denkraum, 107
Derrida, Jacques, 16, 26, 155n119
désœuvrement, 89, 147n66
détournement, xii, 112
discontinuity, xiii, 5, 8, 135n81, 142n17
dishomogeneity, xiv, 5–6, 11, 27, 33, 78, 142n18, 150n89
Duchamp, Marcel, 96, 158n148
Dürer, Albrecht, 80

Ebeling, Knut, 109–12, 172n102
enjambment, 65, 84–86
entwicklungsfähigkeit, xviii, xix, 121n1
episteme, 23–24, 28, 78, 122n2

Feuerbach, Ludwig, xi, xiii
form-of-life, 92
Foster, Hal, 102, 107
Foucault, Michel, xiii, xviii, 5–12, 16, 19–20, 22–24, 26–30, 78, 105, 110, 112, 122n11, 137n90, 142n17, 143nn30–31, 155n119
Freud, Sigmund, 20–21, 30–31, 34–35, 109, 112
Fukuyama, Francis, 104

Giacometti, Alberto, 119
Goethe, Johann Wolfgang von, 14, 18, 27, 57, 100, 160n159
Gourgouris, Stathis, 16–18
Groys, Boris, 115–16
Guillaume, Gustave, 49–51, 56

Hegel, Georg Wilhelm Friedrich, 12, 42, 54, 56, 71, 74, 123n3, 123n6, 134n70, 137n90, 162n4
Heidegger, Martin, 16, 131n48, 138n92, 142n15, 143n20, 153n110, 155n120, 156n126
hermeneutic circle, 71, 152n110
Herodotus, 40
historical a priori, xi, xiv, 15–16, 19, 22, 25–30, 36–37, 57, 127n20, 128n30
historiographic turn, xvi, 100, 104, 106, 113, 117, 168n69
Hofmannsthal, Hugo von, 156n128
Hölderlin, Johann Christian Friedrich, 65, 84

image, 58–59, 64–66, 68, 84, 88, 94, 98, 110, 117; dialectical, xv, 58–60, 64, 66, 69–73, 79, 108, 110, 148n70, 162n7
inoperativity, xvi, 18–19, 47, 55–56, 68, 89–90, 92–93, 143n28, 148n69, 154n111

Jarry, Alfred, 121n2
Jabès, Edmond, 125n15

kabbalah, 94, 125n9, 126n15, 167n57
Kafka, Franz, 160n162
kairos, 43, 48, 53–54, 59, 141n15; ho nym, 44–45, 48–49, 53–54, 147n62, 163n20
Kant, Emanuel, xiii, 1–2, 20, 22, 25, 27–29, 63, 72, 99, 110, 112, 117, 127n20, 128n30, 137n90, 149n79
katargein/katargeo. See inoperativity
Kishik, David, xix, 111
Klee, Paul, 80
Kojève Alexandre, 12–13, 148n69
Kracauer, Siegfried, 105, 139n1, 139n4
Kraus, Karl, 159n159
Kubler, George, 114

Le Goff, Jacques, 170n75
Leibnitz, Gottfried Wilhelm, 87–88, 121n1
Lévi-Strauss, Claude, 121n3, 140n10
Luther, Martin, 56

Marx, Karl Heinrich, 39–40, 42–43, 63, 123n6, 146n57
marxism, 40, 54, 58, 63, 137n89, 151n91
Mauss, Marcel, 28–29
mediator. See middle
melancholy, 64, 79–80
Melandri, Enzo, 30–32, 37, 71, 87
Merleau-Ponty, Maurice, 20
messiah, 46–49, 53–55, 58–59, 65, 87, 139n114, 147n62, 148n69

middle (*meson*), 18, 57, 83, 86, 96, 98, 105, 158n151
modus operandi, xvi, 93, 97
moment of arising, 6–7, 10–12, 28, 30, 32, 35–37, 68, 128n30, 128n35
montage, 64–65, 108, 170n75

Nietzsche, Friedrich Wilhelm, xiii, 4–7, 9, 11–12, 27, 29–30, 32, 41, 122n11, 127n27, 138n92, 143n30, 155n119
Nora, Pierre, 155n124

origin, 2, 5–7, 10–11, 13–19, 21–22, 28–30, 35–36, 44, 57, 61, 63, 67–68, 72, 78, 80–81, 98–99, 128n30, 131n48, 134n69, 145n55, 154n111, 160n159, 169n73
Overbeck, Franz, xiii, 10–12, 27–29, 128n30

paradigm, xiv, 38, 43, 57, 66–68, 71–72, 75, 87, 104, 128n35, 135n80, 139n114, 142n17, 152nn109–11
Paul, Saint, xv, 44–49, 52–56, 58–59, 87, 90, 139n114, 144n54, 148n69, 163n20, 172n101
Plato, 15–16, 40, 45, 63, 71, 116, 125n9, 141n15, 159n159
poiesis, 80–81, 92–93, 95, 166n37
potentiality, xiv, xvi, 4, 50, 55–56, 59, 69–70, 89–95, 98, 105, 111, 118, 143n19, 146n57, 153n111, 156n127, 163n20, 166n31
prehistory. See *urgeschichte*

Raad, Walid, 108–9
ready-made, 79, 96, 111
Rilke, Rainer Maria, 84–85, 90
ruinology, 2, 157n148

sabbath (*sabbatical, sabbatism*), 55, 90, 92

Scholem, Gershom, 144n55, 147n60, 159n159
Schürmann, Reiner, 15–16
signature, xiv, 33, 36, 66, 68–70, 72–73, 75, 153nn110–11
silence, 85–89, 134n70
Sophocles, 84
spatiality, xiv, 20, 51, 160n162; messianic, 83
Spinoza, Baruch, 91, 126n15, 134n70

temporal structure (*of philosophical archaeology*), xiv–xv, 12, 29–36, 57, 127n20
temporality, 14, 18, 49, 97, 110–11, 115–17, 125n14, 127n20, 131n47; conception of, 3, 37, 158n148
Thomas Aquinas, Saint, 118, 171n97
time: chronogenetic, 50–52; conception of, xi, xiv, xvii, 5, 12, 17, 21, 29, 32–34, 39–44, 48–49, 57, 97, 111, 117–18, 127n20, 158n148, 164n21, 165n31, 166n31, 170n75; messianic, xv–xvi, xix, 3, 10, 39, 43–49, 52–59, 81, 90, 97, 117, 139n114, 142n19, 144nn50–51, 144nn54–55, 147n62, 148n77, 161n162, 161n164; operational, 49–53, 56
time of the now. See *ho nym kairos*
Twombly, Cy, 83–85, 91

urbilder, 2
urgeschichte, xiv, 11, 27–28, 30, 36, 128n30
urphänomen, 14, 27, 57, 160n159

Valéry, Paul, 85
Vernant, Jean-Pierre, 18
void, 64, 70, 86, 93–94

Warburg, Aby, 107–8, 143n30, 152n110
Wind, Edgar, 73–74, 125n10

zero degree, 88

www.ingramcontent.com/pod-product-compliance
Lightning Source LLC
Chambersburg PA
CBHW030653230426
43665CB00011B/1078